WORLD WAR I

and the

AMERICAN

NOVEL

BY STANLEY COOPERMAN

THE JOHNS HOPKINS PRESS, BALTIMORE

The section entitled "Believing" appeared in *Western Humanities Review*, Autumn, 1964, as "Christ in Khaki: Religion and the Post-World War I Literary Protest"; "The War Lover" appeared in *Literature and Psychology*, Vol. XIII, No. 3, as "Willa Cather and the Bright Face of War"; and "Death and *Cojones*" appeared in *South Atlantic Quarterly*, Winter, 1964, as "Death and *Cojones:* Hemingway's *A Farewell to Arms*" (copyright 1964 by the Duke University Press). Permission to reprint is gratefully acknowledged.

*for Leon Edel
and Jenifer—the* marinkee
and Esta

FOREWORD

"If you have a clubfoot you learn to live with your clubfoot," remarked John Dos Passos of the populations that fought World War II. Four decades ago, however, the "clubfoot" of total violence, machine civilization, futile terror, and mass death could not be so simply accepted. The impact of World War I was unparalleled; it shattered a cultural universe and in the United States shaped the literature of a generation.

Readers and critics, however, often tend to look back upon the Great Crusade either with nostalgia or impatience. Lauded for its excitement or attacked for its naïveté, the work of post-World War I writers has suffered from the fact that the burden of their protest has been so rapidly and so thoroughly absorbed. In a time of gas chambers, atomic death, and continuing tragi-comedies of death, what shall we say of Verdun?

But Hemingway, Dos Passos, Cummings, Faulkner, and many other American writers of the twenties began their work in a time of unique crisis. In order to understand their development it is necessary to understand the nature of the crisis itself, to see it clearly and without nostalgia. For it was the Great Crusade which gave to American literature an art not simply "influenced" by war, but in a vital sense created by it.

The impact of the war is not a simple thing to recreate, either for new generations of readers or for critics who look back upon the experience of the twenties through a curtain of sentiment. Certainly the post-World War I period has become increasingly sentimentalized; indeed, the popular merchandizing of the "gay twenties" has had its effect even on serious readers and students, who have never known—or who have forgotten—the humanistic faith of the Crusade and its subsequent shattering under the impact of political no less than military absurdities.

World War I for the vast majority of Americans, including the young men who were to produce the literature of the postwar period, was a Crusade in the fullest sense of the term. It was a call to glory, a struggle against the hosts of darkness, a "sovereign disinfectant" to lean-down and revitalize a materialistic society, a prelude to the "Socialist Commonwealth" which many American intellectuals saw as part of the inevitable future of the nation. The explosive enthusiasm, as well as the subsequent disillusion of the war experience, requires an act of retrospective imagination if the literature of the twenties is to be seen clearly for what it was.

In a very real sense we are all creatures of World War I, both in aesthetic and political terms. The great authoritarian movements of our century; the experiments in art and literature against all forms of rhetoric; the triumph of technological civilization—these things were then new, and they were the raw material for art, an art which found its expression not merely in "negativism" or "escapism," but rather in an examination of possible alternatives to a framework of obsolete values and romantic verbiage.

The aim of this study, then, is not merely to "criticize" a literary period, but rather to re-experience it, to get at something of the essence which made of the twenties so vital a decade in American letters. This is not a book for literary men only, or for historians only, but rather—hopefully—for all those who are interested in understanding why Americans do tend to embark on so many crusades, and why they so often manage to trip over their own ideals in the process. This book, in short, represents an attempt to view literature as a dynamic "echo of meaning" within and part of cultural process: what Ezra Pound meant, perhaps, when he defined literature as "news that is always news."

A word on method: the organization is thematic rather than chronological. Convenient but pointless categories are replaced by the more significant themes of social, political, military, and religious developments arising from initial expectations and the impact of war experience. While the focus of attention remains on the fiction, a variety of sources—memoirs, historical studies, military critiques—has been utilized for purposes of evidence and general information.

Sections on the bold journey into war and the broken world of war experience are followed by an examination of representative protagonists of the novels and a discussion of the basic preoccupations of the postwar writers. A section on criticism of war fiction has been included because such criticism has greatly defined—and, for modern readers, has greatly distorted—the nature of World War I impact and the literary expression which followed it. The war against fascism and the continuing Cold War have had their own effect on critics, who too often attempt to explain away what appears as the simple "negativism" of the twenties, or who praise it on very doubtful grounds.

I wish to acknowledge my deep appreciation for the Indiana University Fellowship, and the Simon Fraser University research grant, which made possible the completion of this project. I also wish to express my appreciation to the staffs of the Indiana University Library and the New York Public Library for their kindness and their patience. My debt to Professor Leon Edel, Professor Terence Martin, and Dr. Charlotte Alexander is incalculable; their advice, their criticism, and their personal interest have had no small share in the shaping of this book. And to the many others—both at Indiana University and elsewhere—many thanks for their suggestions and encouragement.

Vancouver, B.C.   *Stanley Cooperman*
Summer, 1966

CONTENTS

WORLD WAR I *and the* AMERICAN NOVEL

I

THE BOLD JOURNEY

*The world is moving away from military
ideals, and a period of peace, industry, and
world-wide fellowship is dawning.*
—Review of Reviews, 1914

*War is the great scavenger of thought. It is
the sovereign disinfectant, and its red stream
of blood is the Condy's Fluid that cleans out
the stagnant pools and clotted channels of
the intellect.*
—SIR EDMUND GOSSE, *Inter Arma*, 1916

*America tore the gag of neutrality from her
lips, and with all the strength of her liberated
lungs, claimed her right to a place in the
struggle. The pacifists crept into their
holes . . .*
—EDITH WHARTON, *The Marne*, 1918

Toward the Crusade

D uring the years preceding the First World War there was a faith seldom doubted by intelligent people, a secular faith of man in man: democracy was coming into its own. As late as 1913 Randolph Bourne saw in Europe only "the most advanced civilization . . . a luminous intelligence that selected and controlled and did not allow itself to be overwhelmed."[1] Pointing to the great intellectual confidence of the prewar years (more than optimism because the future already seemed part of the present), Jules Romains could refer to the conviction that the "bestial periods" of history were behind mankind, that western civilization had at last achieved a moral orientation and mature culture.[2]

The cultural maturity, however, the "luminous intelligence" of which Henry James was the chief American spokesman in literature, was not the only pride of the prewar era. The excesses of the industrial revolution were being arrested; social no less than intellectual awareness was added proof of the progress of civilization. In the United States the business barons had drained one railroad and juggled one stock issue too many, and there was Teddy Roosevelt. Social justice had become respectable and the United States, faced with rapidly increasing industrial and urban populations, welcomed or tolerated modifications of laissez faire unique in its history.

With the continental frontier gone and the robber barons in disrepute, America was taking stock of herself and deciding that material perfection, a standard of life and government equal to anything in the world, might be achieved with improved machinery and continued effort. Nor were the dreams limited to visionaries on the order of Eugene V. Debs, Henry George, and Edward Bellamy. As Richard Hofstadter points out, "The growing enthusiasm of middle-class people for social and economic reform . . . affected in a striking way all the major and minor political parties and the whole tone of American political life."[3] Large circulation magazines such as *Cosmopolitan, Forum and Munsey's,* and *McClure's* (with the publication of Lincoln Steffens'

[1] Quoted by Alfred Kazin, *On Native Grounds* (New York, 1942), p. 184.
[2] Jules Romains, *Verdun* (New York, 1939), p. 155.
[3] Richard Hofstadter, *The Age of Reform* (New York, 1955), p. 5.

"Tweed Days in St. Louis" in 1902) enlisted their presses in the cause of the great housecleaning, and the "muckrake" had begun; in 1906 the *American* was founded by Lincoln Steffens and Ida Tarbell, who had already tilted her lance against the Standard Oil dragon. Protest and reform spilled over into literature, and the naturalists published exposé after exposé. Books such as *The Octopus* (1901) and *The Jungle* (1906) had all but written legislation. The mass was no longer a dirty word. Millions believed, along with Benjamin O. Flower's *Arena,* that "the Republic shall no longer lag behind the march of progress," and with *Everybody's Magazine* that "our public health is being conserved. The money God totters. Patriotism, manhood, brotherhood, are exalted. It is a new era. A new world."[4]

By 1912, when Woodrow Wilson told the Democratic nominating convention that "it is a new age," change was the keynote and the golden era was as sure as the annual boom in population. During the election of that year the Socialists captured the astonishing number of 897,011 votes. Machines were beating the pulse of a civilized future in a civilized world. "It is difficult now," Amy Loveman remarked in 1944, "after the misery of the years that have intervened, to realize how sincerely the men and women of the first decade of the twentieth century believed that humanity was on the march to happiness."[5]

The "march to happiness," however, a material happiness based on better wages, newer goods, and wider stock distribution, was not universally celebrated. As Henry F. May remarks in *The End of American Innocence* (1959), there were many "cracks in the surface" of American prewar society, many elements out of step. For some the very complacency of material progress was stifling, alien; liberal arts culture, for example, was still very much nineteenth-century, and young men educated under the "ether cone" of university life felt themselves wilted by the heat and sweat of vulgar economic machinery.[6] These were the young men who, like Andrews in John Dos Passos' *Three Soldiers,* "were sick . . .

[4] Quoted by Harold Underwood Faulkner, *American Political and Social History* (New York, 1946), p. 576.
[5] Amy Loveman, "Then and Now," *Saturday Review of Literature,* XXVII (August 5, 1944), 45.
[6] See Charles A. Fenton, "A Literary Fracture of World War I," *American Quarterly* XII (1960), 119–132; Henry F. May, *The End of American Innocence* (New York, 1959).

of carrying individuality aloft like a banner above the turmoil."[7] Unprepared for the "march to happiness" by reason of their cultural pretensions, academic and artistic young men retreated into the twin towers of humanism or aestheticism. And other young men, in offices, factories, or salesrooms, were bored despite the better wages, were bored because of better wages, were bored because there seemed no way in the slow roll of solidifying citizenship to prove themselves while still young. When the war did arrive it was seized as the very breath of glory, as the Big Chance, by the young aesthete, humanist, and commercial man alike.

Meanwhile, however, the "New Democracy" continued and with the election of Woodrow Wilson in 1912 reached its crest. The moderate liberalism of Wilson, swept to power by the liberal sentiment of the time, nibbled away at monopoly, at the laws which for decades had favored the concentration of economic power. There was reform after reform, modest but nonetheless basic: among others, the Federal Reserve Act, the Clayton Antitrust Act, a permanent Federal Income Tax, and Federal Aid to Road and School Construction. Young idealists, encouraged by what appeared to be the triumph of an intellectual president, felt that "the world was going in their direction, the new standards were winning out, and America in ten or fifteen years would not only be a fatherland of the arts, but also a socialist commonwealth."[8] War seemed impossible. Norman Angell had proven it impossible because economically unfeasible when he wrote *The Grand Illusion* in 1910. David Starr Jordan made the same point, explaining that "the safeguards against the armies and navies Europe has gathered for war is that Europe is not rich enough to use them, and is too human and humane to want to use them."[9] And as late as January, 1914, the *Review of Reviews* proclaimed that "the world is moving away from military ideals, and a period of peace, industry and worldwide friendship is dawning."[10]

The experts were suddenly proved wrong by events which shattered the certainty of progress, introduced technological slaughter, manipulated mass propaganda to justify mass death, and produced a collective trauma such as the world had never known. The impact of the war on the older writers and thinkers, who were developing

[7] John Dos Passos, *Three Soldiers* (New York, 1921), p. 26.
[8] Malcolm Cowley, quoted by Kazin, *On Native Grounds*, p. 172.
[9] Quoted by Charles C. Tansill, *America Goes to War* (Boston, 1938), p. 18.
[10] Quoted by Walter Millis, *Road to War* (Boston, 1935), p. 15.

a culture of intelligence and reason, literally defies description. The context in which they worked, and in which they were struck by the war, is for most of us remote. We *live* with the barbarity of civilization; many of us have been aware of the barbarity at least as long as we have been aware of living at all. The heartwrack of a man like Henry James, for example (despite his Anglophilism and support of the Entente), can only be hinted at, even by James himself. In a letter to Howard Sturgis in 1914 James wrote that it was "vain to speak as if one weren't living in a nightmare." "The plunge of civilization into this abyss of blood and horror . . . ," he continued, "so gives way the whole long age during which we have supposed the world to be, with whatever abatement, gradually bettering, that to have to take it all now for what the treacherous years were making for and *meaning* is too tragic for words . . . this unspeakable giveaway of the whole fool's paradise of our past—this is what we were so fondly working for!"[11]

War—the fire in which heroes had been forged throughout man's history—drained Europe and drew in America. But in place of fire there was mud; in place of heroes there were faceless masses of men butchering each other with little or none of the personal tests celebrated in epics reaching back to the origins of language itself. There were no identifiable gestures of nobility in this war; and a young man named Ernest Hemingway, who later was to make a fetish of "dying well," had not forgotten that when in 1923 he wrote a snatch of verse bitterly titled "Camps d'Honneur" for *Poetry Magazine*:

> Soldiers never do die well:
>   Crosses mark their places—
> Wooden crosses where they fell,
>   Stuck above their faces.

[11] Quoted by Robert Cantwell, *New Republic*, XCI (June 23, 1937), 178. For a slightly different text of the same letter, dated August 4, 1914, see *The Letters of Henry James*, ed. Percy Lubbock (New York, 1920), p. 132. The enormous lack of preparation on the part of intellectuals for the outbreak of the war is indicated by another letter, dated August 6: "Everything is of the last abnormalism now, and no convulsion, no historic event of any such immensity can ever have taken place in such a turn-over of a few hours and with such a measureless rush—the whole thing being, in other words, such an unprecedented combination of size and suddenness. There has never, surely, since the world began, been any suddenness so big, so instantly mobilized, any more than there has been an equal enormity so sudden. . . ."

> Soldiers pitch and cough and twitch—
> All the world roars red and black;
> Soldiers smother in a ditch,
> Choking through the whole attack.[12]

The scientific century had produced what was probably the first of the scientific wars and, as John Peale Bishop remarked, "The most tragic thing about the war was not that it made so many dead men, but that it destroyed the tragedy of death."[13]

Land, power, and trade are familiar causes of war. For thousands of years these were reasons enough for fighting. By 1914, however, the peoples of the western world, proud of their civilization, were looking forward to innumerable decades of peace and ever-increasing prosperity. In such a context material reasons alone were not capable of evoking the mass support necessary for total mobilization. National leaders found it necessary to wrap war purposes in a compelling war rhetoric, and in the United States the need for this rhetoric was especially urgent. With traditional hostility toward European involvement, with booming hopes for continued growth and peace, Americans could not easily be drawn into war for lands in which they were not interested or for power which they might well feel was part of their destiny as a nation. On August 2, 1914, for example, the *New York Times* represented strong public opinion when it referred to the conflict as "the least justified of all wars since man emerged from barbarism." As late as September 9, despite its Anglophilism and subsequent war enthusiasm, the *Times* was still sneering at "the first press-agent's war."

Why did this people—who re-elected Wilson in 1916 because "he kept us out of war"—swing on a pendulum from neutrality to total involvement? How was it possible to forge this disparate, sprawling, provincial, at once idealist and materialist population into a war machine which quoted the most grandiose verbiage on freedom and democracy while discouraging political and intel-

---

[12] *Poetry*, XXI (January, 1923), 19.
[13] Quoted by John Alfred Atkins, *The Art of Ernest Hemingway* (London, 1952), p. 116. There might be some justification, from the standpoint of technical military history, for considering the closing period of the American Civil War as marking the development of scientific methodology. However, the intervening years—and the growth of nostalgia after the conflict—served to revitalize the "gentleman" concept of warfare. This, of course, had important results in the Crusade itself—especially when combined with the vast technological developments of the interwar period.

lectual deviation? Why did the people of the United States, after resisting every seduction of European diplomacy, respond to their ultimate seduction with explosive enthusiasm? The reasons—often paradoxical, none simple—related to economic pressures, to the enormous growth of propaganda-as-science, to the need of organized religion for Holy Cause, and to the concept of battle as the personal proving ground for manhood.

The first of these reasons, the pocketbook, has perhaps been given the most attention of all. Money, trade, jobs, and dividends. These were not the private concern of that species of monstrosity branded by Socialists and pacifists alike as "warlords of munitions." It was true enough, as Walter Millis points out, that in creating an industry from 1897 to 1914 to build the complex new armaments "we had inevitably created new pressures to expand the armaments in order to sustain the industry."[14] But the fact remains that the United States profited enormously during the early years of the war, almost entirely because of trade with the Entente. The experience of Claude's father with the British purchasing office in Willa Cather's *One of Ours*, or that of Caleb in Steinbeck's *East of Eden*, was repeated on many economic levels throughout the country. The blockade of Germany was successful, so successful that the United States soon had an impressive financial stake in Allied victory.

Again, it must be stressed that the change in war attitudes took place throughout the nation, with a vehemence by no means limited to particular groups or classes. When, for example, Congress appeared ready to support the Gore-McLemore resolution (to keep American passengers off belligerent ships and to squelch, once and for all, the submarine issue as a possible cause for war), it was popular opinion that was outraged. The national legislature, in other words, was defeated less by a war-profiteering minority than by a militant popular majority. Certainly the political chaos of 1916 cannot be clarified simply by means of class-and-mass formulas. Ultimately the entire nation became in effect the prowar party, until pacifist politicians and pacifist capitalists alike (Henry Ford, for example) were forced to give way.[15]

[14] Walter Millis, *Arms and Men* (New York, 1956), p. 148.
[15] Even the Socialists were stymied by the general war prosperity, which made their attacks on "money masters, profit seekers" an absurdity to labor itself. See Upton Sinclair's *Jimmy Higgins* (Racine, Wisc., 1918). Jimmy's dilemma

Despite the widespread belief in perpetual progress, the United States at the beginning of the conflict was caught in a downward swing of the economic cycle, a descent arrested largely by war business which resulted in sudden prosperity. The importance of this bread-and-butter factor has often been overestimated, but it must not be ignored. Ambassador Walter Hines Page, for example, an Anglophile, handed his trump card to Wilson before renewed submarine warfare "forced" America into the war. "It is not improbable that the only way of maintaining our present pre-eminent trade position," he said, "is by declaring war on Germany."[16]

The "pre-eminent trade position" stressed by Ambassador Page gives a rather ironic dimension to Wilson's rhetorical idealism (and this most certainly helped to create cynicism and revulsion after the Crusade had ended). J. P. Morgan's raising of 500 million dollars in unsecured loans to Britain, for example, which netted the financial wizard and vehement patriot a fat cash profit, swelled British purchasing power and "passed into the hands of American business, until prosperity returned to the United States."[17] By 1917, furthermore, the United States had a two-billion-dollar stake in Allied victory with munitions shipments alone. The entire pattern of Anglo-American financial relationships during the period of technical neutrality from 1914 to 1917 makes a fascinating study. There was Colonel House's abortive peace attempt in 1916, which not only threw the stock market into complete panic but actually evoked concrete protests from Secretary of State Lansing. So-called military atrocities themselves produced public indignation and private rejoicing; while the United States press was denouncing Germany for the submarine-sinking of the *Arabic*, to cite but one example, Morgan cabled his office that "conditions may have improved toward favoring a new unsecured loan."[18]

---

was not unique; indeed, it was the dilemma of the ideological left in both Europe and the United States: "The enthusiasm for these [war] contracts became as it were the religion of Leesville; it spread even to the ranks of Labour, so that Jimmy found himself like a man in a surf, struggling to keep his feet against an undertow" (p. 46).

[16] Frederick L. Paxon, "Pre-War Years, 1914–1917," *American Democracy and World War* (4 vols.; Boston, 1936), I, 135. Theodore Ropp, in *War in the Western World* (Durham, N.C., 1959) notes that "by the end of 1916 the United States had become an Allied arsenal" (p. 238).

[17] In a telegram to Wilson dated March 5, 1917, quoted by Faulkner, *American Political and Social History*, p. 606.

[18] Quoted by Tansill, *America Goes to War*, p. 108.

Occasionally, however, the contradictions between rhetoric and mercenary interest did clash in public, and when this happened the situation approached farce. American shipbuilding for the Allies, for example, reached enormous proportions soon after the outbreak of hostilities; parts were sent to Canada for final assembly despite pontifical government instructions to the contrary. But Charles M. Schwab of Bethlehem Steel chose an unfortunate moment to be self-righteous in support of neutrality; he issued a public denial of his own shipbuilding program at the very moment the British government saw fit to issue a public citation of Bethlehem Steel's war production record.[19]

There were, of course, protests against the specious nature of American neutrality. But men like LaFollette and Bryan, while correct in assuming that Americans would not support a war for what Charles C. Hyde called "commercial privilege," underestimated the role of Wilsonian rhetoric and the developing science of public relations. Certainly the economic factor alone would have had insufficient weight with the man in the street, who was not ready to go to war to protect investments or "pre-eminent" trade positions. Life was generally comfortable, or at least hopeful; prosperity (although to a large extent prosperity based on someone else's war) was proceeding according to plan. Francis Winwar's remark that "the people of the United States . . . on the whole lived a complacent, carpet-slipper existence," reflects the spirit of an age in which major upheavals were neither anticipated nor desired.[20]

Despite the "cracks in the wall" of American culture, the nation as a whole was far too comfortable for Armageddon, and Entente propagandists, closely advised by Anglophiles and Francophiles within the United States, soon perceived that economic interest alone would not produce an adequate war fever. Their subsequent propaganda sought to induce an emotional infection following three lines of least resistance: the disaffection of the young educated classes with the material standards and money worship of the time, a disaffection that could be translated into fervent embrace of a Great Cause; the lack of excitement and basic anonymity of the new economic machinery, which could be contrasted with the op-

[19] Tansill points out that not only was Schwab lying, but he obviously could not have continued his war production "except upon intimations from government officials that such a violation would be construed favorably" (p. 45).
[20] Francis Winwar, "The World War and the Arts," *War in the Twentieth Century*, ed. Willard Waller (New York, 1940), p. 195.

portunity for glory afforded by great battles; and the tremendous resources for vicarious suffering (accompanied by disinterested generosity) possessed by the American population in general and the American female population in particular. It was in this last area that the opinion experts achieved an unparalleled success: the distribution of atrocity stories became a major weapon of the war.

Propaganda: The Machine, the Crusade, and the Teutonic Beast

Atrocities had occurred; their commission—by both sides—was inevitable in a war that was the first of man's machine wars. As James Morgan Reade points out in his unimpassioned study of atrocity propaganda, the new scientific weapons were themselves atrocious.[21] Events which produced unbelieving terror and enraged headlines during World War I would hardly produce surprise, much less passion, today. The involvement of civilian populations through long-range bombing, the strafing of cities, the use of mines and submarines, the frequency of "no quarter" engagements in which prisoners were killed as quickly as they were taken, the tremendous revolution in morality (or immorality) that occurred when great masses of men were concentrated in minute and devastated geographical areas—these factors constituted immediate horror for populations essentially unprepared for them in either military or moral codes.

Perhaps the most obvious example of the manner in which atrocious machine warfare could be translated into atrocities was the repeated horror evoked by stories of the "handless children." The Germans, it was said (by Entente propagandists), were cutting off the hands of little children. Both Reade and H. C. Peterson point out that this was proved only as it might be proved: the Germans—and the Allies as well—were cutting off the heads, noses, genitals, or legs of enemy soldiers. These things happened, but for the first time in the history of warfare they happened without individual action.[22] An exploding bomb was no respector

[21] James Morgan Reade, *Atrocity Propaganda* (New Haven, Conn., 1941). See especially pp. 1–78.
[22] H. C. Peterson, *Propaganda for War* (Norman, Okla., 1939). Both Peterson and Reade emphasize the terror aroused by machine war itself.

of age, sex, or human anatomy. In traditional warfare a beheading or a mutilation had been a matter of barbarism and savagery; because of the impersonal nature of modern warfare, it became a matter of course.

The impact of machine war, however, was soon to be appropriated as "one of the . . . chief means of [propaganda] operation against a belligerent army."[23] Feeding upon the fact that atrocities were indeed occurring, Entente propagandists formulated the methods of what is now known more respectably as public relations and carefully magnified every possible atrocity under the glass of mass distribution. With the press reaching phenomenal circulation and the cinema coming into its own, propaganda could be used as a weapon to sharpen public opinion and military *esprit de corps*. Reade describes graphically the technique—then new, now familiar—of the public relations expert: a single bloody event, whether or not deliberately committed, could be photographed and reported until it became one thousand similar events; any of these, if challenged, could be verified by reference to the first.

Propaganda, of course, was not discovered in 1914; it is as old as warfare itself. What was new in 1914 was propaganda as science. The tremendous development of modern communications enabled the experts, in the frank words of the English Brigadier General Crozier, to "alter completely outlook, bearing and mentality . . . and bring about the brute-like bestiality which is so necessary for victory."[24]

Besides a perfected technique, propagandists had a concurrent advantage in the lack of preparation on the part of their audience for the opinion campaigns. The very term propaganda itself was new; its victims hardly knew what the word meant. This was especially true of Americans, who lacked the acquired caution of the Europeans. Even granting the fact that, as Charles de Gaulle later pointed out, "the mass movements and mechanization to which men and women were subjected by modern life had preconditioned them for mass mobilization," the European's political skepticism could offer at least partial insulation against the rhetoric of unselfish fury and the Humanitarian Crusade.[25] But Americans were provincial not only in regard to European politics; their pro-

[23] Ralph D. Casey, "Propaganda and Public Opinion," *War in the Twentieth Century*, p. 446.
[24] Quoted by Reade, *Atrocity Propaganda*, p. 6.
[25] Quoted by Ropp, *War in the Western World*, p. 221.

vincialism extended to include the nature of war itself. The lives of women and children were still regarded as sacred, and anything which threatened such noncombatants was taken to be the result of savagery. One difference between the Apache and the white man, after all, was that the latter—as a civilized Christian—understood what noncombatancy meant. Certainly disasters such as that of the *Lusitania*, with eye-witness accounts of women and children dying at sea and heart-rending illustrations in Sunday supplements, produced a nationwide reaction of authentic horror.

In addition to other advantages (such as control of transoceanic communication and a virtual monopoly of press dispatches), Allied propaganda benefited by certain technological developments. "The American press," Millis remarks, "which like everyone else had lightly talked and thought of war so long, was stunned by the dread visage of [machine] war itself. It could not be war which was responsible for these horrors; it must be the Germans."[26] The role of the submarine, for example, that dramatic illustration of Prussian inhumanity, of skulking Teutonic cowardice, was a far more effective propaganda target than the blockade employed by the British against entire populations.[27]

Ironically enough it was the British, with Sir Edward Grey as their spokesman, who first formulated the concept of total combatancy which was to bear so rich a harvest in World War II. Justifying his redefinition of contraband to include all foodstuffs and medicines in addition to actual war materials, Grey pointed out that the German government had instituted food rationing for the purpose of supporting its armies; the German civilian population had accommodated itself to this program and therefore could be regarded as a "belligerent population" which—within the frame-

---

[26] Millis, *Road to War*, p. 67.

[27] Poison gas also provided—temporarily—a focus for Entente propaganda. "The first chance to exploit fully the propaganda value of the use of new methods of warfare," Peterson remarks, "was the introduction of gas at Second Ypres. This enabled Wellington House to publicize the 'inhuman' methods employed by the enemy. Some of the heat in this controversy may have resulted from professional jealousy, for the French had been working on a gas and were not yet ready for its trial. When they did perfect it, there was a good deal of satisfaction expressed in the newspapers over the just retaliation. Very soon there was an easing up on the talk about 'inhuman warfare' in regard to gas, because the prevailing winds favored the Allies, and they found gas a most useful weapon" (*Propaganda for War*, pp. 63–64). After noting that both the French and British were heavily in the market for liquid chlorine as early as September, 1914, Peterson also remarks that months before the gas attack at Ypres, the French had introduced liquid fire.

work of existing international law—could be "starved into submission." Women and children, in other words, who persisted in eating according to government regulation, would henceforth be considered "combatants differing only in the weapons they carried."[28]

Such reasoning rendered international law absurd and made Wilson's later rhetorical excommunication of the submarine ludicrous. There were, however, sharp protests from the United States immediately after the British formulated the idea of total contraband. Indeed, public opinion went so far as to support a "Milk for German Babies" campaign. Ambassador Page warned solemnly that American opinion would not tolerate a policy which would keep food from noncombatants. Something had to be done, and done quickly.

British response was twofold: first, a program was immediately announced for "total purchase" of American foodstuffs. Anything produced by the American farmer would be bought and paid for in cash. Allied purchasing agents with unlimited funds were soon offering unbelievable prices in market towns throughout the country. Ambassador Page also played a part, and an astonishing part it was. After handing the British an American note strongly protesting the total embargo, he actually consulted with the British as to the wording of that government's reply, hastening into print with assurances that the United States would do very well with trade limited to the Entente. Page's willingness to serve as ex officio member of the British Foreign Service was sharply reprimanded by Washington, especially as it became obvious that American shippers had no choice in the matter and that the American flag was no protection against confiscation on the high seas. But Page's reprimand itself occasioned a notable outburst from his counterpart in the United States, Sir Cecil Spring Rice, who sounded an alarm regarding German "treachery in high places" within the American government, an alarm which—reflecting the "deepening shadows of war insanity"—included religio-racial denunciation. "The German-Jewish bankers," said Sir Spring Rice, "are toiling in a solid phalanx to compass our destruction. . . . The *New York Times* . . . has been practically acquired by Kuhn, Loeb and Co. and Schiff, the arch-Jew and special protege of the Emperor . . . since Morgan's death the Jewish banks are supreme and they have captured the Treasury Department."[29] The English ambassador's

[28] See Paxon, I, 218 for discussion of Grey's position.
[29] Millis, *Road to War*, p. 116.

16

despair was ill-grounded: with farmers no less than businessmen discovering the difficulty of quarreling "with a nation that had literally dragged America from a deep slough of economic despond," total embargo soon ceased to be a major issue.[30]

But Germany was still making a strong defense of submarine warfare by pointing to the disastrous effects of total blockade on her home population. The British had to obtain a focal point for emotional protest against the submarine, and this was provided by what was, perhaps, the most effective single propaganda issue of the war, the sinking of the *Lusitania*.

The episode of the *Lusitania*—a name which was to become a slogan of the Great American Crusade—in retrospect seems surrounded with ambiguities. Shortly before the sinking, for example, Sir Edward Grey asked Colonel House what would happen if an "ocean liner" were sent to the bottom. "A flame of indignation would sweep across America which would in itself carry us into the war," Colonel House replied.[31] The sinking of the *Lusitania*, then, had actually been envisioned before the event. The liner herself was carrying six million rounds of small-arms ammunition; German warnings, and the repeated pleas of men like Bryan that a ship carrying contraband should not rely upon passengers to protect her from attack, were ignored. And the course of the *Lusitania* was most peculiar: completely without convoy protection she made no use of the zigzag, which by then had become standard for ships in enemy waters, but hugged areas which were known to be favorites for German submarines. To climax a long list of coincidences, the fully completed Bryce Report on German atrocities was issued to the American press within one week after the

[30] Tansill, *America Goes to War*, p. 133. One must note how frequently the volume by Tansill, a revisionist scholar, agrees with the more objective work of Paxon. Certainly revisionist scholarship is still vitally necessary to students of war literature, since studies of the First World War do not always offer a full examination of the political and military realities of the time. As recently as 1960, for example, Pierce G. Frederick's *The Great Adventure: America in the First World War* repeats the merest rhetorical superficialities. And Barbara W. Tuchman in *The Guns of August*, published in 1962, takes the Entente atrocity-reports with far more solemnity than they deserve. Reviewing her book, indeed, Cyril Falls—himself a pro-Entente military historian (*The First World War*, 1960)—remarks that "the German atrocities, abominable as they were, are somewhat overdone in this account. . . . A good many of the charges launched during the war have since been found grossly exaggerated, if not entirely false" (*New York Times Book Review*, January 28, 1962, p. 26).
[31] Quoted by Millis, *Road to War*, p. 160.

Lusitania was sunk. The stage was now set for the rhetoric describing German bestiality.

Horrified by episodes such as that of the *Lusitania,* primed by atrocity dispatches from London or Paris, American clergymen eagerly embraced the concept of Holy Cause, Jesus in khaki, and represented the war as a test of spiritual righteousness. God was confronting the devil, and under the circumstances pacifism or "hyphenated Americanism" was not only unpatriotic but blasphemous. Like other educated persons in the United States, many ministers had been slowly alienated from the growing monolithic structure of secular values. The eruption of war demanded spiritual justification; the development of machine war, with unparalleled horrors, provided spiritual justification in the form of a crusade against the antichrist. And religious rhetoric flowed with a heat unequaled before—or since.[32] A survey of newspapers and periodicals gives repeated examples of this sort of invocation, which is typified by the Louisville *Courier-Journal* (May 8, 1915): "This holy sabbath," the paper urged, "every pulpit in America should send a prayer to God in protest . . . and more than all—the Christian President of the United States, a cool and brave man, sprung from a line of heroes and saints—ceasing longer to protest, should act, leaving no doubt . . . that he is . . . a leader of men and nations, and that he holds aloft the sword of the Lord and Gideon!"

Ministers of the major denominations set out upon the Crusade that at last permitted militant Christian action against a definable target, against Satan become vulnerable because identifiable in the flesh. English clergymen like Father Bernard Vaughan aroused their American colleagues: "Not content to crucify Canadians, mur-

[32] It is interesting to recall the effect of the American government's "peace note" of 1916, which called for all belligerent powers to state their war aims. Not only were General Woods, Theodore Roosevelt, and the entire Anglophile group outraged at the suggestion that there was little to choose between the war aims of the Central Powers and those of the Entente (the tragic conviction of which Wilson had been, privately, voicing for several months), not only did every Allied source respond furiously ("The Allies, unfortunately, could not state their real war aims. Their own peoples would have refused to go on fighting for all the territorial spoils they had been compelled to pledge each other." [Millis, *Road to War,* p. 368])—more than these, a prompt call by Mr. George C. Pepper, to the "Christians of America," resulted in an enormously Christian response, via public signatures, against efforts to secure a "premature peace" when the antichrist was ravaging Europe.

der priests, violate nuns, mishandle women and bayonet children," he reported, "the enemy torpedoes civilian-carrying liners and bombs red-cross hospitals."[33] And in this country men like Samuel McCrea Calvert, Assistant Secretary of the General War Time Commission of Churches, merely echoed clerical opinion prevailing since the *Lusitania* when he defined the war as a "conflict between forces that make for the coming of the Kingdom of God, and forces that oppose it."[34] Small wonder that popular wartime novelists like Arthur Train followed the lead of the clergy and summoned every resource from both the Old and New Testaments in depicting "a struggle between . . . a cruel and inhuman paganism and the teaching of Jesus Christ."[35] The pulpits of the nation and of the army as well were issuing the sort of "fighting sermon" which James Stevens was later to satirize so effectively in *Mattock* (1927). Writing in the first-person dialect narrative of a boy from Indiana, Stevens adopts a stance of naïveté to achieve judgments no less bitter than those of John Dos Passos, Thomas Boyd, E. E. Cummings, or Lawrence Stallings. An army chaplain, Stevens writes, "swung into the rousingest exhorting sermon I'd ever heard in all my born days":

He had started his sermon with a fearful picture of the hellishness of the Huns who would fight us when we got to the trenches, and . . . the minister called down upon them the wrath of Almighty God.

He told us about the wicked Kaiser, the vile Crown Prince, the monsters of Hun officers and Junkers and the savage Hun soldiers who raped girls and butchered babies. And on all of their loathsome tribe the minister called down the wrath of Almighty God . . .

'Be willing instruments, that Almighty God's fierce and vengeful wrath may sweep the hellishness of the Huns from his beautiful earth: Onward, Christian Soldiers!'[36]

The fighting sermon, however, was not the only kind of exhortation; many were wrapped in sentimental fiction and delivered for the home front during or before America's official entry into the war. Novel after novel, usually by lady authors such as Mary Raymond Shipman Andrews, Temple Bailey, or (unfortunately) Edith Wharton, seriously portrayed God-fearing boys blondly car-

[33] In *The Collected Cartoons of Louis Raemaker* (New York, 1917), p. 30.
[34] Quoted by Ray H. Abrams, *Preachers Present Arms* (New York, 1933), p. 57.
[35] Arthur Train, *Earthquake* (New York, 1918), p. 306.
[36] James Stevens, *Mattock* (New York, 1927), pp. 39–40.

rying the banners of Christian faith against a simian foe. In Temple Bailey's *The Tin Soldier* (1918), for example, Drusilla sings to the soldiers:

"I must go out to them," Drusilla said . . . her voice roared:
"In the beauty of the lilies Christ was born across the sea,
With the glory in his bosom which transfigures you and me.
As he died to make men holy, let us die to make men free,
While God is marching on."
Tired and spent, they saw in her . . . America coming fresh and unworn to fight a winning battle to the end. So they turned their faces toward Drusilla. She was more to them than a singing woman. Behind her stood a steadfast people. And God was marching on.[37]

And in Mary Raymond Shipman Andrews' *Joy in the Morning* (1919), a novel written during the first flush of victory, a mother's doubts are swept away by the epiphany of purification through Holy Cause:

It began to rise before her, a distant picture glorious through a mist of suffering, something built of the sacrifice, and the honor, and the deathless bravery of millions of soldiers in battle, of millions of mothers at home. The education of a nation to higher ideals was reaching the quiet backwater of one woman's soul. There were lovelier things than life; there were harder things than death. Service is the measure of living. . . . More and more entirely, as the . . . vision crowded out selfishness, this woman, as thousands and tens of thousands all over America, lifted up her heart—the dear things that filled and were her heart—unto the Lord.[38]

The triumphant endorsement of the war by religion, however, caused a revulsion against the assumptions and rhetoric of religion itself; such revulsion was, as we shall see, a basic theme of the postwar novel of protest. For many young men serving either in the trenches or in auxiliary detachments, for soldiers like William March (holder of the Distinguished Service Cross) no less than for volunteers like Dos Passos or Cummings, anything which claimed divine sanctification for what they saw and experienced was at best an expression of fantastic ignorance and at worst a calculated swindle. While the rhetoric of the Holy Crusade issued from pulpits at home and in YMCA huts in France, while Jesus was dressed in khaki by clergymen who pictured the Saviour as

[37] Temple Bailey, *The Tin Soldier* (Philadelphia, 1918), pp. 455–56.
[38] Mary Raymond Shipman Andrews, *Joy In The Morning* (New York, 1919), pp. 215–16.

20

joyfully firing machine guns against the Hosts of Darkness, such young men had discovered death without dignity, violence without purpose, politics without meaning, and—very often—sex made available like a public latrine. They had found, as Frederick J. Hoffman remarks, "an irrational world in which vulgarity, filth, confusion, and unreason were the rule instead of the unpleasant exception";[39] juxtaposed with such a world, the religious endorsement of the war helped create subsequent revulsion against values which seemed to be set in quicksand.

The facts of living no less than the facts of dying made the wartime role of religion a horror of absurdity for the novelists who would create an image of the war. " 'He ought to realize that in urging young men to go into this cockeyed lunatic asylum of war he's doing everything he can to undermine the principles and ideals he most believes in,' " writes Dick Savage to the wife of a clergyman in *1919* (1932).[40] And in one brutal paragraph of *The Enormous Room* (1922), E. E. Cummings reduces religion to the senseless mechanism of war itself:

The shrinking light which my guide held had become suddenly minute; it was beating, senseless and futile, with small fists upon a thick enormous moisture of gloom. To the left and right burst dirty burglars of moonlight. The clammy, stupid distance uttered dimly an uncanny conflict—the mutterless tumbling of brutish shadows. A growing ooze battled with my lungs. My nostrils fought against the monstrous atmospheric slime which hugged a sweet, unpleasant odour. Staring ahead, I gradually disinterred the pale carrion of darkness—an altar, guarded with the ugliness of unlit candles, on which stood inexorably the efficient instruments for eating God.[41]

Religious rhetoric was rendered absurd by more than the battle-front alone, or by the impersonal obscenities of machine warfare. The Protestantism of the American soldier fared no better in non-combatant areas, where the official or semi-official view of American troops as Soldiers of Christ (a characteristic of the A.E.F. discussed more fully in Chapter II) created those situations of religious asininity later dramatized so extensively in literature. Protagonists of the postwar novel usually set out on their crusade only to find, as Fred Summers does in *1919*, a war that appears

[39] Frederick J. Hoffman, *The Twenties* (New York, 1949), p. 54.
[40] John Dos Passos, *1919* (New York, 1954), p. 216. (The first edition of *1919* appeared in 1932.)
[41] E. E. Cummings. *The Enormous Room* (New York, 1934), p. 58. (The first edition of *The Enormous Room* appeared in 1922.)

to be " 'a goddamm whorehouse.' " Fuselli, in *Three Soldiers* (1921), acting by the standards of prewar America, proposes marriage but contracts only syphilis; Irwin, in Elliot Paul's *Impromptu* (1923), is completely coarsened; Zorn, in Theodore Fredenburgh's *Soldiers March!* (1930), is perhaps the archetype of the young man for whom the shock of impersonal sex is almost as great as the shock of "invisible death" on the front lines. In context, the virginal proclamations of ministers and the vacuously cheerful "Y" men were to be equally despised.

The religious endorsement of the conflict, however, had been something of a revolution. Not since the days of the crusades and religious wars did the ministers of western civilization demand, with such enthusiasm, killing for the greater glory of God and justice. Writers such as Dos Passos, Cummings, Boyd, March, or Fredenburgh were later to protest bitterly; James Stevens could resort to mockery by making his hero into a sardonic image of religious fatuity (essentially the same image as the hated "Y" men). But the religious endorsement was by no means ineffective at the time of the Crusade itself; contributing enormously to the concept of enemy-as-beast, a new concept in modern war between civilized nations, religious verbalism was often indistinguishable from racial cause.

Once the war was given an ideological basis there was no room for chivalry, for any concept of the "gallant foeman"; and this ideological basis was the only one which the American people would accept in the years from 1914 to 1918. Primitive wars were limited because they were fought for limited ends; the reason for fighting was immediately apparent to combatants and noncombatants, most of whom usually stood to gain directly if victorious.[42] Given abstract reasons, however, the war could be justified only on ethical grounds, and this in turn demanded total capitulation on the part of the enemy, who was literally branded an inferior species. "The attack," Reade indicates, "began with historical analogies and ended with anthropological and biological inferences."[43]

Distinctions between nationality and race, certainly, were blurred and often nonexistent at the time of World War I. Both scholars and laymen assumed "the validity of common racial and instinctive doctrines" and could therefore build easily upon stereo-

[42] L. L. Bernard, *War and Its Causes* (New York, 1944). See "Changing Attitudes Toward War," pp. 115–41; "The Ideologies of War," pp. 141–65.
[43] Reade, *Atrocity Propaganda*, p. 17.

types.[44] The new, scientifically organized propaganda gave what passed as scientific justification for war against inherently evil or pernicious races. Men like Willa Cather's Claude (in *One of Ours*) found it difficult to hate Germans; they could, however, defend humanity against the Teutonic Beast. To cite another example in fiction: even as early as 1915, when Mary Raymond Shipman Andrews was still hopefully awaiting Anglo-Saxon victory and maintaining her precarious and short-lived neutralism, a central protagonist in *The Three Things* could see the war as "civilization against barbarism! Gentlemen against Huns; Englishmen and Frenchmen whom we know to be straight and clean against—the unspeakable Germans! From the Kaiser down—seventy millions of canaille. . . ."[45] The increasingly abstract nature of war propaganda tended to submerge the individual—ally no less than enemy—beneath broader classifications of biological and cultural categorization.

But the views of wartime writers, the novelists of war sentiment, had been reinforced by respected men of science or belles-lettres. In Paris the Doctors Le Bon, Berillion, and others produced "scientific" papers defining the inherent racial degradation of the German mind; *Le Temps* revealed that Germans were possessed of a "sclerotic fascination which loves the agonized cries of little children," while from England G. K. Chesterton, reflecting both the imperatives of racial cause and the disgust evoked in the breast of a literary person by machine warfare, compared "German war" to "German eating and drinking." "Anyone who has been in a German restaurant during that mammoth midday meal which generally precedes a sleep akin to hibernation," he remarked, "will understand how that same barbarous solemnity has ruined all the real romance of war . . . butchering is not necessary for a good army any more than gobbling is necessary for a good dinner . . . it is possible to both fight and eat like a gentleman."[46]

The Entente opinion experts developed race propaganda to its highest extent; they distributed it more widely and wrote it more imaginatively than did their German counterparts, picturing the

[44] See Charles H. Shafer, "The Causes of War in American Popular and Professional Literature" (unpublished Ph.D. dissertation, University of Maryland, 1955).
[45] Mary Raymond Shipman Andrews, *The Three Things* (New York, 1915), p. 1.
[46] Quoted by Reade, *Atrocity Propaganda*, p. 17; see Raemaker, *Cartoons*, p. 22.

enemy as "inhuman fiends who had to be eliminated, like germs or monsters, from all influence on world affairs."[47] The pestilent muck heap of no man's land, John Hoag points out in *Word Warfare* (1939), "was the shallow veil between civilization and barbarism. Beyond that barrier lay territory where inhuman things occurred—where an implacable blood-stained tyranny reigned, where men of an almost simian savagery gloated over disgusting cruelties."[48] It was, indeed, a "propaganda of damnation," a total indictment in which clergymen, scientists, and literary gentlemen joined forces against "malign spirits steeped in depravity and lewdness."[49] We need not wonder that even so objective an observer as Hervey Allen regarded Germans as "the same Goths and Vandals who left their graves in Egypt, unchanged since the days of Rome, and still fighting her civilization. . . . Somehow everything German gave me the creeps. . . . It seemed then as if we were fighting some strange, ruthless insect-being from another planet; that we had stumbled upon their nests after smoking them out."[50] Ironically enough, the World War II weapon of genocide, raised officially to an ideal, was forged in the Entente rather than the German propaganda mills of the first conflict.

And so the rhetoric poured forth: "We are going to save civilization," the people were told, by means of a war—in Wilson's own words—against a "natural foe to human liberty." The United States government's wartime Committee of Public Information provided propaganda stimuli for motion picture screen, press, and pulpit. George Creel, chief of the committee and a public relations man prefiguring Dos Passos' Ward Moorehouse, was later to write a volume impressively titled *How We Advertised America* (1920). Certainly the job Creel did, along with Britain's Cecil Parker, was in many ways a pioneering effort; the two men, for example, virtually introduced the "PR packet"—a vividly written, ready-for-printing news package, complete with interviews, news accounts, features, photographs, and maps. But even before this country entered the war Parker's "news service" was especially welcomed by American editors; it was free, it was exciting, and it often carried exotic datelines.[51]

[47] Reade, *Atrocity Propaganda*, p. 17.
[48] John Hoag, *Word Warfare* (London, 1939), p. 14.
[49] Peterson, *Propaganda for War*, p. 67.
[50] Hervey Allen, *Toward the Flame* (New York, 1934), pp. 113, 115.
[51] As the Allied armies fell back during the early months of the war, U.S. newsmen "were naturally barred from reporting what was really going on. The atrocity story filled the void" (Millis, *Road to War*, p. 68).

One of the most successful cinema propaganda pieces (or, rather, declarations of war) in neutral America, was Commodore J. Stuart Blackton's *The Battle Cry of Peace*. The film was based on Hudson Maxim's *Defenseless America* (1915), a blood-curdling cry for the expansion of American armaments. Maxim, incidentally, was the brother of a major arms manufacturer who only a few years earlier had produced enormous quantities of guns, especially machine guns, for the Kaiser. At any rate the film, widely distributed early in 1916, "thrilled and horrified by its portrayal of an unprepared America overrun by the brutal and licentious soldiery of a foreign power which, although unnamed, uniformed its troops in a strangely close imitation of the Germans. Assisted by tons of smoke power and regiments of supers, Miss Norma Talmadge and Mr. Charles Richman personified the nation in an invasion more horrible—and more exciting—than anything depicted in the censored films of the real war in Europe."[52]

Preparedness was itself a cause. America was depicted as being in immediate danger of invasion by the Central Powers, despite the Entente's complete mastery of the seas. Respectable young ladies from Boston to Kansas City were both flattered and horrified to learn that they too might share the fate of helpless Belgian Womanhood, debauched by the insatiable Teutonic Rapist. "Without question," says Vane in Mary Raymond Shipman Andrews' *Old Glory* (1917), "there is no secret about the stretches of our shore which lie open to an invader":

"I'm going to throw every pound of power I have, body, brains, and substance, into the work of arousing and preparing my country so that she may be ready to meet—not England—God forbid!—but any power on earth. . . . I have a vision of my country"—his eyes gazed over the audience of hypnotized listeners, eyes dark and shining, yet keen—"as of a beautiful young mother going out in a gauzy costume into a hailstorm, confident and gay and foolish." He straightened, flashed about a glance like a blow. "Her sons will arm her and clothe her. They are to see to it. Now. Not later. One is not to risk—America."[53]

Supplemented by the British Bryce Report, which had been published in 1915 and utilized sex atrocity as a chief propaganda resource, the wartime Committee of Public Information hammered at public sensibilities until soldiers and civilians alike regarded

[52] Millis, *Road to War*, p. 217.
[53] Mary Raymond Shipman Andrews, *Old Glory* (New York, 1917), p. 62.

Christianity, sexual purity, and political freedom as interchangeable aspects of the Great Crusade. The postwar novelists, indeed, were to remember the defense of purity as perhaps the most effective cause of all; and if a soldier in Thomas Boyd's *Through the Wheat* (1923) cries for the blood of " 'the Huns that raped the Belgians, Huns that would have come over to the good old U.S.A. and raped our women if we hadn't gotten into the war,' "[54] his vehemence (and his preoccupation) is no more notable than that of the opinion experts themselves, or of wartime novelists like Arthur Train or Dorothy Canfield Fisher, for whom the defense of purity was outranked only by the defense of christianity as an emotional battle cry.

It was in connection with the Bryce Report that Creel almost outdid himself. The committee, determined to acquire scholarly evidence for its atrocity campaign, assigned Princeton Professor Dana Carleton Monroe to check the authenticity of the Bryce atrocities. Failing to uncover any usable evidence, the Professor was reprimanded by having his appointment abruptly cancelled. Similarly, a group of American newsmen (Harry Hansen, John T. McCutcheon, Roger Lewis, O'Donnell Bennet and Irvin Cobb) had earlier issued a joint cable to the Associated Press emphatically denying atrocity reports and news stories.[55] But nothing was to interfere with the committee's opinion warfare, and the mood of the United States, as Roland H. Bainton remarks in *Christian Attitudes Toward War and Peace* (1960), was hammered into "a blend of hysterical nationalism and crusading idealism. . . . The Lord God of Battles was rolling up the hosts of Armageddon to destroy the great beast of the abyss. . . ."[56] A young crusader in Dos Passos' *First Encounter* (1920) dramatizes something of this emotional climate: " 'If there are any left after the war they ought to be chloroformed. . . . The curse! the Huns! Oh, I don't see why they take any prisoners; I'd kill them all like mad dogs.' "[57] Such enthusiasm, certainly, had been growing not only among soldiers but among civilians as well, and the war rapidly took on all the trappings of a crusade against Moloch, the eater of children.

[54] Thomas Boyd, *Through the Wheat* (New York, 1923), p. 14.
[55] For text of this cable see Millis, *Road to War*, p. 217.
[56] Roland H. Bainton, *Christian Attitudes Toward War and Peace* (New York, 1960), p. 210.
[57] John Dos Passos, *First Encounter* (New York, 1945), p. 16. (The original U.S. edition was published in 1920 as *One Man's Initiation*.)

In addition to sermons, or sometimes along with them (notably in the case of the YMCA), men in the front lines were often fed a diet of atrocity stories and exhortations designed to eliminate any remnant of traditional military attitudes; studies of World War I propaganda emphasize the fact that dehumanization of the enemy in sexual, racial, and military terms was a basic purpose rather than an incidental result of the propaganda itself.[58] The postwar novelists were to offer sardonic and extensive recapitulation of the rhetoric hurled at troops by officers (usually with civilian backgrounds) or YMCA men. In *Mattock*, for example, an officer harangues his men before they go "over the top":

'Remember that the Boche is the worst devil ever let loose on the world! Remember the girls he raped and the babies he butchered in Belgium! Remember his submarines and his devilish slaughter of innocent women and children on peaceful ships! Remember the *Lusitania!* Remember his mutilation of captured American soldiers! Remember it all now . . . and imagine that you have the vile Boche, the worst criminal and coward in history, before your naked steel!'[59]

In Charles Yale Harrison's *Generals Die in Bed* (1930), an officer tells his troops that a hospital ship has just been sunk by German submarines and reminds them of their duty to " 'avenge the lives of our murdered comrades. An enemy like the German— no, I will not call him German—an enemy like the Hun does not merit humane treatment in war. . . . I'm not saying for you not to take prisoners. That's against international rules. All that I'm saying is that if you take any we'll have to feed them out of our own rations.' "[60] After this mixed exhortation the men begin a total slaughter. Harrison portrays a group of disarmed Germans, "mostly youngsters," who cower in a crater and attempt to surrender. They are slaughtered "like target practice"—and when the men discover that the hospital ship had been carrying more munitions than wounded and that the British had been warned repeatedly by the Germans, the reaction is guilt followed by anger, anger by the deepest cynicism, a pattern which indeed came to define much of the World War I literary protest; the emotional excitement of "Remember the *Lusitania!*" curdles into a skepticism no less extreme than the original propaganda cry. Fredenburgh's

[58] See Reade, Peterson, Abrams, Bainton, and Harold Lasswell, *Propaganda Technique in the World War* (New York, 1927).
[59] Stevens, *Mattock*, p. 96.
[60] Charles Yale Harrison, *Generals Die in Bed* (New York, 1930), p. 247.

Soldiers March! (1930) dramatizes something of this process; " 'Why, in the name of humanity, didn't the British prevent the Americans from sailing on the *Lusitania?*' " a soldier demands:

"The Germans gave public warning that it was a marked ship. Why didn't they? I'll tell you why. Because the sinking of a ship like the *Lusitania* was what they needed to get American men and money into the war. What a grand opportunity! . . . Murder a few hundred Americans and gain the support of the world's most powerful nation. In the hue and cry and bitter wrath at German inhumanity the sly cynics of Downing Street could raise their glasses and, tongue in cheek, give solemn thanks to God and Wilson that the depravity of Germany had at last been made manifest."[61]

The intensity with which the propaganda had been first accepted, however, was a vitally important factor in the subsequent revulsion against all verbalized value, what Frederick Hoffman notes as a "sharp distinction" in postwar literature "between words used vaguely to inspire or coerce and words used to designate objects, persons, and acts."[62] After World War II, the Korean conflict, and the continuing Cold War, the rhetoric of World War I may well seem transparent and cliché ridden. It is easy to underestimate the success this same propaganda enjoyed in shaping American attitudes from 1914 to 1918 and difficult to remember that such attitudes persisted among many civilians for years after the armistice, when writers like Willa Cather or Edith Wharton continued to regard the war experience either in the military context of the Alamo, or in terms of a struggle against racial and moral vulgarity. Miss Wharton, indeed, in 1923 still earnestly waved the banner of the *Lusitania*: "Now indeed America was in it," she writes in *A Son at the Front;* "the gross tangible proof for which her government had forced her to wait was there in all its unimagined horror. Cant and Cowardice in high places had drugged and stupefied her into the strange belief that she was too proud to fight for others; and here she was brutally forced to fight for herself."[63]

On one hand Europe—the war itself—was seen as a picture postcard affair with quaint peasantry and clear-faced, bold Allied soldiers; on the other there was the Teutonic Beast. Many historians have remarked upon this country's general naïveté as to what the political structure of Europe actually represented; Peterson

[61] Theodore Fredenburgh, *Soldiers March!* (New York, 1930), p. 30.
[62] Hoffman, *The Twenties*, p. 54.
[63] Edith Wharton, *A Son at the Front* (New York, 1923), p. 255.

and—more recently—Charles A. Fenton emphasize the equally naïve Anglophilism and Francophilism among the literary or leisured gentility of America.[64] In his introduction to *The Full Measure of Devotion*, for example, a sentimental wartime novella by Dana Gitlin published in 1918, *McClure's* editor Charles Hanson Towne hails the book as "one of the few stories to live forever," pontificates on "the beauty and grandeur of this war," and regurgitates not only the usual atrocity verbiage, but the nobilities of Lafayette and "French Motherhood" as well. As late as 1922 the energetic Miss Andrews was still gushing over the Crusade in all its glories of purity, sacrifice, and Sunday-school pageantry: " 'If war comes I want you to be the first to go,' " says the dearest woman in Jimmie's life, who—inevitably—is his mother; " 'I couldn't bear it if you weren't fighting.' All over America boys' mothers were saying such words. Perhaps it was one reason that America's four million soldiers were known as a singing army."[65]

The novelists of protest were to remember the naïveté, the emotion, and the pageantry; and Fuselli's daydream in *Three Soldiers* (after a propaganda film) combines all three elements:

He was in a place like the Exposition ground, full of old men and women in peasant costumes, like the song 'When it's Apple Blossom Time in Normandy.' Men in spiked helmets who looked like firemen kept charging through, like the Ku Klux Klan in the movies, jumping from their horses and setting fire to buildings with strange outlandish gestures, spitting babies on their long swords. These were the Huns. Then there were flags blowing very hard in the wind, and the sound of a band. The Yanks were coming. Everything was lost in a scene from a movie in which khaki-clad regiments marched.[66]

It had indeed been a strangely theatrical crusade. Villains were horrible and victims were pitiful, while Americans were pictured by wartime clergymen and novelists alike as antiseptic adolescents untouched by battle and polite to women, Boy Scouts doing their good deeds on a global scale. The pastel unreality of the fiction and propaganda produced during the war must be understood as a central factor in the later impact of the war's realities. Certainly much of the fiction portrayed army life with little more depth than did the recruiting poster. Willa Cather's *One of Ours*, for

[64] Fenton, "A Literary Fracture of World War I."
[65] Mary Raymond Shipman Andrews, *His Soul Goes Marching On* (New York, 1922), p. 36.
[66] Dos Passos, *Three Soldiers*, p. 37.

example, while published after the armistice and in many ways superior to the work of "belligerent women on the home front," nevertheless is often typical of wartime writing—of the books of Temple Bailey, Ida Alena Ross Wylie, Mary Raymond Shipman Andrews, and a host of others.[67] The rhetoric of the Crusade did not end with the signing of the armistice—a fact which may help explain the violence of those novels written by young men who had been overseas.

One of Ours, which received the Pulitzer Prize for 1922, is effective only when Miss Cather limits herself to the subject she knew so well: the dead weight of midwestern farm and town life upon a young person of sensitivity and intelligence. Claude, her central figure, embraces the "opportunity" for war largely as a means of escaping from the strait jacket of his environment. This was a common motivation not only for Americans during the Crusade as it had rapidly built up after 1915, but also for the protagonists of postwar realistic novels; the heroes of Dos Passos, Fredenburgh, Boyd, or Paul initially welcome war, or at the very least accept it, as a bold new direction to their lives.

Once the action of the book leaves the midwestern town for the army, however, Miss Cather falls back upon the stereotypes of war rhetoric, the picture of clean-cut American boys marching to save the world. There is the Colonel with "little twinkling eyes and a good natured face . . . without a particle of arrogance or official dignity." There is the soldier dying "in perfect dignity . . . a brave boy giving what was not his to keep." There is the perception of the war as a great parade in which young men prove themselves to their own glory and the glory of their country: "Wooden ships! When great passions and great aspirations stirred a country, shapes like these formed along its shores to be the sheath of its valour. . . . They were the very impulse, they were the potential act, they were the 'drawn arrow, the great, unuttered cry,' they were Fate, they were Tomorrow!"[68]

The book is especially notable for the manner in which Willa Cather presents the American soldier as a good-natured hired hand, whose pre-eminent quality—whether in ship, battlefront, or army camp—is a pleasant mien and thoroughgoing willingness to do all assigned chores:

[67] See "Reading and Fighting," unsigned editorial, *Saturday Review of Literature,* VI (April 12, 1930), 918.
[68] Willa Cather, *One of Ours* (New York, 1922), p. 268.

They all came to give and not to ask, and what they offered was just themselves; their big red hands, their strong backs, the steady, honest, modest look in their eyes. Sometimes, when he had helped the medical examiner, Claude had noticed the anxious expression in the long lines of waiting men. They seemed to say, "If I'm good enough, take me. I'll stand by." He found them like that to work with; serviceable, good-natured, and eager to learn.[69]

Throughout the book Miss Cather introduces unnamed individuals who *look* at Claude or the brave boys. Adopting the point of view of such an individual to alleviate the burden of rhetoric she places on her narrative, Miss Cather can render a highly inspirational account of scenes such as this embarkation of troops:

A Staten Island ferry-boat passed close under the bow of the transport. The passengers were office-going people, on their way to work, and when they looked up and saw these hundreds of faces, all young, all bronzed and grinning, they began to shout and wave their handkerchiefs. One of the passengers was an old clergyman, a famous speaker in his day, now retired, who went over to the city every morning to write editorials for a church paper. He closed the book he was reading, stood by the rail, and taking off his hat began solemnly to quote from a poet who in his time was still popular. "Sail on," he quavered,

"Thou too, sail on, O Ship of State,
Humanity, with all its fears,
With all its hopes of future years,
Is hanging breathless on thy fate!"

As the troop ship glided across the sea lane, the old man still watched it from the turtleback. That howling swarm of brown arms and hats and faces looked like nothing but a crowd of American boys going to a football game somewhere. But the scene was ageless; youths were sailing away to die for an idea. . . .[70]

It was not only the idealization of the Crusade that Miss Cather and the sentimental novelists presented. The men themselves were pictured as boys who "detested the idea of trifling" with their sexual impulses, as an army of virgins setting out to purify the continent while saving it from the Hun. To be sure, there is the American who pilots for the British and spends weekends with loose women, but he is estranged from the American conscience and therefore set apart. Claude and the "boys" in his company are forever fresh faced, ruddy, and preferably Nordic. And in the trenches they think as well as speak rhetorically: "Claude's appear-

[69] *Ibid.*, p. 248.
[70] *Ibid.*, p. 273.

ance on the parapet had attracted no attention from the enemy at first, but now the bullets began popping about him; two rattled on his tin hat, one caught him on the shoulder. The blood dripped down his coat, but he felt no weakness. He felt only one thing; that he commanded wonderful men. . . . They were to stay until they were carried out to be buried. They were mortal, but unconquerable."[71] The quotation speaks eloquently for itself; there would, certainly, be a great deal to protest.

Another characteristic of sentimental fiction produced during or immediately after the war was the spectatorial attitude. This is not to be confused with the attitude which, as Malcolm Cowley points out, was the result of the alienation of the fighting man from his cause, a noninvolvement and revulsion to be seen in Hemingway's Frederic Henry, Dos Passos' Andrews, or in its extreme form, in the walking death of Boyd's Hicks and Faulkner's Mahon. For novelists like Miss Cather, who in *One of Ours* exploited the vein of military sentiment already exploited by others, including such writers as Samuel H. Adams, Arthur Guy Empey, Ruth Dunbar, and Credo F. Harris, the war *was* spectacle; it was authentically stirring, replete with trumpets, "dignified death," the red badge of courage, cheering populations, and bronzed warriors of tomorrow.[72] Such writers not only looked at the war, but looked at it as if it were taking place on a motion picture set; their attitude reflected the general naïveté in this country concerning both the realities of technological warfare and the role that American troops would actually fulfill. "Common opinion held it that the American force was to be sent to France chiefly for the purpose of parade," Paxon notes;[73] even as far back as 1914 so eminent a figure as Edward D. White, Chief Justice of the Supreme Court, had exchanged judicial calm for a public flush of war enthusiasm, ardently wishing "that he could be young again so he could go to Canada and volunteer."[74]

[71] *Ibid.*, p. 453.
[72] From the start of hostilities war books by English writers were eagerly contracted by American publishers. Writers like Coningsby Dawson, Rev. W. H. Leathem, Beatrice Harraden, William J. Locke, and others dramatized the Entente position in novels, memoirs, and monographs; their work, no less than books by American writers, helped shape the literary environment both before America's entry into the war and during the Crusade itself.
[73] Paxon, "America at War," *American Democracy and the World War*, II, 10. The nature and fate of such expectation is discussed more fully in Chapter II of this study.
[74] Quoted by Tansill, *America Goes to War*, p. 24.

It was the fife and drum of the local military exercise rather than the filth of no man's land which captured and delighted American imaginations; so difficult, indeed, was it for Americans to grasp the nature of machine combat and mass transportation that the earlier attitudes persisted long after the armistice. Even in 1922 Miss Cather could write: "The Americans went through every village with march step, colours flying, bands playing. . . ." This is much the same vision as Fuselli's daydream, but with one vital difference: where the naïveté in *Three Soldiers* represents dramatic irony, the naïveté in *One of Ours* represents Miss Cather herself:

they were bound for the big show, and on every hand there were reassuring signs: long lines of gaunt, dead trees, charred and torn . . .
"Begins to look like we're getting in, Lieutenant," said Sergeant Hills, smiling behind his salute.
Claude nodded, and passed forward.
"Well, we can't arrive any too soon for us, boys?" The sergeant looked over his shoulder and they grinned, their teeth showing white in their red, perspiring faces. Claude . . . thought they were the finest sight in the world.[75]

The sentiment will strike the modern reader as obvious; it is hardly necessary to belabor the point. It is, however, necessary to emphasize that during and immediately following World War I such sentimentality was not always calculated or dishonest. Romance was widely taken for reality, a fact which profoundly influenced the novels of protest written by young men whose own romantic expectations had been clawed away in a broken world of actual experience. The producers of literary sentimentality were themselves products of older, more sentimental concepts of war, and their work must be understood clearly—perhaps even harshly—if we are to understand the mental framework of disgust and mockery from which young writers created their testaments of disillusion. And the very fact that war sentiment had been characteristic of literature, that it continued after the armistice, helps account for the fact that the protest itself so electrified American readers. Only after World War II could realistic war fiction be taken in stride by a public long since educated to the nature of technological combat, a public for which technology, political ambiguity, licentiousness, and mass suffering had been newspaper copy for decades.

[75] Cather, *One of Ours*, p. 358.

An innocent public at the time of World War I, to be sure, offered a rich ground for propaganda, and the British, almost with the outbreak of hostilities, mobilized the publishing industry as they had already mobilized the press. "The Allied propaganda . . . enjoyed the inestimable advantage of being self-financing," Walter Millis remarks. "Our public clamoured for the books, articles, and motion-picture films which conveyed it. Old established American publishing houses found it profitable, and did not think it unpatriotic, to enter into agreements with the Entente governments for the distribution of propagandist war books, and there was a huge trade in volumes on French life from the French and British standpoint." Commenting on the wartime book trade Archibald G. Ogden, in *Publishers' Weekly*, notes that "England was flooding this country with propaganda of all sorts and making it ridiculously easy (and profitable) to import such titles as 'Life in a German Crack Regiment,' by Baron von Schlicht, 'Germany's War Mania,' by Sir George Forrest, and 'I Accuse,' by Dr. Richard Crelling. . . . [Book] imports rose tremendously during the last six months of 1914. . . . During 1914 and 1915 there was great demand for history books dealing with the war, and England was turning them out as fast as they could be printed."[76] The Entente actually proved far more progressive in this respect than did the Germans, who in addition to suffering considerable disadvantage because of the Anglophilism of American publishers, simply failed to realize that mass communications media—including fiction— could play a vital role in shaping American attitudes toward war and European involvement. The success of scientifically organized Allied propaganda in the United States, which helped create much of the subsequent opposition to political and aesthetic rhetoric, was certainly not matched by German efforts.

Whether directed at the United States or at home-front populations, German propaganda lacked both the scope and imaginative urgency of the Entente program. One might note that, unlike their American and British counterparts, German postwar writers attacked propaganda as a weapon developed largely by the other

[76] Millis, *Road to War*, p. 202. Archibald G. Ogden, "The Book Trade in War Time," *Publishers' Weekly*, XXXVI (July 8, 1939), 96. Peterson notes that of the two million books and articles on war causes, "guilt," and atrocities, an overwhelming number was produced by the Entente. In the United States, he adds, the "veritable flood" of this literature reached "unbelievable proportions"—nearly all of which "presented the British point of view" (*Propaganda*, p. 49).

side.[77] There was, even among German novelists of war protest, no revulsion against rhetoric as such; there was no disgusted sense of betrayal, of being "sold out" by large-scale abstractionism manipulated on a broad cultural canvas. For this reason the major German novelists dealing with the war experience could and did utilize rhetoric, even anti-war rhetoric. Major American works of the twenties and thirties, on the other hand, written by men who remembered a literary establishment captured and debased by a vast propaganda system, tended toward the obliteration—through formal structure no less than philosophical emphasis—of any rhetorical statement whatever, including the statement of disillusion.

Under the direction of Sir Gilbert Parker the British had drawn up a program for the publishing industry which for the time was vast indeed. Parker's appropriation in 1914 was the sum of one million dollars; the program was so successful that his budget was increased to four million dollars by 1917. Writers for Parker's office included such famous names as G. K. Chesterton, Conan Doyle, E. J. Trevelyan, Mrs. Humphrey Ward, Alfred Noyes, Cardinal Mercier, and Hilaire Belloc. A special committee was formed to prime the American literary pump, and authors like J. M. Barrie and John Masefield were sent to the United States "to meet the people, especially those connected with universities, and explain the British case."[78] Contrasting "our Anglo-American heritage" with Teutonic barbarism, using Shakespeare as a cultural-linguistic rallying cry, drawing heavily upon the Bryce Report and the work of scientists to prove that the Germans were "degenerates, brutes, baby-killers, and Anti-Christs," such emissaries of civilization found a ready market for their wares.[79]

Their task was made easier by the fact that in the United States "the men of letters . . . were hungry for drums and rhetoric." All of the allegiances of the belles-lettres group were toward England and France, Mr. Fenton notes; and many men of culture went so far as to denounce German art as intrinsically and necessarily "alien."[80] Among war enthusiasts a vehement but by no

[77] See Helen Istas, "French and German Attitudes to the First World War As Reflected in Novels and Memoirs" (unpublished Ph.D. dissertation, Indiana University, 1951).
[78] Millis, Road to War, p. 29.
[79] Burton Rascoe, "What They Read during the Last War," Saturday Review of Literature, XX (September 23, 1939), 3.
[80] Fenton, "A Literary Fracture of World War I," p. 124.

means unrepresentative example was Thomas Sergeant Perry, the Boston littérateur, who "like so many American men of letters during World War I had become almost as demented as his abolitionist ancestors."[81] From the start of hostilities, what passed as the literary establishment of the United States left no doubt as to the nature of its enthusiasm. The National Institute and American Academy met in joint session on November 19, 1914: "On a stage fringed with garlands of laurel and balanced at either side of a green bay tree, they applauded each indictment of Teuton barbarism."[82]

Although the lecture tours he arranged with the co-operation of Anglophile elements within the United States were enormously effective, Parker's chief area of operations remained the printed page. A good example of one of his more successful efforts is the collected edition of Louis Raemaker's cartoons (1917). In addition to Raemaker's own illustration of German bestiality, there are texts by Chesterton, Belloc, and many other respected personages, including clergymen, lawyers, and scientists. Perhaps the most memorable—and pathetic—selections are those written by the literary men like Belloc, who from a sort of medievalism and equally obsolete romanticism, blamed the Germans for ending the image of war as a recreation for gentlemen:

The feature that will stamp Prussian war forever . . . is the *character* of its murder and pillage.

Of all the historical ignorance upon which the foolish pacifist's case is founded, perhaps the worst is the conception that these abominations are the natural accompaniment of war. They *have* attached to war when war was ill-organized in type. But the more subject to rule it has become, the more men have gloried in arms, the more they have believed the high trade of soldier to be a pride, the more they have eliminated the pillage of the civilian and the slaughter of the innocent from its actions. Those things belonged to violent passions and lack of reason. Modern war and the chivalric tradition scorned them.

The edges of the Germanies have, in the past, been touched by the chivalric tradition: Prussia never. That noblest inheritance of Christendom never reached so far out into the wilds. And to Germany . . . soldier is no high thing, nor is there any meaning attached to the word "glorious." War is for that nation a business. . . .[83]

---

[81] *Ibid.*, p. 123.
[82] *Ibid.*, p. 121.
[83] Raemaker, *Cartoons*, p. 18.

Belloc's statement is a virtual checklist of prevailing attitudes toward warfare, toward the Hun, and toward machine war (the impact of which on such a sensibility necessarily involved horror and hate). There is special irony in Belloc's mention of "civilians"—it was, again, the British who formulated the concept of "belligerent populations" as a legal justification for total blockade. And perhaps the crowning absurdity in this particular volume, and most telling comment upon American neutrality, is Prime Minister Asquith's dedication: "Mr. Raemaker's work gives form and colour to the menace which the Allies are averting from the liberty, the civilization, and the humanity of the future. He shows us our enemies as they appear to the unbiased eyes of a neutral."

For many postwar novelists of disillusion the warfare of the printed page was a special source of irritation. Bayard Schindel, for example, in *The Golden Pilgrimage* (1929), relates how the son of a professional army officer comes to despise the new war of machines and hysteria, a war in which the resources of literature have been debased into propaganda and used as weapons:

Brentano's . . . was filling up with books which were supposed to portray the German occupation of Belgium and France. The books bore fantastic titles: *The Blonde Beast, The Hun Conqueror, The British Black Eagle*. There was one in particular which seemed to Peter an instance of treachery to the gentleman's profession of arms. On the jacket was a picture of a woman sitting up in bed, while a German officer, with a twisted and sneering face, leaned over the foot of the bed and smiled dreadfully. . . . Gentlemen fought with each other and did not do this woman's trick of talking behind backs.[84]

But "talking behind backs" with a fascinating blend of sentiment and shrillness had been a pre-eminent quality both of wartime fiction and of books produced during the brief period after the armistice when writers whose emotions had not been tested by war experience could still regard the Crusade as a triumph rather than a catastrophe. In *Home Fires in France* (1917) Dorothy Canfield Fisher dramatizes almost *in toto* the catalogue of Bryce atrocities: Germans destroy villages as a sort of recreation, rape women (preferably fair-haired young mothers) as a matter of policy, and rob churches as a matter of course. And to make possible a maximum communication with her audience, Miss Fisher draws upon the Christian suffering of such a book as *Uncle Tom's Cabin:* " 'Why Auntie, this might have been written about us, mightn't

[84] Bayard Schindel, *The Golden Pilgrimage* (New York, 1929), p. 54.

it?' " says a young French girl sighing over the Stowe classic. " 'It tells about things that happen to us all the time—that we have seen. The men who are flogged and starved and killed, the mothers trying in vain to follow their daughters into captivity, the young girls dragged out of their fathers' arms—it's all just like what the Germans do to us, isn't it?' "[85]

The Teutonic Beast, however, was not a target merely as a soldier. The German-American community came in for its share of literary attention. In E. Phillips Oppenheim's *Pawn's Count* (1917), for example, written before America's official entry into the war, Pamela Van Teyl, the all-American girl, exercises a delicious indignation over German sex atrocities; heaps scorn upon all who prefer desk work to fighting; waxes highly emotional on the subject of Anglo-American culture; denounces German-Americans who, from misplaced racial loyalty, refuse to see the Entente as Guardians of Civilization; and emerges, in all her glory, as a fictional counterpart of those "belligerent women" whom later novelists were to remember with such cynicism.[86]

Another and perhaps more striking example of the manner in which propaganda fiction—even after the Armistice—dealt with the Teutonic danger on the home front is the work of a very popular novelist—Samuel H. Adams. Mr. Adams' *Common Cause* (1919) is remarkable not only for its patriotic solemnity, but for its sustained hysteria. An exposé of "Deutschtum" in America, the book tells the story of a German-American community in Fenchester, a city in the midwestern state of Centralia. During the course of the book the German-Americans are finally convinced that everything pertaining to Germany (including the language) is a product of the "mad wolf." Those who are not altogether convinced, who persist in reading German-language newspapers or wondering vocally if the war is really necessary, are squelched by various political or economic pressures. The book is especially notable as one of the first novels to absorb the ideological policeman as hero, the quiet-voiced Secret Service man who goes about warning people to "talk American." And when the crescendo is reached:

Through the murk and fumes of alien treachery, enemy propaganda, and the reckless self-seeking of petty partisanship, had burst a clear,

---

[85] Dorothy Canfield Fisher, *Home Fires in France* (New York, 1917), p. 129.
[86] Pamela Van Teyl ("I am for America first, America only, America always.") is more than vicariously belligerent; triumphing over Teuton traitors and Negroid spies, she becomes a sort of racist supergirl.

high, consuming flame of Americanism . . . Centralia, 30 years before marked by Deutschtum to be the Little Germany of the New World, was slowly, doggedly establishing its birthright of Americanism.

But poison still lurked in its system. There were whisperings in dark corners. The German-language press still gave heart-service to the Kaiser . . . the German pulpit, preaching an eradicable Germanism by the very use of the German tongue. . . .[87]

Whether directed against "Deutschtum" at home or Teutonic depravity abroad, a large quantity of such fiction was written and read for indictment and inspiration.[88] Like some novels of present-day ideological contexts, the books reflected horror upon a specific target and reduced tragedy to a single cause. In this manner the most soul-shattering events—the ravaging of women or desecration of churches—gave, in their own way, considerable comfort: above all, they gave reassurance that the reader was hating the right people. Propaganda novels now, however, must take into account a vast increase in political and ideological sophistication on the part of the reading audience. For this reason there is some control of rhetoric, and at the very least, a posture of objectivity—of dealing with the complexities of motivation and situation. Simple epithets no longer possess the efficacy they did during the first war; they have been used too often.

During the first war, however, the epithets worked. For the American audience (as well as for many American writers), emerging suddenly from provincialism to the complexities of world power and mass warfare, "there was vast ignorance . . . as to the background of the context and the diplomatic history which preceded the call to arms."[89] In literature the patriotic poster novels preceded and helped provoke the subsequent reaction; the scream of "Hun!" which had captured so many imaginations during the

[87] Samuel H. Adams, *Common Cause* (Boston, 1919), p. 462.
[88] The postwar novelists were to remember such agitation as one of the least palatable aspects of the Crusade. Edward Harris Heth's *Told With a Drum* (Boston, 1937), for example, is a rather moving account of a German-American patriarch who looks upon the war as a *Beleidigung*, a nightmare. Grasping at the false straw of American neutrality and hoping desperately for an early armistice, he is at first outraged and then ruined by the propaganda hurled at his neighbors through every means of public communication. Even with a book like *S.O.S.* (Indianapolis, 1928), a novel of war acquiescence rather than protest, John D. Whiting notes the rapid growth of home-front hysteria from 1915 onward, a hysteria in which German-Americans came to be viewed as "callous creatures" whose "treachery" was not merely political, but cultural and racial.
[89] Amy Loveman, "Then and Now," *Saturday Review of Literature*, XXII (September 7, 1940), 8.

war was afterward followed by protest and exposé. "Gifted writers such as Edith Wharton and Dorothy Canfield Fisher," George Snell remarks, "can, in time of war, produce novels glorifying destruction. The air is electric with false shibboleths; a mind-cast is prevalent that distorts our view of reality. And when the war is ended, the illusions of a frenetic time seem to be the result of betrayal. Then we have fiction which condemns the attitudes previously extolled and reflects hostility to all idealism."[90]

The "idealism," in fiction no less than in other areas, did not concern itself simply with political or national cause. Blood became a reason unto itself, the proof of racial superiority, purge for decadence, and sign of moral health. Writers like Arthur Train or Arthur Guy Empey, with their celebration of unselfish death as a means of physical and spiritual purification, could be more than matched by a literary gentlewoman like Edith Wharton, who in 1923 was still proclaiming that "the great turning points in progress" had been created by blood, and that "the efficacy of the sacrifice" depended upon "the worth [and quantity] of the victims."[91] Certainly such war enthusiasm played a vital role in shaping postwar disillusion; if there was an unusually sharp break between the older writers and the younger, one reason was "the extraordinary willingness of the older writers to lend their prestige and talent to the most bloodthirsty aspects of the war"—a willingness which repelled those who had seen the futile butchery for themselves. "In the case of World War I," Mr. Fenton remarks, "the war itself becomes a genuine dividing line between the literary generations."[92]

The hostility to idealism in the years following the war produced or accentuated a flight from all abstraction, evidenced, for example, in the dictum of Hemingway—and Pound—that the object, the thing, the experience-in-itself, stated boldly and without rhetorical flourish, would recreate truth to an extent far beyond even the idealism and abstraction of protest. Hemingway's insistence upon the tangible and single proved self-limiting in his attempts to explore interpersonal drama. But there is a close relationship between Hemingway's cinematic tautness and Pound's ideogram, and a direct line leads from both to the reaction against World War I abstraction and sentiment. Dos Passos' objective withdrawal of self

[90] George Snell, *The Shapers of American Fiction* (New York, 1947), p. 307.
[91] Edith Wharton, *A Son at the Front*, p. 255.
[92] Fenton, "A Literary Fracture of World War I," p. 119.

in his later, collectivist novels also belongs in this pattern, as does the cross-sectional technique of the French *roman-fleuve*.

It must be emphasized that not all the propaganda literature of World War I was produced cynically, simply as a good thing for a ready-made market. Although Grub Street was feeding well and richly on the national emergency, there were sincere writers, editors, critics, and scholars for whom the involvement in wartime hysteria was completely authentic. If their naïveté was profound, it nevertheless produced vivid results. Whether they possessed the literary American's awe of Paris and horror at the thought of its destruction (and the new weapons seemed to make that possible for the first time in a thousand years); whether their emotional associations with England ruled out rationality; or whether the lurid news dispatches and the Bryce Report took root in sensibility, they contributed to a spate of novels which substituted categorization for analysis, and, at the lowest level, used the war to provide the simplest progression of plot continuity.

One might hardly expect a novelist like Edith Wharton to succumb to the temptation of writing this kind of fiction. With *The Marne*, however, published in 1918, Miss Wharton combined gentility with bloodthirst, the mannerisms of the social novelist with the matter of a recruiting poster. Troy Belknap, a slender, rather pale young man who spends much of his childhood in France, simply lives for the day when he will be able to take his place among "scenes of anguish and heroism . . . a name of glory and woe was attached to every copse and hollow."[93]

As Troy waits impatiently to become old enough to enter the fray, he discusses and defends his ambitions in earnest conversations with a young lady who doubts the moral and political justification of war. The method is reminiscent of James's use of the confidante, except that here the passages are less conversations than exercises in rhetoric. As in most novels of propaganda, one argument—Troy's—wins because the reader agrees with his premises; the key of hate is provided through regularly recurring phrases such as *"Lusitania," "La Belle France,"* and *"Glory."* Finally even the gesture of analysis ends, stopped by a simple proclamation that antiwar sentiment is nothing more than a rationalization for cowardice, for materialism and selfishness: "Troy . . . perceived with disgust and wonder that at the bottom of the anti-war sentiment, whatever specious impartiality it put

[93] Edith Wharton, *The Marne* (New York, 1918), p. 27.

on, there was always the odd belief that life-in-itself—just the mere raw fact of being alive—was the one thing that mattered and getting killed the one thing to be avoided. . . . This new standard of human dignity disgusted him. . . ."[94]

Like Temple Bailey or Mary Raymond Shipman Andrews, Miss Wharton saw American troops as Boy Scouts out on a field trip, serious about killing Germans, gay among themselves, polite to women, and giving their lives as a sort of good deed for the day, with the merit badge of "Glory" for their reward. "They wanted to kill Germans, all right, but hanging around Paris wasn't what they'd bargained for." And in the rear areas: ". . . everybody was smoking and talking . . . young women in trim uniforms with fresh innocent faces moved among the barrels and boxes, distributing stamps or books, chatting with the soldiers and being generally home-like and sisterly. The men gave them back glances as honest and almost as innocent."[95]

It would be simple to dismiss such fiction as unimportant. The significance of *The Marne*, however, is that a novelist of Miss Wharton's stature cannot be dismissed. If she exhibited provincialism and sentimentality toward the war, it was because provincialism and sentimentality were basic characteristics of the American journey into battle. This journey, furthermore, was shaped by a pre-existing national attitude toward the glories of war. Certainly enormous quantities of literature from the Spanish-American War to World War I imaged "the soldier-American, heaven-blessed . . . bearing his burdens aggressively, asserting his conviction of his superiority, and citing freedom, inalienable rights, the American Eagle, the Fourth of July, the Star-Spangled Banner as symbols of a tradition qualifying him to march forward as Palladium of the liberties of less fortunate peoples of the world."[96]

Only as part of such a framework may readers come to understand the basis of Miss Wharton's rhetoric: "America tore the gag of neutrality from her lips, and with all the strength of her liberated lungs, claimed her right to a place in the struggle. The pacifists crept back into their holes. . . ." "The faces leaning from the window of the train glowed with youthful resolution. . . . As

[94] *Ibid.*, p. 43.
[95] *Ibid.*, p. 92.
[96] Frank T. Phipps, "The Image of War in America, 1891–1917" (unpublished Ph.D. dissertation, Ohio State University, 1953), *Dissertation Abstracts*, XX, 2298.

Troy looked down at them, so alike and so innumerable, he had a sense of a force inexorable and exhaustless, poured forth from the reservoirs of the new world to replenish the wasted veins of the old."[97] After the revolution-in-morals of the 1920's, it is not always easy to remember that the soldiers setting out in 1917 were leaving what was an essentially puritan, Victorian society, modified by frontier-developed emphasis on the virtues of righteous struggle, for a world in which every standard seemed torn apart.

Many of the later antiwar novels were written with an inverse lack of reality. The direction was different, but the quality of the work was no higher. While novelists such as Dos Passos (in *First Encounter* and *Three Soldiers*) and Stallings used elaborate rhetoric, they managed to produce a realistic examination of war and postwar experiences.[98] During the 1920's and 1930's, however, writers like Hector Lazo viewed the war with no more depth than did Miss Wharton, although the cause had changed: the national mood had shifted from war enthusiasm to war disgust.

In Lazo's book, *Taps* (1934), a college student named Gordon Mason becomes a leader in welcoming the war, calling for his class to enlist together: "War! A glorious chance for the newest nation to show the world the practical vision that made this nation great, a glorious chance to right the wrongs of the world—to reestablish the rights of the meek and the humble—to save humanity from the hands of militarism gone mad!"[99] Gordon, however, is called upon to sacrifice his reputation by becoming a Secret Service agent, posing as a pacifist while spying upon "Conchies" and Socialists. As a result of this mission he is disowned by his heartbroken father and despised by the girl he loves. During the course of his work, however, he finds that the pacifists and Socialists he has been spying upon are fine human beings, and after an impassioned two-page discussion with a disillusioned classmate who had already seen battle, he embraces the pacifist cause.

Gordon had been captain of his college debating team; with a certain amount of narrative logic he proceeds to make literate and effective antiwar speeches. But the Secret Service is still under the impression that he is carrying out his assignment, and the

[97] Edith Wharton, *The Marne*, pp. 45, 79.
[98] Although Stallings' novel, *Plumes* (New York, 1924), is overshadowed by his more famous dramatic work, it is an interesting study of the plight of a returning war veteran (or rather, war victim).
[99] Hector Lazo, *Taps* (Boston, 1934), p. 19.

final irony occurs after the boy dies of influenza while aiding soldiers during an epidemic. Decorated as a war hero by the government he disowned, Gordon is honored in the name of a cause he rejected. And at his funeral, crowded with relatives and military officers,

Fate—the Inexorable—smiled as the procession reached the cemetery, lifted her finger and with that signal blew ten thousand more men upon the blood-soaked battlefield. Then she turned her gaze once more upon the flag-draped casket and hissed:

"*Sic Transit Gloria Mundi.*"[100]

Like the press and pulpit, American literature during World War I had been placed at the service of the propaganda machine, and the willing assent of older writers to such indentured service helped shape postwar disillusion in two directions: a rhetorical protest by young men who utilized their war experience as material for fiction, and a form of antiwar propaganda no less absurd than the pseudo-literature of the Crusade itself. Ultimately reaction struck at both. A movement of counter-rhetoric developed during the twenties and early thirties, bringing into articulate focus the general cynicism represented by the work of Elliot Paul, the anesthetized "I" of Hemingway's heroes, and the broad, objective, scientific noninvolvement of Dos Passos' collectivist novels. For the most serious craftsmen, value inflated by rhetoric was suspect, whether it celebrated or protested against the glory of democracy at war.[101]

All the brave young men

Propaganda—the rhetoric of atrocities, of religious cause, of race hate, and of glory-through-battle—was only a single factor in the bold journey which was to stall and turn back in mud and blood. Propaganda was a stimulant, but young men at the time of World War I were often looking for a stimulant and were bored for lack of it. Their idealism was real enough, whether or

---

[100] *Ibid.*, p. 145.

[101] See the MacLeish-Cowley debate on war literature in the *New Republic* (September 20, October 4, 1933) and Kenneth Burke's intriguing suggestion in his *The Philosophy of Literary Form* (New York, 1947) that antiwar rhetoric actually may have stimulated rather than inhibited willingness to fight.

not provoked by opinion campaigns; but the idealism of war was embraced all the more enthusiastically because it sanctioned a release from a world increasingly set and materialistic. And novelists of the next decade recalled and recreated the quality of this idealism. Jerry Towers, for example, in Larry Baretto's *Horses in the Sky* (1929), welcomes war as a glorious release from a small-town banking future; Richard Plume in Stallings' novel seizes upon it as an escape from a small, sectarian college environment; Willa Cather's Claude is motivated by a combination of erotic frustration and material boredom; Dos Passos' Andrews is typical of the young aesthete embracing a cause as a means of obtaining some concrete direction to his life, even to his death.

In *The End of American Innocence* Henry F. May points out that while "the first world war was, clearly, an enormous experience for the peaceful and optimistic country," during the years preceding the war there were numerous cracks in the "official surface" of "intolerable placidity and complacency."[102] This is an important insight, for there can be no doubt that new currents in art, philosophy, economics, and politics were already in evidence before the impact of World War I speeded up the process of change. The war, however, was seized upon by precisely those elements most disaffected with their time—it was taken, indeed, as a means for escaping materialism, for achieving personal nobility and social mobility, for carrying the banner of disinterested justice, for "living life to the hilt." All these hopes were reduced to ashes in the savage absurdity of the war. Mr. May correctly indicates that America's loss of "innocence" was, even if World War I had never occurred, inevitable; that so many Americans innocently embraced battle as an antidote for their dissatisfactions, however, accounts for much of the shattering impact of the war itself. Far from being a corrective for, the war was discovered to be an excrescence of, hypocritical values and a tragically flawed society. This was the final—and unforgivable—disillusion. And it was this disillusion which brought new pressures on what Mr. May calls "cracks in the surface" of an American culture still (he grants) very much nineteenth-century. The cracks, in other words, were there; but only the intense pressure of war—or rather, of its failure—brought the walls tumbling down.[103]

[102] Henry F. May, *The End of American Innocence* (New York, 1959), p. x.
[103] Mr. May takes careful note of the enormous distance separating the prewar avant-garde from the postwar movement: "In the new, more complex, and less cheerful climate of post-war dissent, nearly all the chief leaders of the pre-war movement found themselves feeling strange and uprooted" (p. 396).

In the better liberal arts colleges young men were going through the process Maurice Barrés calls *deracination*—alienation from a society for which their education rendered them useless, at least until the gloss of culture they had acquired could be quite rubbed off. There were, Malcolm Cowley says, the aesthetes and the humanists, both equally estranged from the productive thrust and material values of prewar America: the aesthetes

were apparently very different from the Humanists . . . and yet, in respect to their opinions, they were simply Humanists turned upside down. For each of the Humanist virtues they had an antithesis. Thus, for poise they substituted ecstasy; for proportionateness, the Golden Mean, a worship of *immoderation;* for imitating great models, the opposite one of *living in the moment.* Instead of decorum, they mildly preached a *revolt* from middleclass standards, which led them toward a sentimental reverence for sordid things; instead of the Inner Check, they believed in the duty of *Self-Expression.* Yet the Humanist and aesthete were both products of the same milieu, one in which the productive forces of society were regarded as something alien to poetry and learning.[104]

For these young men the war was a call to adventure enveloped in and sanctioned by idealism; an adventure, in turn, which Martin Howe and other aesthetic protagonists are able to think of as "the flame that would consume to ashes all the lies in the world."[105] Such an attitude may well seem naïve and provincial, and it was both. But it was still possible for the young men setting out on their bold journey in 1916 or 1917, backed by rhetoric and traditional ideas of what was involved in fighting, to think of war in terms of traditional heroism and a chance for a free visit to a Europe they knew largely from novels. In the prewar period, furthermore, going abroad was both cause and effect of culture; to go abroad with the opportunity of becoming a hero was no less than a golden chance.[106]

The chief literary antecedent in the matter of war heroism was the work of Stephen Crane. Despite his ironic deflation of the grosser aspects of war rhetoric—the sentiment of unselfish sacrifice, brave boys, and exhilaration in combat—Crane could and did use

[104] Malcolm Cowley, *Exile's Return* (New York, 1951), pp. 35–36.
[105] Dos Passos, *First Encounter*, p. 14.
[106] "A picture that was shattered past repair in 1914," Mr. May remarks, "and a picture that had been more deeply imprinted on the American consciousness than most Americans realized, was the picture of a united European culture" (*The End of American Innocence*, p. 362).

war itself as a symbol of life experience, of confrontation. He saw in battle an opportunity for shaping human identity. Thus Henry Fleming becomes a man through confrontation, fear, cowardice, resignation, and courage; Crane includes fear and cowardice as part of the process by which courage is ultimately achieved. War, for all Crane's irony, is still the magnificent proving ground, an area where cause is internal rather than external, affected by individual will rather than by political, economic, or (perhaps most important in terms of World War I combat experience) technological determinism.[107] There is perhaps no sharper indication of the general naïveté toward warfare than the fact that *The Red Badge of Courage* was an image of reality for young men, especially college-educated young men, setting out in 1917 to earn their own badges of courage and manhood.

But there was no "Tall Man" falling like a great oak tree amid the technological slaughter and trenches of World War I. Good soldiers and bad soldiers alike, men like the Frederic Henrys and Zorns of the postwar novels, or the Andrews and Howes, came not only to reject the absurdity of external causes, but also the absurd role of the individual soldier. Correctly estimating the influence of Crane, students of war literature have tended to underestimate the enormous contrast between the symbolic combat experience he described (war as the achievement of manhood) and the actual experience of World War I—a contrast rendered all the more psychologically and emotionally damaging precisely because of Crane's influence. What Crane saw in warfare writers like Hemingway had to find elsewhere—if they found it at all; the latter's "moment of truth" could come only in other spheres of action where the individual *could* take a stance, even that of loser, and preserve the nobility of his manhood. Only at the beginning of the war did young men on both sides of the Atlantic see in conflict

[107] In his later work as a correspondent at the Greco-Turkish war, Crane was to see—and record—something of the futile slaughter which in World War I was to become a basic strategy rather than failure of military policy. In his account there is also something of the spectatorial attitude, the sense of alienation from a tragic absurdity, so notable in the World War I literature of protest. The battles Crane describes, however, with their "roll of musketry fire," with their incoherent but clearly *watchable* infantry and cavalry attacks, can by no means be equated with the trenches, the long-distance artillery, the protracted attrition, and the mass grinding together of World War I armies. See "Stephen Crane at Velestino," *New York Journal*, May 11, 1897; E. R. Hagemann, " 'Correspondents Three' in the Greco-Turkish War," *American Literature*, XXX (1958), 339–44.

the values achieved by Henry Fleming. In "A Letter from a British Soldier," for example, published in the *London Mercury*, personal reasons are simple enough: "Don't tell me war does no good. . . . What do we gain? I think we gain the one thing that every man has wanted from his boyhood up—opportunity. Opportunity to show what he's made of. Opportunity to show *himself* what he's made of."[108] It was this entire concept of the proving ground that was broken in World War I; and it was broken violently enough to affect permanently the literature of a generation.

The great enthusiasm for exchanging the "uniforms of culture for military uniforms" was not, Cowley points out, as radical for the young men in universities as it might seem. American patriotism, he says, differed from that of French peasants, who were defending their own fields and farms. Amercian patriotism was abstract: it "concerned world democracy and the right to self-determination of small nations, but apparently had nothing to do with our daily lives at home, nothing to do with better schools, lower taxes, higher pay for factory hands (and professors) or restocking Elk Run with trout."[109] The war seemed abstract enough to avoid the taint of utilitarianism; based on disinterested ideals, it provided a means to action without the vulgar economic distractions of the market place. War was a gentleman's means of proving himself and at the same time saving a beautiful lady (*La Belle France*).[110] War was an activity in which individuals tried to defeat other individuals by superior strength, cunning, or marksmanship. It was the test, the exercise in manhood, at once the prerogative of selfless youth and—an idea widely held and widely voiced—the most reliable method of toughening a flabby society.

For the young men were restless under the "ether cone" of their education. They could feel, like Boyd's William Hicks in *Through the Wheat* (1923), that "in conflict . . . would arise a reason for his now unbearable existence."[111] They could agree with the English scholar, Sir Edmund Gosse, that "war is the great scavanger of thought":

[108] Quoted by Clennell Wilkinson, "Back to All That," *London Mercury*, XXII (1930), 544.
[109] Cowley, *Exile's Return*, p. 36.
[110] There was, for example, Henry Van Dyke's hit tune, "The Name of France": "Give us a name to fill the mind/With stirring thoughts that lead mankind,/A name like a star, a name of light—/I give you, France!"
[111] Boyd, *Through the Wheat*, p. 4.

It is the sovereign disinfectant, and its red stream of blood is the Condy's Fluid that cleans out the stagnant pools and clotted channels of the intellect. . . . We have awakened from an opium-dream of comfort, of ease, of that miserable poltroonery of the "sheltered life"; our wish for indulgence of every sort . . . our wretched sensitiveness to personal inconvenience, these are suddenly lifted before us in their true guise. . . . We have risen from the lethargy of our dilettantism, before it is too late, by the flashing of the unsheathed sword.[112]

War, again, could be "good" in the sense that Gosse had pointed out, good in the same sense that justified Roosevelt's sneers at "pacifist theory" or Bourne's proclamation of war as the health of the state. But since 1865 Americans had had no real opportunity to test themselves on the fields of battle; "the Spanish-American War, for all Stephen Crane had made of it, was really only an incident. Young men at Harvard, at Princeton, or in Kansas City were anxious to get to France where the guns were booming and armies maneuvering."[113] And combined with the thirst for adventure was the fact that Darwinian views which had shaped so much of American naturalist fiction were accompanied by the Spencerian translation of these views into sociological thought, postulating the beneficent or life-giving results of struggle.[114]

Some young dilettantes, however, were not interested in the war as a proving ground or a cure for social decadence; they were motivated by a more personal need for Grand Gesture, a gesture also known as "going to join the Foreign Legion." Sickened by writing or reading poems to love goddesses, arguing about form, scribbling music reviews, or floating in a many-colored dream of beauty, such young men embarked on their journey to "get away from it all," to find a solid basis of real experience with common people. The Ivy League universities, for example, contributed a very heavy percentage to such auxiliary services as Norton-Harjes or Lafayette Escadrille, both before and after America's official entry into the war; the sole preparation of such volunteers for the technological slaughterhouse had been an education geared to aesthetic or literary pursuits. Dos Passos' Andrews, in *Three Soldiers*, embodies perhaps the most memorable dramatization of this

[112] Sir Edmund Gosse, *Inter Arma* (New York, 1916), p. 3.
[113] Hoffman, *The Twenties*, p. 51.
[114] Roosevelt, indeed, proclaimed bluntly that "the diplomat is the servant, not the master, of the soldier" (Henry Pringle, *Theodore Roosevelt* [New York, 1931], p. 172).

group. We shall examine Andrews more closely later, but it is necessary to understand that the beginning of his journey arose from a basis of *gesture:*

> They were all so alike, they seemed at moments to be but one organism. This is what he had sought when he enlisted, he said to himself. It was in this that he would take refuge from the horror of the world that had fallen upon him. He was sick of revolt, of carrying his individuality aloft like a banner above the turmoil. . . .
>
> He seemed to have done nothing but think about himself, talk about himself. At least at the bottom, in the utterest degradation of slavery, he could find forgetfulness, and start rebuilding the fabric of his life, out of real things this time, out of work and comradeship and scorn.[115]

The search for adventure, on the other hand, was by no means limited to the educated classes. The young men of office, farm, and factory welcomed the war with equal enthusiasm. It must be remembered that American attitudes toward struggle—whether or not shaped by the frontier imagination so essential to this country's cultural growth—had always been ambiguous. One might say that the "Onward Christian Soldiers" complex typified a national, emotional schizophrenia regarding questions of war and peace; from the days of Manifest Destiny to the glories of the Spanish-American War and Rough Riders, American history was a narrative of what had been surely the most pugnacious peace-loving nation on earth. By the turn of the century, furthermore, America was feeling her oats as never before. She had taken her place as a new and major international power; she had acquired territories even in the distant Pacific; the orations of her politicians were all but battle cries on every national holiday, which inevitably were celebrations of military victories. As Frank T. Phipps has suggested, "Although most Americans believed they hated war, what they did not realize was that they were committed to an admiration of war: for on the level of the imagination they consistently imaged America (and Americans) as honorable, courageous soldiers marching, with divine guidance, toward a destined future."[116]

A specific case in point, and one which illustrates the enormous pressures toward war building up in the United States despite the verbiage of idealism, was the Mexican crisis of 1913. Walter Millis points out that "moral force, however attractive in the domestic

---

[115] Dos Passos, *Three Soldiers*, pp. 26, 31.
[116] Phipps, "The Image of War in America, 1891–1917."

sphere, was less popular when applied in Foreign Affairs. An ethical foreign policy seemed to lack the glamour of the old-fashioned and more martial variety."[117] There was irresistible public demand and support for military action after General Huerta "insulted" the U.S. flag at Vera Cruz; and when American troops suffered casualties in the invasion of that city, Washington excitement reached fever pitch with "the deep thrill of war running through the nation."[118] The fact that there was no full-scale war with Mexico evoked a sense of national disappointment rather than relief.

It is this peculiar quality of aggressive pacifism—what Count von Bernstorff called "the juxtaposition in the American people's character of pacifism and an impulsive lust of war"—which made the presidential campaign of 1916 so remarkable and chaotic an ideological episode in American history. For if Wilson, reluctantly, campaigned on "keeping us out of war," his victory was made possible only by the determined extension of the arms program supported and originated by his arch foes, the triumvirate of General Woods, Senator Lodge, and Theodore Roosevelt. Proclaiming the irresistible war might of the American eagle, Wilson reassured the American public—that same public which had denounced its Congress for pacifism—that the glories of martial power without the blood of twentieth-century battle was his goal. Balancing national pride, chauvinism, and demand for a parade of arms with the equally strong national distrust of entanglement and an unawareness of what the consequences of such entanglement would be, Wilson's complex position reflected the complexities and anomalies of America's position as a nation.[119] And in this connection one can understand the inability of men like General Woods and Theodore Roosevelt, the former a professional militarist and the latter a military romanticist, to tolerate what appeared to them as despicable hypocrisy. But the hypocrisy—or rather, the schizophrenia—was part of the very fabric of American politics, especially the idealism of reform.[120]

In *One of Ours* Willa Cather utilizes the war drive seething beneath the peaceful surface of American life during these years as a major aspect of Claude Wheeler's journey into meaning-

[117] Millis, *Road to War*, p. 12.
[118] *Ibid.*, p. 16.
[119] Hofstadter, in *The Age of Reform*, also speaks of the combination of "nationalist belligerence," "crusading credulity," and "Christian pacifism" (p. 271).
[120] See Hofstadter, pp. 273–74, on the relationship between progressivist idealism and Wilsonian war rhetoric.

through-violence. Claude, indeed, is typical of the midwesterner reaching for war as a means of achieving what his society simply ruled out as unthinkable (unless for missionary work): adventure, daring, "the bright face of danger." Life in the small town had hardened into noneventfulness; the frontier was one, and with it the eruptions of violence, of break in routine, which could quench the fire of young men, especially young men who—like Claude— were frustrated in love and prosperous enough so that their energies were not taken up with the basic problems of earning a living.

For Claude the war came as a release from rigidity and the unsubmitting will of his wife. Certainly the small-town morality permitted no corrective for restlessness. Like thousands of other respectable young farmers, Claude had "dreams that would have frozen his young wife's blood with horror." When the war broke out in Europe, Claude broke out in a great emotional flush; the means of escape was at hand. He knew it even while others were talking about neutrality. He felt it. He often brooded about it: "All the dreary, weary, ever-repeated actions by which life is continued from day to day. Actions without meaning. . . . He wondered how he was to go on through the years ahead of him, unless he could get rid of that sick feeling in his soul." The war provided the purgative. It was a cosmic prescription: the opportunity to join the men of history books, the brave soldiers of destiny, doing something more vital than putting in a crop and wondering what the prices would be next harvest time. Paris was the fabled city: "There was nothing else he would so gladly be as an atom in that wall of flesh that rose and melted and rose again before the city which had meant so much before the ages."[121]

There were, however, difficulties: Germans had never seemed raving beasts, militarists, or Huns. They were not the sort of people from whom it should have been necessary to save civilization. "He had always been taught that German people were preeminent in the virtues Americans most admire; a month ago he would have said they had all the ideals a decent American boy would fight for. The invasion of Belgium was contradictory to the German character as he knew it in his neighbors and friends." Before the adventure of war could be justified, therefore, a reversal of attitude was necessary, an abstract indictment had to be formulated. And this in turn provided its own difficulties, for the provincial American midwesterner was not accustomed to dealing with words and

[121] Cather, *One of Ours*, pp. 173, 223.

abstractions. If there must be an act, the cause was no less obvious than the effect, and neither rhetoric nor explanation was necessary. Faced with the terrible need for his adventure, with the fact that his adventure had to be justified abstractly if it was to be justified at all, Claude—and the thousands of other Claudes—simply used what abstractions were provided. They read the atrocity stories, the stories were horrible, and it was clear that " 'the world simply made a mistake about the Germans all along. It's as if we invited a neighbor over here and showed him our cattle and barns, and all the time he would come at night and club us in our beds.' "[122]

From the moment the reason was provided to justify the adventure, no complexities needed to be discussed. Belgium, the *Lusitania*, Edith Cavell could be spoken of (often sincerely) as public reasons, and young men could treasure their dreams of glory as private, more vital reasons. Claude could be justified in saying, " 'I never knew there was anything worth living for, until this war broke out.' " When challenged, he could provide the sanctioned rhetoric, but privately there would be another: "He would give his adventure for no man's. On the edge of sleep it seemed to glimmer like the clear column of the fountain, like the new moon—alluring, the half-averted, bright face of danger."[123]

The desire for adventure was equally entrancing for young men who were bound neither by small-town rigidity nor deracinated by over-education. Since the material standard of value was, increasingly, the major standard of value in the United States, those in subordinate positions were deprived of status, self-status no less than social status. Unlike the aesthetes, these young men themselves used the yardstick of material wealth. And the war, for men of the factory, salesroom, and office, was more than adventure; it was a means of achieving the stature they could obtain in no other way. " 'Whoever likes it can run for a train every morning and grind out his days in a Westinghouse works,' " a soldier in *One of Ours* says, " 'but not for me any more!' "[124] There was no way to prove oneself in a Westinghouse works—or in an optical store, or a haberdashery. This theme, the hope for social and material stature-through-glory so tragically reversed by the war experience itself, was to be a major one in the postwar novel of protest. In *Three Soldiers*, for example, Fuselli earns an importance simply

[122] *Ibid.*, pp. 166, 270.
[123] *Ibid.*, p. 466.
[124] *Ibid.*, p. 278.

by donning his uniform: "The man had added fervently, 'It must be grand, just grand to feel the danger, the chance of being potted any minute. Good luck to you, young feller.' . . . The words had made him stride out of the office sticking out his chest, brushing truculently past a group of men at the door. Even now the memory of it . . . made him feel important, truculent."[125] And there is the vision of Zorn, in *Soldiers March!*: "Before him lay the great adventure. A legendary country called France, and a host of men at grips. Adventure; glory; death . . . he felt small before his vision of the future. Would he play the man? Would he be a great figure, medals for valour on his breast, a good soldier?"[126]

Before it was shattered by technological combat and mass death, the mental world of the young men who fought the war (and later wrote the books protesting the war they had fought) was a different world indeed. To Gilbert Seldes, for example, writing in 1925, both the "progress" of prewar democracy and the melancholies of prewar aestheticism were equally absurd. "As for the faith lost by the intellectuals," Seldes writes, "there is room to wonder what sort it was. . . ."

Creative forces of the last 100 years: active belief in democracy, respect for science, hope for education, general faith in progress. Progress ended in the war, science in machinery; democracy died two deaths, in Bolshevism and KKK Fascism. . . . Of the vaguer assumptions, liberty and love of humanity remain in the cocked hat where they landed between 1914 and 1919. . . . The pessimism of the 1890s was personal. The world . . . provided no habitation for the aesthete, the man of feeling, the wit. But the world was also perfectable; beauty and Pagan love and Renaissance glamour could be saved. . . . Nothing of that hope remains.[127]

"The green fields shriveled in an afternoon," Parrington remarks of the Great Crusade; "the moral and philosophical structures of the earlier society collapsed," writes Frederick Hoffman; "you could have supposed the whole of Europe had been tilted up with all of its anciently established things being upended and tilted into the sea," notes H. M. Tomlinson; "the sanctified values had

---

[125] Dos Passos, *Three Soldiers*, p. 11.
[126] Fredenburgh, *Soldiers March!*, p. 11.
[127] Gilbert Seldes, "Notes and Queries," *New Republic*, XLIV (October 21, 1925), 231.

become sheer nonsense," Lloyd Morris reminds us.[128] The very fact that there had been "sanctified values," however, and that at the time of the Crusade such values remained generally intact, indicates the vast gulf separating the World War I experience from that of the second conflict, when young men who "got their idea of the world during the depression years . . . drank in the brutalities of Europe with their breakfast coffee."[129]

The impact of World War I must be seen not only in terms of the military and political realities for which soldiers and civilians alike were unprepared, but in terms of a naïveté so profound as to require an act of retrospective imagination only a few decades afterward. It was a naïveté in which war for most Americans was defined by the Vera Cruz expedition or by the picnic exercises of the local militia and Fourth of July celebrations; it was a naïveté in which educated Americans viewed Europe as the united base of western civilization and uneducated Americans regarded it as a fascinating combination of immortal traditions and sexual sophistications, of proud aristocracy and colorful peasantry. And it is the quality of this naïveté which sets up the dramatic process of disillusion and impact in the post-World War I novel. " 'Is the stars the same over there, overseas, as they is here?' " asks Fuselli in *Three Soldiers*. And in *One of Ours* there is the image of Paris which, for young men leaving the backwaters of midwestern existence, seems Babylon itself:

The Seine, they felt sure, must be very much wider there, and it was spanned by many bridges all longer than the bridge over the Missouri at Omaha. There would be spires and golden domes past counting, all the buildings higher than anything in Chicago, and brilliant, dazzlingly brilliant, nothing grey and shabby about it. . . . They attributed to the city of their desire incalculable immensity, bewildering vastness, Babylonian hugeness and heaviness—the only attributes they had been taught to admire.[130]

After the second conflict and the continuing threat of atomization, such naïveté may well seem as fantastic as a belief that the world was flat. In no World War II novel do protagonists

---

[128] Vernon Louis Parrington, "The Beginnings of Critical Realism in America," *Main Currents in American Thought* (New York 1930), III, 412; Frederick J. Hoffman, "The Temper of the Twenties," *Minnesota Review*, I (1960), 40; H. M. Tomlinson, "War Books," *Yale Review*, XIX (1930), 449; Lloyd Morris, *Postscript to Yesterday* (New York, 1947), p. 1491.

[129] John Dos Passos, introduction to 1945 edition, *First Encounter*.

[130] Cather, *One of Ours*, p. 341.

set out with a comparable mixture of innocence and baroque expectation. "To Americans of my generation," Dos Passos remarks, "raised as we were in the quiet afterglow of the nineteenth century, among comfortably situated people who were confident that industrial progress meant an improved civilization . . . , more freedom, a more humane and peaceful society . . . , the European war of 1914–1918 seemed a horrible monstrosity, something outside the normal order of things, like an epidemic of yellow fever in some place where yellow fever had never been heard of before."[131] It was precisely this expectation of progress, together with the concept of war as a lance-and-plume affair and Europe itself as both cultural monument and picture postcard, which resulted in so sharp a recoil in the World War I literature of disillusion. Machines had turned dying into an obscenity ("the self-grinding and ubiquitous mill of death")[132] and politics had turned the crusader into a pawn; reality broke the rhetoric, the memories of storybook warfare, and the hope for adventure. And what was true of warfare became for young writers true of an economic and social system which had presented war as a cure for social ills. The world itself was broken. It was still broken when World War II began, but by then the family china had long been cracked.

[131] Dos Passos, *supra* n. 129.
[132] Henry Seidel Canby, "War Books and 'All Our Yesterdays,'" *Golden Book,* XI (March, 1930), 96.

II

THE BROKEN WORLD

It is God who has summoned us to this war.
It is His war we are fighting. This conflict is
indeed a crusade. The greatest in history—
the holiest. It is in the profoundest and truest
sense a holy war . . . Yes, it is Christ, the
King of Righteousness, who calls us to grapple
in deadly strife with this unholy and
blasphemous power.
—from a sermon by REV. RANDOLPH H. McKINN,
Washington, D.C., 1917

Dear Madam:
Your son, Francis, died needlessly in Belleau
Wood. You'll be interested to know that at the
time of his death he was crawling with
vermin and weak from diarrhea. His feet
were swollen and rotten and they stank. He
lived like a frightened animal, cold and
hungry. Then, on June 9th, a piece of
shrapnel hit him and he died in agony,
slowly. You'd never believe he could live
three hours, but he did. He lived three full
hours screaming and cursing by turns. He
had nothing to hold on to, you see: he had
learned long ago that what he had been
taught to believe . . . under the meaningless
names of honor, courage, patriotism, were all lies.
—WILLIAM MARCH, *Company K*, 1933

Clemenceau
Lloyd George
Woodrow Wilson.
Three old men shuffling out the pack,
dealing out the cards: . . .
machinegun fire and arson
starvation, lice, cholera, typhus;
oil was trumps.
—JOHN DOS PASSOS, *1919*, 1932

I n *The Century of Total War* (1954) Raymond Aron, one of the most objective students of World War I, attempts to steer a middle course between the revisionist and antirevisionist debates which have continued among historians ever since the mid-twenties. Viewing the war itself as the result of worldwide political, economic, and social pressures, Mr. Aron absolves leaders of both the Entente and Central Powers from actually desiring an outbreak of hostilities.

The tragedy of 1914 (and later wars as well), however, is that while no one actually wanted war, a great many individuals and groups had urgent desires which could not be gratified without it. Young men wanted glory and young women wanted excitement; the Kaiser wanted a navy and the British wanted supremacy of the seas; farmers wanted better prices and industrialists wanted government contracts; clergymen wanted a holy cause and generals—whether named Woods or Von Clausewitz—wanted to convince a world grown "soft" with peace that the profession of arms represented the health of the state. The ultimate irony was not that national leaders—and populations, for that matter—"wanted" a war, but rather that they did not want the war they got.

What they did get—cynic or idealist, profiteer or patriot, clergyman or militarist ("The diplomat is the servant, not the master, of the soldier," thundered Roosevelt)—was a juggernaut that could no more be controlled by its drivers than by its victims. Certainly European statesmen had small inkling of the blood bath toward which they were driving their world in the years before 1914. By 1915 Ambassador Walter Hines Page, for example, whose views in many ways were typical of the Anglophile and prowar enthusiasts in the United States, strikes an almost poignant note in his letters: "When there's 'nothing to report' from France that means the regular 5,000 casualties that happen every day. . . . A member of the Cabinet . . . told me so much military bad news which they prevent the papers from publishing or even hearing, that tonight I share this man's opinion that the war will last till 1918. That isn't impossible." And in 1916, after great engagements like Verdun had proven nothing except that a million men could die in a single battle without changing so much as the front line,

Ambassador Page (in a fit of horror prefiguring that of the post-World War I novel) could despair of "a crazy world—a slaughterhouse where madness dwells."[1]

"A crazy world," Mr. Page said; and diplomats no less than professional soldiers were like men trying to find their way by consulting a map on which all names had been erased. International law, international protocols, international military traditions still existed, but only as formulas which simply could not be applied to existing realities. When these formulas were applied, the result was only a deepened confusion and a more profound absurdity. When Captain Kruger, to cite but one example, made his triumphal entry into Baltimore, declaring his unarmed submarine to be a merchantman with a cargo of dyestuffs, Lord Grey immediately protested on the grounds that any vehicle traveling beneath the surface of the sea was inherently illegal and uncivilized. And the "defensive arms" on merchantmen represented another aspect of the problem, since the guns were deadly to submarines surfaced for any reason whatever. Wilson himself, before he eliminated the submarine by fiat, suffered continual misgivings: "It is hardly fair," he wrote to Colonel House as early as 1915, "to ask submarine commanders to give warnings by summons if, when they approach as near as they must for that purpose, they are fired upon, as Balfour would have them fired upon." In a rather plaintive note the President added, "It is a question of many sides."[2] Wilson's private uncertainties, always academic in tone and inevitably concerned with lack of precedents, still make vivid reading when set beside his God-struck and revivalist public declarations. These private doubts, however, no less than the facts of Ambassador Page's collusion or Morgan's hopeful survey of ship sinkings, were published only after the war, when the public declarations were still an essential part of the nation's cultural and political environment. One need not wonder at the resultant cynicism and revulsion, on all levels of the population, against rhetorical idealism.

Professional soldiers were equally unprepared for the technological warfare of attrition and machine. The officers of western Europe, convinced that war had at last become a science, looked forward to a neat and surgical conflict;[3] so sure were they that

[1] Quoted by Walter Millis, *Road to War* (Boston, 1935), pp. 251, 314.
[2] Quoted by Charles C. Tansill, *America Goes to War* (Boston, 1938), p. 415.
[3] In *Arms and Men* (New York, 1936) Millis points out that "the democratic and industrial revolutions between them had provided enormously increased

the war would be a sort of Franco-Prussian exercise to change (or confirm) the earlier decision, that "at the beginning of the winter of 1915 everyone was running short of supplies. Even Germany had not stocked ammunition for a long war or correctly estimated the enormous ammunition requirements of the new rapid-fire weapons."[4]

The failure to stock ammunition, however, was only one symptom of a wider failure to cope with the vastly increased fire power of machine war. Only in World War II did the machine achieve mobility; in 1914 officers thought in terms of infantry, of cavalry, of "flanking," of "advance," of "engagement." The pathetic butchery of French cavalry in William Scanlon's *God Have Mercy On Us* (1929); the anachronistic epitaph by General Assolant in Humphry Cobb's *Paths of Glory* (1935) on a company of soldiers blown to pieces by a long-distance shell; the absurd "protection" afforded to American troops, in Thomas Boyd's *Through the Wheat* (1923), by tanks that literally provided German artillery with helpless targets of flesh and blood—such episodes are dramatizations of events repeated on all sectors of the front, until the sole strategy of military leaders became the strategy of death itself, of attrition. Nothing else worked. "Their carefully planned war," J. C. F. Fuller remarks, was "smashed to pieces by fire-power. . . . There was no choice but to go under surface. . . . Armies, in their own lack of foresight, were reduced to the position of human cattle."[5]

The military leaders of both the Entente and the Central Powers, however, did not take kindly to going "under surface." There were protracted experiments with direct attack, repeated examples where—given virtually unlimited manpower—armies were hurled

---

potentials of violence and devastation." These potentials were increased by "the managerial revolution . . . which was to reach its unexpected and terrible climax in the First World War": military leaders had to cope with "new problems of metallurgy, ballistics, electrical equipment, military and marine engineering [to say nothing of what would now be called 'public relations']." The result was an attempt, through the General Staff system, to create a science: "With scientific study and careful advance planning, war would become, like surgery, an almost clinical instrument. . . ." The tragedy, of course, was that management managed neither technology nor ideological war, and far from achieving a "clinical instrument," World War I leaders were forced to rely on attrition of the enemy, a laborious process that itself demanded increased emotional stimulation via propaganda. With enormously increased technology in both weapons and communication, there was attrition on an unparalleled scale (pp. 122–23).

[4] Theodore Ropp, *War in the Western World* (Durham, N.C., 1959), p. 226.
[5] J. C. F. Fuller, *War and Western Civilization* (London, 1932), pp. 227–28.

at each other, or rather, at each other's machines. The cult of the offensive still had many followers:

Many generals could not see that these tremendous artillery bombardments sacrificed mobility and surprise for mass and concentration. The guns destroyed all communication in the GAP—roads, paths, even the topsoil—leaving crater-pocked deserts as bad as the barbed wire and trenches, and making surprise impossible. War was mechanized behind the lines; reserves brought up in trains or trucks could plug the GAP while the attackers were laboring through it. The nineteen-day British bombardment at Third Ypres (1917) used 321 train loads of shells, a year's production for 55,000 war workers. The whole battle area reverted to a swamp in which the British army took 45 square miles at a cost of 370,000 men. . . . Never before had so many men been under such fire. The shock was greater because they had known nothing of war and had been taught that it would be a short, though dangerous adventure.[6]

The generals, in other words, had no concept of the tactical application of their own weapons, and—as Céline remarks in *Journey to the End of the Night* (1934)—"everyone queued up to go and get killed."[7] It was this war of determined but absurd blood letting, a senseless reiteration of futility and callousness, that was to give David's story in *The Enormous Room* (1922) a dimension of symbolic truth:

[6] Ropp, *War in the Western World*, p. 231. A recent English novel of the Somme campaign by John Harris, *Covenant with Death* (New York, 1961), communicates something of both the ignorance and futility which marked the "fighting" of World War I. In reviewing Mr. Harris' book for the *New York Times*, Leon Wolff remarks that "the slaughter on the Western Front was, and is, unique in warfare. . . . It was not fighting in the normal sense. Of the millions who died, few ever saw an enemy soldier. In their trenches, in their dugouts, on no man's land, they were mostly killed by unseen agents: hidden machine guns, camouflaged mortars and distant artillery." (See "Senseless Slaughter," *New York Times Book Review*, [October 22, 1961], p. 49.)
[7] Louis-Ferdinand Céline, *Journey to the End of the Night* (New York, 1960), p. 26. Ropp gives us an insight into the mass death of World War I with statistics on just a few battles: the Marne cost each side 500,000 lives; at Verdun the Allies lost 362,000 and the Germans 336,000; the Somme cost the Allies 614,000 and the Germans 650,000. "Essentially," Mr. Ropp says, "both sides had accepted the French Staff's conclusion that 'breakthrough' followed by exploitation is impossible until the enemy has been so worn down that he has no reserves available to close the gap." (p. 230) The result: 10,000,000 dead. In this respect one might note that military leaders on the Italian front, setting for Hemingway's *A Farewell to Arms*, also managed quite well. By September, 1917, the Italians had lost almost a million men, with the situation still indecisive. "One cabinet had been forced out, but General Cardonna was still in command of the army, Colonel Douhot, an artillery officer interested in transport and air power had been court-martialed and imprisoned for circulating criticism of Italian tactics" (p. 230).

> "Il volait au-dessus des lignes, et s'etonnait,
> un jour, de remarquer que les cannons français
> ne tiraient pas sur les boches mais sur les
> français eux-mêmes. Précipitamment il atteris-
> sait, sautait de l'appareil, allait de suite
> au bureau du général. Il donnait le salut, et
> criait, bien excité: Mon général, vous tirez sur
> les français! Le général le regardait sans
> intérêt, sans bouger, puis il disait tout
> simplement: On a commencé, il faut finir."[8]

And it was this war that provided the background for the brief march of Colonel Dax's men to the line in *Paths of Glory:*

> The 181st had lost thirty-two men, the Tirailleurs seventeen. It wasn't a bad record for a relief made during a heavy bombardment, nor did it make the slightest difference to the conduct of the war. Every day and every night men were being killed at the rate of about four a minute. The line remained the same—uniforms, equipment, faces, statures, men. . . . Forty-nine men had been killed, and one set of collar numerals had been replaced by another. Rats weren't interested in collar numerals, so it made no difference to them either.[9]

The war of stasis and futility, however, was only one breaking factor in the combat environment. Equally important was the fact that "fighting" became a passive rather than an active procedure; the vast majority of casualties on both sides was incurred among soldiers who at the moment of their deaths were either groveling on the earth, fighting desperately among themselves for shelter, or playing interminable games of cards in trenches or rear-echelon posts. The man was separated from the act; the potential hero could be—and often was—splattered by a stray shell under circumstances that had nothing whatever to do with soldiering. In the Meuse-Argonne offensive, for example, one of those in which American troops played a central part, 75 per cent of all casualties were caused by shell fragments and 2 per cent by gas; only 23

---

[8] E. E. Cummings, *The Enormous Room* (New York, 1934), p. 179.
[9] Humphry Cobb, *Paths of Glory* (New York, 1935), p. 46. In *The Literary Situation* (New York, 1954), Malcolm Cowley insists that the World War I protests were justified by the facts: "Even a professional soldier would admit that . . . rebellion was based on a valid complaint, since the Western battles of World War I were most of them useless and stupid from the military point of view. Until 1918 the commanding generals on both sides had no military objectives. Their imaginations were deadened by the sheer quantity of manpower and material at their disposal. They planned their massed offensives merely to gain terrain, when yielding it might have been the wiser strategy, or merely to inflict losses upon the enemy" (p. 38).

per cent of the casualties earned their red badges of courage in any sort of direct encounter with the Hun.[10]

The result of this passivity was a psychic emasculation inherent in the combat environment itself, a sense of violation which had such vitally important results as the subsequent preoccupation of Hemingway with death-and-*cojones*; its importance is also indicated by the reiteration of castration images in the work of March, Cobb, Harrison, Boyd, Fredenburgh, and others. Survivors, furthermore, were often individuals who did survive only by perfecting the virtues of cleverness rather than of intelligence—the latter, according to the almost universal testimony of postwar novelists, resulting in either desertion or death. Hence protagonists like Mattock, Irwin, or Eadie cultivate a certain expertness in flattery, a subtle disobedience of suicidal orders, or a strategic involvement with the delicacies of personal effacement. "Veterans are not men who have learnt how to charge obstacles more furiously than others," Alden Brooks comments, "but men who have learnt, rather, how to avoid obstacles more furiously than others, and so too, men who have learnt how to disobey orders—or they would not be veterans."[11] It was Mattock, and not Captain Johnny Hard, who survived.

The war of stasis, of course, did not affect American troops as heavily as it did their European counterparts. Except for a conviction that the Frogs and Limeys were a shiftless, spiritless, defeatist, and opportunist lot, the American soldier, with an enthusiasm born of ignorance and propaganda,[12] was spared the long years in which

[10] See Conrad Lanza, "The Artillery Support in the AEF," *Field Artillery Journal*, XXVI (1936), 62–86.

[11] Alden Brooks, *As I Saw It* (New York, 1929), p. 299. On the matter of "survival" L. L. Bernard (*War and Its Causes* [New York, 1944]) notes that "when men fought with clubs, spears, bows and arrows, and swords, only men of courage, skill and strength could hope to win. As a consequence, the battle was in no small degree a selective factor in the development of the population type. In modern war, however . . . most of the fighting . . . is by machines which operate against other machines or against troops, fortifications or other objectives which are invisible" (p. 68). Hence Hervey Allen's comment in *Toward the Flame* (New York, 1934) on a dead soldier: "Fletcher . . . was a better man physically than most; a fast runner, a good shot, handsome, a keen thinker, deeply conscientious, with a broad sense of humour and a catching laugh. He should have lived to have children instead of being snuffed out later in a miserable garret in Fismes by a chance shell" (p. 167).

[12] General Herman von Giehrl refers—half in admiration and half in pity—to American "ignorance of . . . and therefore indifference to danger." See his "The A. E. F. in Europe, 1917–19," *Infantry Journal*, XX (1922), 144.

grinding attrition became the basic strategy of the war. In certain respects, however, the harsh realities of mass movement; of cattle-car transportation; of lice, filth, influenza, and veneral disease; of labor battalions and military police; of alcohol and whores; and—certainly not least important—of battles such as Soissons, Montfaucon, and Meuse-Argonne had an even sharper impact for the American soldier than for Entente or German troops.

What was true of European military leadership—a lack of prepa-ration for the machine they had created—was woefully true of American forces on all levels and all ranks. Military leaders, in-deed, had assumed from the first that if American troops were to be sent overseas at all, they would be sent for auxiliary duties only; when the War Department was "face to face with the ques-tion of sending an army to Europe," General Pershing remarks in his memoirs, they found that "the General Staff had never con-sidered such a thing. No one in authority had any idea how many men might be needed . . . how they should be organized or equipped."[13]

American army leaders were unprepared not only for the role they had to play, but also for the war in which they had to play it. The Mexican adventure (Vera Cruz) provided a few weeks of enjoyable excitement for Washington and the nation as a whole and gave a baptism of fire to an extremely limited number of regular troops, but its lessons had to be unlearned in France. In a very real sense the Mexican campaign rendered the necessities of the Western Front more incomprehensible than ever: unsolved problems of ballistics and liaison resulted in a bloody chaos, the "madhouse" theme that runs through so many World War I novels.[14]

The battle of Soissons, for example, provided several of the

[13] John J. Pershing, *My Experiences in the World War* [I] (New York, 1931), p. 78. Note that in James Stevens' *Mattock* (New York, 1927) the protagonist remarks: "I argued with Pa that the war would certainly be over by Spring, anyway, and that only the riff-raff regular army soldiers would get into the fighting" (p. 32).
[14] Failure of liaison, of course, was a problem on all sides. Céline, for example, writes of the perpetual stumbling which rapidly developed into a major charac-teristic of the war: "He told me two or three times that it was as black as your bottom and then he died; killed, quite soon after that, on leaving a village which we mistook for another, by some Frenchmen who mistook us for someone else" (p. 24). And Allen, in *Toward the Flame*, relates how "in one place the Germans arrived on a train and got off almost in our lines—where they were immediately taken prisoner. They did not know we had moved up so far" (p. 171).

"breaking" incidents later used as material by writers such as March, Fredenburgh, and Boyd: United States officers, for one thing, ordered a frontal assault on machine-gun defenses, and the result was a butchery. In addition, there was a breakdown in medical services,[15] and artillery support was so unreliable that American soldiers wondered, and military historians are still wondering, whether German or American guns did the heavier damage. "Possibly the worst feature of the attack," John W. Killigrew remarks (maintaining a certain euphemistic professionalism), "was poor artillery-infantry liaison. Observation posts were not forward enough to see the targets which were being fired upon, and as a result, many short rounds were fired which contributed to the general lack of confidence among front line troops in American artillery."[16]

Other factors contributing to postwar mockery of "the military mind" were inadequate army intelligence and chaotic transport. Officers, indeed, often had no idea where the enemy actually was, so that "the entire advance from the Marne . . . seemed to be a hit or miss affair."[17] Infantry commanders "knew little as to the location of their subordinate units. Attack orders were duplicated, superseded, and then ordered again"—with troops milling aimlessly, often under fire.[18] And in addition to lack of liaison between American detachments and between American and Allied groups, transport difficulties turned into veritable nightmares.[19] De-

[15] Incompetent or discriminatory medical service is a minor theme of several novels, including March's *Company K* (New York, 1933) and Boyd's *Through the Wheat* (New York, 1923).

[16] John W. Killigrew, "A Critique of American Military History" (unpublished Ph.D. dissertation, Indiana University, 1952), p. 13. See also Leonard R. Boyd, "Will It Happen Again?," *Infantry Journal*, XX (1922), 145–47. Lanza, in "Third Battle of Romagne," *Field Artillery Journal*, XXIV (1934), remarks that liaison officers with the infantry were notably lacking in observation efficiency (see 334–46). In "The Artillery Support in the AEF," published in *F.A.J.* two years later (see n. 10), Mr. Lanza becomes more sharply critical of American military ignorance. "Neither staffs nor line officers were aware of the long range and power of modern artillery," he points out. "They did not know how to use it. . . . Our pre-war instruction had taught the limitation of artillery; but its possibilities were almost unknown. . . . Bloody losses assisted in proving that driving the enemy back a few kilometres did not necessarily mean that he would be on the run" (pp. 71, 84).

[17] Killigrew, "A Critique of American Military History," p. 18.

[18] *Ibid.*, p. 82.

[19] An example of chaotic liaison: the march of the 1st Division to Sedan from the center of the First Army across the area of the entire Corps and into the French Zone produced confusion, delay, and actual blockage of the French advance.

scribing the situation at Soissons, the historian Frederick Palmer departs from his pro-Allied orientation and waxes almost as dramatic as the war novelists themselves:

They were a rumbling jam of pressing and varied transport, with the guns and ammunition and machine guns on the front demanding right of way. Rain began to fall. This intensified the darkness of the woods under the overhanging tree tops. Within the woods, a man was not visible at the distance of a pace. Commanding officers had to scout the line in the midst of this inky, drizzling night. . . . Troops, in threading their way past and around that weaving, straining mass of transports . . . stumbled off into sloughs, bumped into wheels and mules and found themselves off the road colliding with trees. It was a groping, blindman's bluff kind of business.[20]

It was men rather than machines, certainly, that suffered from transport chaos, and this not only at the front. The "Forty and Eight" now sentimentalized every year by conventioneering veterans were very often box cars crowded with lice-ridden, exhausted, or nauseated Soldiers of Democracy, who were frequently demoralized before they had suffered so much as a single casualty in actual combat. One remembers that Zorn, in Fredenburgh's novel, formulates his survival-through-strength theory long before his company arrives at the front.

Faced with fire power greater than anything they had ever experienced, with fixed-front warfare and a chaos in liaison, American military leaders, even more so than their Allied colleagues, evolved one strategy of operation—the direct advance. Military historians repeatedly remark upon the high-density concentration and the inexperience of American troops advancing upon fixed positions, the vast ignorance on the part of their officers as to tactical behavior, and the concomitant ignorance on the part of troops as to what they were getting into. Even so objective an observer as Hervey Allen in *Toward the Flame* notes futile troop movements under fire, "frightful" orders to advance under conditions in which the only result was "murder": ". . . what was left of the companies returned. The loss had been terrific. Some of the companies were down to a few men. The gain had been nothing."[21] And General Pershing's basic strategy of attrition, of "continued pressure unremittingly applied,"[22] was accompanied by trag-

[20] Frederick Palmer, *America in France* (New York, 1918), pp. 336–37.
[21] See Allen, *Toward the Flame*, pp. 269, 272.
[22] Killigrew, "A Critique of American Military History," p. 70.

ically inaccurate intelligence: the untried Fifth Corps at the Argonne, for example, advanced under "information" that the Germans were retreating, while the enemy had actually mounted a full-scale counterattack.[23] The fact that such episodes did occur must, certainly, help us understand the sense of impact in a novel like *Through the Wheat*—where troops are thrown into a major battle while under the impression (shared by their noncoms and many of their officers) that they are on the way to a rest area.

These difficulties were further compounded by the fact that United States army training was often vastly inadequate. "The old militia theory—the plow left in the furrow and the long rifle taken from the wall—was to be reinforced by the idea that industrial capacity alone guarantees adequate preparation for modern mechanized war."[24] As a result the atmosphere of training camps themselves suggested nothing more dangerous in store for troops than the exercise at Vera Cruz. Indeed, many troops, in what Harry W. Caygill calls a "ghastly administrative error," were shipped overseas with six weeks of actual training.[25] They were then kept penned in replacement depots or in "rest" camps where close-order drill made up the bulk of the military diet, regaled by YMCA enthusiasm and martial sermons on Sunday, and sent into the line expecting "a good fight" along the lines of some vaguely imagined Indian skirmish. In *Through the Wheat*, Captain Powers, with his dreams of saber charges, who almost before Hicks' rapidly benumbed eyes was to become a bit of uniform, a leg, and a pile of brains modestly contained in a battered helmet, was a historical type no less than the creation of a writer's imagination. There

[23] See Lanza, "Three Battles in One," *Field Artillery Journal*, XIV (1934), 119.
[24] Ropp, *War in the Western World*, p. 243.
[25] Harry W. Caygill, "Operations of Company M., 23rd Infantry," *Infantry Journal*, XL (1933), 135. The lack of adequate training reiterated in many war novels is satirized in *Mattock:* "We were long past the rookie and camp-guard stages. We were veteran soldiers who had been having intensive training for a solid six weeks, and now we were soldiering right. We were toughened to drilling eight hours and hiking six miles every day. We had fired twenty rounds apiece on the rifle range. We had learned how to throw hand grenades and shoot rifle ones. . . . We still had considerable trouble deploying into wave formation and following the platoon leader's complicated hand signals, but that was only Frog army stuff, and we didn't think much of it anyway . . ." (p. 88). Troops resent "tactics" in *Mattock* first, because they expect shells to pass over them; second, because they have been taught that the Germans are cowards: "What's the use of it anyway? When all we need to do is to get out and give 'em the cold steel?" (p. 103).

were many men—of all combat ranks—who suffered the same fate in either physical or psychological terms. And many of those who did not, who survived, did so only by developing the scar tissue of Zorn, the numbness of Hicks, the broken indifference of Irwin, the professional veteran Babbittry of Mattock, or the clever indirections of Sergeant Eadie.

Add to these qualities the inner vacuum and outer materialism of Richard Savage in *1919;* the pro-Fascist worship of "strength" of the "Futurist" Italian officer in the same novel; the political bitterness of Richard in Stallings' *Plumes;* the retreat into aesthetics of Andrews or Cummings; the flight from *nada* of Frederic Henry—and we have the post-World War I literary attitudes in their broadest outlines.

Fighting

I n Leonard Nason's *Sergeant Eadie* the protagonist wonders "what kind of a war was this anyway, with no enemy? He wanted to see some of them, to shoot off his pistol at them."[26] Nason's book, in no way a novel of protest, reflects the fact that expectations of a "good fight" were basic to American military attitudes at the onset of World War I. Professional soldiers, even noncoms like Eadie, found all too suddenly that they had been "polishing their pistols" in vain; Eadie, indeed, finds that under his new military environment the chief task, even virtue, for a man is to "find a good, deep cellar." Certainly the impact of technological warfare was by no means confined to draftees and volunteers; the professional soldier no less than his amateur counterpart was disgusted by a war which rendered the facts of military life obsolete. Hence Urquhart, in *Company K*, after "thirty years as a professional soldier" and after watching "the reactions of many men to pain, hunger, and death," takes back from France a bitterness equal to that of any disillusioned idealist, a bitterness resulting both from the shattering of the combat-as-a-proving-ground idea, and a close view of the politics within mass warfare. "There should be a law," Urquhart says, "in the name of humanity, making mandatory the

[26] Nason, *Sergeant Eadie* (New York, 1928), p. 136.

execution of every soldier who has served on the front line and managed to escape death there."[27]

The transitional nature of the American army (an essentially nineteenth-century establishment plunged, with an impact that shocked its own leaders, into a twentieth-century war environment) created moments of absurdity as well as horror, and both qualities proved to be major resources of the postwar novel. Dutch, for example, in Elliot Paul's *Impromptu*, is officially given the rank of "Horseshoer" and is humiliated when "a comrade with a talent for drawing made a cartoon of Dutch nailing a horseshoe on the Major's Dodge car."[28] But only in training camp did such episodes seem amusing; in the front line, where officers and men alike were still expecting "horseshoes," death itself took on the element of absurdity. The reaction of many men was the laughter of a rictus.

In *First Encounter* the view of the war as an Alice-in-Wonderland situation, as a "solemn inanity" of both life and death, resembles the descriptions also to be found in virtually every novel of the war except those written for purposes of outright propaganda. So great was the gulf between military theory and practice (as between political rhetoric and reality), that a writer like Cummings was to give up direct protest altogether and use a deceptively casual, metaphoric mockery throughout *The Enormous Room* (itself a symbolic enactment of the Crusade): "Whistling joyously to myself," he writes, "I took three steps which brought me to the door end. The door was massively made, all of iron and steel. . . . It delighted me. The can excited my curiosity. . . . At the bottom reposefully lay a new human *t . . d.*"[29]

The horror, however, cannot be underestimated, even—or especially—for those involved with a belief in war as an exercise in manhood. "We lay there like newly castrated sheep," says a soldier in *Company K*—a novel written by an author who had himself earned the Distinguished Service Cross. And Bayard Schindel, in *The Golden Pilgrimage*, typifies postwar attitudes toward mechanical combat, giving a vivid emotional portrait of the disgust aroused in a professional soldier by a war he could no longer respect:

War had become the profession of the mechanic, a person in greasy overalls who merely worked the machines that killed better men. . . .

[27] March, *Company K*, p. 178.
[28] Elliot Paul, *Impromptu* (New York, 1923), p. 82.
[29] Cummings, *The Enormous Room*, p. 23.

It was a coward's way of making war, this crouching in sewer excavations and daring the other fellow, who is crouching in a similar excavation 200 yards away, to stick his head above the earth. . . . To hell with this machine war, he thought, this soulless grubbing in the dirt.[30]

But the Uncle Toby complex died hard. Obsessed with the Winchester-on-the-wall frontier tradition, or with military romanticism personified by Teddy Roosevelt, Americans remained unperturbed by news of unparalleled casualties in Europe. Richard Plume, in Stallings' novel, scion of a southern family with a history of military achievement dating back to the Revolutionary War ("there was not a coward among them"), is exposed to the martial rejoicing of his father, who—after congratulating his son upon enlisting—opens his own scrapbook: "There he was [as a member of the "Fulton Light Hussars"], white infantry cross-belts over a blue pouter's chest, epaulettes burnished, wide crimson sash bellied faultlessly and shako at the faintest angles. . . . He would give his soul to be with his boy and watch his face the first time Richard went 'over the top.' . . ."[31]

What going "over the top" actually meant was a mystery to the vast majority of the American public, and it remained a mystery until returning veterans began writing books. Only then would a sense of World War I fighting be brought home dramatically to the American mind. For novelists like Edith Wharton (*A Son at the Front*, 1923), or Willa Cather (*One of Ours*, 1922) had pictured the experience as something of a cross between the Alamo and Bunker Hill. That military officers on their way to France in 1917 had been under the same impression is indicated by the fact that the Germans often regarded the action of United States troops (the Marines at the Marne, for example) with a mixture of awe, hatred, and pity; German military commentators at the

[30] Bayard Schindel, *The Golden Pilgrimage* (New York, 1929), pp. 93–94.
[31] Laurence Stallings, *Plumes* (New York, 1924), pp. 25, 27. Richard's reactions become especially bitter when he thinks either of military environment of the past or military cheerleading in the present: "I come from a long line of shiftless men who welcomed the opportunity to leave their wives," he says while visiting Mount Vernon. "What a pleasure it must have been to have a few horses shot from under you as George in there did, and then come home to this delightful barony" (p. 204). As he lies on the ground wounded, Richard curses the local military romanticists: "Parades and parades and parades. Esme. He had given her up and she had given him up, and back home thousands of loose-lipped seriously drooling sons of bitches were talking pompously of supreme sacrifices made pompously" (p. 244).

time, indeed, felt that such action could only be the result of total ignorance.[32] Just as Hervey Allen describes the administrative chaos and poor liaison that heavily increased American casualties, so Thomas Boyd, in *Through the Wheat*, portrays the gradual wearing away of soldiers—even good soldiers like Hicks—under conditions of total attrition, with direct combat the exception rather than the rule. In Boyd's novel a visiting general addresses a battalion consisting mostly of replacements and proclaims with heavy rhetoric that "you" have shown that "you" cannot be beaten by the Hun. Hicks then remarks:

"But it all seems so damned ridiculous. Take our going over the other day. A full battalion starting off and not even a fifth of them coming back. And what did they do? What did we do? We never even saw a German. They just laid up there and picked us off—direct hits with their artillery every time. . . . Think of being sent out to get killed, and the person who sends you not knowing where you're going. . . . It'd be all right if we could go up and clean things up with one big smash, but . . . you go up and come back, go up and come back, until you get knocked off. . . .

"Where the hell is it all going to end? Gimme another drink."[33]

Having begun his journey anxious for combat and proud of his "marksmanship badge," Hicks—like Irwin in *Impromptu*—finds battle in which "nobody knew what they were doing," and artillery barrages exploding "like bubbles bursting through the scum of a great cauldron."[34] The similes used most often by World War I novelists to describe combat convey a mixture of inanity and sordidness, indignity and a sense of personal violation—like the castor oil torture perfected in World War II by Italian Fascists, who understood only too well the double death suffered by a man dripping away his life along with his bowels. It is this quality of personal violation by death which, again, accounts for the sense of physical or psychological emasculation so often evoked by the novelists.

If patriots found the nature of technological war difficult to imagine, they found the results impossible to stomach. "The wounds and scars of ancient warfare," L. L. Bernard points out in *War and Its Causes*, "were regarded as evidence of courage and therefore

---

[32] See George Viereck (ed.), *As They Saw Us* (New York, 1929), for German reaction to American troops. Also Von Giehrl, "The A.E.F. in Europe, 1917–19."
[33] Boyd, *Through the Wheat*, pp. 214–15.
[34] Paul, *Impromptu*, pp. 185, 187.

counted as badges of honor. But the disfigurements of modern warfare are looked upon with aversion, and their bearers are in large measure disqualified socially in the struggle for existence, their economic efficiency is weakened and their social acceptance diminished."[35] Such "aversion" provides the dramatic unity of Stallings' *Plumes* and makes the ballroom scene in Faulkner's *Soldiers' Pay* so effective. " 'All your suffering,' " says Gary to Richard in the former novel, " 'comes to exactly the same thing that might have been gained from a fall under a freight train.' "[36] And in *Company K*, Mrs. Steiner, determined to do her bit by helping a few brave boys, says to a nurse: " 'We want you to send soldiers wounded in action . . . but nothing gruesome, you understand: nothing really revolting or gruesome.' "[37]

The impact of twentieth-century fire power on the American troops first exposed to it helped produce the combination of absurdity, protest, and numbness which were to become characteristics of the antihero in the post-World War I novel. American experience, indeed, was perhaps all the more violent because Americans lacked the expensive but thoroughgoing education provided by the early years of the war; the British and French soldiers who had suffered initial impact had already been consumed, and their replacements or survivors had, by 1917, some understanding of the machine to which their lives and deaths were being committed. Not so with the Americans, who had virtually no knowledge of the machine at all. "All the men disappeared; that is, the French did," Allen writes of a sudden artillery barrage. "The Yanks went wandering around like a plumbers' picnic until they had enough men killed off to get wise."[38]

What Herbert Warren described as the "derelict rubbish" of the World War I battlefield ("death unredeemed, death with . . . no hint of heroism, none of heroic action, little even of heroic passion, just death, helpless, hopeless, pointing to nothing but decomposition, decay, disappearance, anéantissement, reduction of the fair frame of life to nothingness")[39] received detailed testimony in the American war novels, even those novels—William Scanlon's *God Have Mercy On Us*, for example—which were not

---

[35] L. L. Bernard, *War and Its Causes* (New York, 1944), p. 68.
[36] Stallings, *Plumes*, p. 128.
[37] March, *Company K*, p. 136.
[38] Allen, *Toward the Flame*, p. 13.
[39] *The Collected Cartoons of Louis Raemaker* (New York, 1917), p. 26.

"protest" books as such. A collation of the more lurid descriptions—decapitations, castrations, remnants of uniforms and anatomy cascading over soldiers still hiding in their holes, pieces of the cook being blown into the very coffee he has just brewed—such details would be out of place in the present study. It must, however, be emphasized that the reaction to horror, indecency, squalor, chaos, and filth was especially violent in the work of American novelists precisely because of the more naïve expectation, and subsequent impact, of the American experience.[40]

No less shocking than technological combat for American troops was trench strategy and a battle area which had taken on all the attributes of an open burial ground. The trenches running almost completely across Europe were, as Boyd remarks, "gigantic latrines built for monsters": lice, boredom, the stench of sewerage and unburied or half-buried corpses, trench rats, the thick, infested mud—these were in some ways even more shattering to initial expectations than machine fire power. Words like "putrefaction," "stench," "decay," "nausea," "infested" are reiterated in the war novels, and for good reason: one remembers Zorn, a "good" soldier, tasting the Glories of Battle by vomiting into his gas mask and sitting with "the filthy stuff slopping about his mouth" all during a barrage. Fredenburgh describes the front line, where "patrols skirmished amid the putrefaction of the valley":

On all sides lay great holes, half-filled with water. The chalky soil had been churned and rechurned until its vitals were spewed to the surface. Fragments of stained and rotten uniforms projected from the ground. The dirty bones of corpses reached despairingly from the soil that gave them no rest. . . .
On the floor of the valley a sickly stream flowed. Its banks of yellow mud looked slimy and unclean in the sun. As far as the eye could reach the valley continued—a yellow, pestilent muck-heap.[41]

---

[40] In William Scanlon's *God Have Mercy On Us* (Boston, 1920) new troops identify themselves as "The First Marine Replacement Battalion." The narrator's reaction reflects American expectations: "It was the first time we had heard the word 'replacement', but we knew what it meant. Replacements were something we had not figured on" (p. 74). And General von Giehrl, who in his article for *Infantry Journal* is impressed with both the bravery and ignorance of American troops, remarks of one division at the Marne: "The fact that the 3rd Division had to undergo its baptism of fire without having been in a quiet sector for training purposes is particularly worthy of attention" (p. 143). The major technological weapons, of course ("mustard" gas and "vomiting" gas, flame-throwers, heavy artillery, and air bombardment), also proved a shock for American troops.

[41] Theodore Fredenburgh, *Soldiers March!* (New York, 1930), p. 112.

It is small wonder that the very image of mountains could become for writers like Hemingway, Cummings, and Barbusse the symbol of something clean and fine.[42]

Fredenburgh's description of the front line is echoed by other writers of fiction and nonfiction alike, who deal both with the "muck-heap" of trench warfare and the fact that casualties accumulated far beyond the capacities of medical sections to treat them, or burial details to put them away. Allen, for example, whose *Toward the Flame* is an explication rather than a protest, simply notes "the immense amount of decay all along the front . . . dead horses, dead men, the refuse, excrement and garbage of armies. The ground must have been literally alive with pus and decay germs. Scratch your hand, cut yourself while shaving, or get a little abrasion on your foot, and anything could happen."[43] Harrison, in *Generals Die in Bed*, remembers most vividly the lice and trench rats "fat and sleek with their corpse-filled bellies";[44] Scanlon remembers half-decayed corpses being dug up by men deepening or repairing shelters; Dos Passos in *First Encounter* refers to the "gangrened soil" and "pulpy masses" of soldiers ("Have you ever seen a herd of cattle being driven to an abattoir?" asks the French aspirant.);[45] and Cobb describes the survivors of trench warfare in a passage whose chief horror is its detailed indignity:

"Look at their faces. See that sort of greyish tint to their skin? . . . Then look at some of those jaws. See how the lower jaw looks sort of loose, how it hangs down a bit? . . . Take a look at their eyes.

---

[42] A clear imagistic pattern emerges in the World War I novels as a group: human beings are seen as animals (sheep, cattle, even—as in Scanlon's book—goats) or insects; the war environment is seen as machine, or monstrous organism (dragon, prehistoric bird, lion). The war is also viewed in terms of absurdity as a "circus" or fly-paper.

[43] Allen, *Toward the Flame*, p. 112. Allen's description of a delayed burying detail is notable for its horror and absurdity, together with a detailed, understated narrative: "Lieutenant Glendenning and I took some men and went back to the 4th platoon trench. We took shelter halves and blankets and went through the ditch and picked up arms and hands and everything else. Some things we just turned under, and the most we buried in a great shell-hole. Then we pulled out the men that were smothered in the dirt; some were cut in pieces by the shell-fragments and came apart when we pulled them out of the bank. Lieutenant Quinn . . . was so mixed with the two men who had lain nearest to him that I do not know yet whether we got things just right. . . . We did not feel this so much at the time . . . you get numbed after a while" (p. 49).

[44] Charles Yale Harrison, *Generals Die in Bed* (New York, 1930), p. 53.

[45] John Dos Passos, *First Encounter* (New York, 1945), p. 130.

They're open, but they have the look of not seeing much of anything. They're nearly all of them constipated, of course. . . .

"The Germans have all our trench latrines registered. And we've got theirs too. Now a soldier doesn't like to go to a place that's registered. What's more, he doesn't like to take his breeches down, because when his breeches are down, he can't jump or run. . . ."[46]

And then, of course, there was the mud—an intrinsic part of a war in which protracted and concentrated fire power literally stripped topsoil from the earth. It is difficult to convey the sense of disgust which, the novelists insist, was produced by mud. It was a situation where (unlike World War II) not only was the rationale for operations often incomprehensible to officers and troops, but where futility was rivaled only by filth as a major characteristic of "battle." Allen describes troops "moving over the heavy mud like brown flies over fly-paper";[47] Harrison writes that "down a duckboard road what is left of the battalion dribbles toward the rear. We pass corpses stuck in the mud—walking wounded who became dizzy and fell into the black ooze and were drowned."[48]

It is interesting to compare such accounts with those of Miss Cather, who in 1922 was able to describe trench war in a somewhat different light. Miss Cather's dugout is "clean"; the land, though bleak, is "quiet"; dawn comes up "saffron and silver"; even shell holes are delicately described as "opaque." The importance of Miss Cather's view of World War I combat, however, lies not in its own limitations, but rather in the fact that similar limitations have persisted ever since 1918 and have, indeed, through a burgeoning nostalgia abetted by the necessities of continuing world conflict, actually conditioned critical attitudes toward World War I fiction as a whole. Readers of Hemingway, for example, have often assumed a continuum of violence-in-the-north-woods to violence-in-war to violence-in-the-bull-ring; as recently as 1960 John Killinger, in *Hemingway and The Dead Gods*, could actually see Nick's war experience as a "moment of truth." That such assumptions are made is an indication of how completely the World War I impact has been blunted by time and a sense of continuing crisis. Hemingway, in his later career, was preoccupied with the formalization

[46] Cobb, *Paths of Glory*, p. 5.
[47] Allen, *Toward the Flame*, p. 165.
[48] Harrison, *Generals Die in Bed*, p. 201.

of death because his war experience showed him violence without truth, without will, and—perhaps most important—without virility. To understand his work, and the work of authors who found their own solutions in political protest or aesthetic retreat, the impact of World War I combat must be seen clearly for what it was.[49]

Soldiering

Shortly before the battle of Waterloo, the Duke of Wellington is said to have remarked of his troops: "They are the scum of the earth, but by God, they can fight." While the remark is apocryphal, the reality behind it was not. The fact that Europe maintained such attitudes toward military service—"the aristocratic and professional concept"—is one reason why the military realities of World War I resulted in widespread demoralization among troops of all combatant powers.[50] For in terms of army organization (if not in the sermons, political speeches, and journalism of ideological warfare), the "common sodjer" was indeed scum; his discipline, his life, and where necessary or convenient his death, were set in rigid patterns of bonded servitude. That such servitude rather than "service" existed must be remembered if the World War I literary protest is to be understood.

The nature of mass warfare, of course, merely reinforced notions of troop expendability. But even under the war of attrition, when divisions rather than companies became expendable, military leaders remained tragically unaware that the unparalleled manpower at their disposal was the result of an ideological revolution. A soldier was a soldier; "scum" remained scum; military codes perfected in the Foreign Legion or colonial labor battalions would obviously serve for the Western Front as well. For this reason the violently negative attitude of novelists toward the armies of World War I cannot be dismissed merely as adolescent protests; if such protest was lacking in the books of World War II, it was not simply because writers were more sophisticated, but also be-

[49] See Chapter V for a more intensive examination of Hemingway and *A Farewell to Arms*.
[50] Millis, *Arms and Men*, p. 65.

cause the army environment itself had undergone vast changes since 1914–18.

In *Paths of Glory*, Humphry Cobb formulated one of the most dramatically effective indictments of military leadership in World War I. But despite the bitterness of his novel, Cobb understood the plight of army leaders caught in a technological situation they could not control and in a human situation they could not comprehend. Even as a villain General Assolant is not without a degree of personal integrity and military idealism. A veteran of many campaigns, possessed of a fierce pride in the fighting qualities of his men and the accuracy of his own judgment, Assolant vehemently opposes the suicidal attack on the impregnable "Pimple."[51] And yet he is forced to capitulate: political rather than military considerations (an error in a communiqué already issued to the press) make the attack essential.

Even as he capitulates to political pressure, however, Assolant remains unchanged from the "fighting officer" he has been throughout his career—and this is the essential tragedy of the novel. For in dealing with the men under his command as though they were Foreign Legionnaires, Assolant is being true to the facts of his own military experience and untrue to the facts of a new military environment: "If those bastards won't face German guns, they will French ones!" he proclaims—a logical conclusion for a colonial army of social dregs, and a terrible miscalculation for a civilian army representing all elements of the population.[52]

Assolant's determination to demand execution-for-example is a dramatization of military attitudes which had come to prevail in all combatant armies during World War I. That "professional" concepts of discipline, combined with mass warfare and technological casualties (shell shock, for example), resulted in enormous numbers of punitive executions or courts-martial is one reason why the military police emerge as such objects of hatred in all accounts

[51] Millis, in *Arms and Men*, notes that the pressures of mass communication and national publicity created new problems for army commanders during World War I. The basic action of *Paths of Glory* (the attempt to capture the "Pimple," the resulting slaughter, and senseless court martial) is necessary because of just such pressures. Hence Assolant's complaint: "You are going to ask me to take with my bayonets what a GHQ ink-slinger had already inadvertently captured at the point of his pen . . . GHQ is no longer satisfied with attacks for the purpose of window-dressing their communiqúes. They must now go the limit and make their infernal literature an objective in itself" (p. 21).
[52] Cobb, *Paths of Glory*, p. 136.

of the war, including fictional ones. As Céline remarks, "They began to shoot troopers by squads, so as to improve their morale, and the M.P. began to be mentioned in dispatches for the way in which he was waging his own little war, the really genuine war, the most desperate of all."[53] Malcolm Cowley points out that the attrition, punitive executions, and battle-by-compulsion later used by postwar novelists as material for their books had played a vital role in shaping the general despair and hopelessness of the World War I combat environment. "Death, not victory, was in the air," he remarks. "I happened to be quartered for two weeks with a battalion of chasseurs that deposed its officers and marched toward Paris. From that one battalion of 1,800 men, the Germans had killed or wounded 15,000 [sic] in the course of three years fighting. . . . After the mutiny the ringleaders were shot by the French. The survivors marched back toward the front, where many of them fought with the spirit of steers being driven to the abattoir—there might be a chance of life if they went ahead, but there was sure death if they ran away."[54]

Soldiers were there to die; that was their function. When any plan miscarried—when any offensive or retreat failed to take place according to schedule (Caporetto, for example)—those soldiers who survived were by that very fact suspect. Since manpower was totally expendable and the objective was all important, military leaders tended to be concerned only with where and how men died rather than with the less relevant question of whether their deaths were necessary at all. Assolant is therefore reflecting a basic tenet of World War I military logic when he dismisses Dax's passionate defense of the 181st (that the men had already suffered more than 50 per cent casualties) by reminding him querulously that "the men had failed to advance. They should have gotten themselves killed outside the trenches instead of inside."[55] Assolant's attitudes, indeed, are recapitulated in a recent novel of World War I, *Promenade in Champagne* by David Johnson. Far less rhetorical than Cobb's, Johnson's novel embodies a more subtle and powerful protest. Aiguillon, the narrator, assents to slaughter even while realizing its futility, defines military "honor" solely in terms of military death, and fails completely to understand the attitudes

[53] Céline, *Journey to the End of the Night*, p. 26.
[54] Malcolm Cowley, "The Dead of the Next War," *New Republic*, LXXVI (October 4, 1933), 214–16.
[55] Cobb, *Paths of Glory*, p. 144.

of civilian soldiers. It is almost as though Assolant, gentled by the years, is remembering his World War I experience:

By 1917 it was quite impossible to turn an enemy's flank, for there were no flanks to be turned. The staffs of Europe's greatest armies were committed to bloody frontal assaults, of a kind which intelligent commanders had discarded a century before. One laid down one's barrage then, hoping that the enemy wire was sufficiently disarranged, launched one's infantry into the waste of shell holes. And by the time the enemy had laid down a counterbarrage and thrown in his reserves, all one had to show was a few kilometers of France and a pile of corpses.[56]

It is this same military logic that ultimately convinces Frederic Henry (in *A Farewell to Arms*) that the war has deserted him; and after the Caporetto retreat punitive execution reduces whatever remains of military duty to a final absurdity. So too Cummings (who had volunteered for Norton-Harjes because of extravagant Francophilism and—at the time of his arrest—had been trying to arrange his own enlistment in Lafayette Escadrille) is educated into the meaning of World War I military death. First the Little Belgian tells him of English, French, Belgian, and German corpses dumped into the river to provide foundations for a bridge. Then the Little Belgian describes a bloody and indecisive battle:

'We Belgians did not see any good reason for continuing. . . . But we continued. O indeed we continued. Do you know why?'
     I said that I was afraid I didn't.
     'Because in front of us we had *les obus allemands, en arrière les mitrailleuses françaises, toujours les mitrailleuses françaises, mon vieux.*'
     '*Je ne comprend pas bien.*' I said in confusion, recalling all the highfalutin rigmarole which Americans believed—(little martyred Belgium protected by the Allies from the inroads of the aggressor, etc.)—'why should the French put machine-guns behind you?'
. . . .
     'To keep us going forward. At times a company would drop its guns and turn to run. Pupupupupupupupup . . .' his short unlovely arm described gently the swinging of a *mitrailleuse* . . . 'finish. The Belgian soldiers to the left and right of them took the hint. If they did not—pupupupupupupupupup . . . O we went forward. Yes. *Vive le patriotisme.*'[57]

So too Dos Passos' protagonists make similar discoveries:

[56] David Johnson, *Promenade in Champagne* (New York, 1961), p. 60.
[57] Cummings, *The Enormous Room*, pp. 186–87.

80

The poilus said la guerre was une saloperie and la victoire was une sale blague and asked eagerly if les americains knew anything about la revolution en Russie. . . . "Fellers," Fred Summers says before turning in, "this ain't a war, it's a goddamn madhouse. . . ."

It rained all day and all night; all day and all night camions ground past the deep liquid putty of the roads carrying men and munitions to Verdun. Dick used to sit on his cot looking out through his door at the joggling mudspattered faces of the young soldiers going up for the attack, drunk and desperate and yelling a bas la guerre, mort au vaches, a bas la guerre. Once Steve came in suddenly, his face pale above the dripping poncho, his eyes snapping, and said in a low voice, "Now I know what the tumbrils were like in the Terror, that's what they are, tumbrils."[58]

The fact that such revelations appear in the vast majority of post-World War I novels can be too easily dismissed; John Aldridge, for example, in *After the Lost Generation*, sees in these novels "the distillation of other men's despair."[59] One must remember, however, that a romantic Francophilism (or, personified by Frederic Henry, an equally romantic love for Italy), had been a basic element of the bold journey itself. The high pitch of crusading idealism that had shaped American attitudes toward the war depended to a great extent upon *"La Belle France,"* "Classic Italy," "Our Anglo-Saxon Heritage," and various racial manifestoes pointing to the rescue of everything fine in European civilization from the menace of the Teutonic Beast. " 'Ever seen a French soldier yet that didn't have a photograph of a baby stowed away somewhere in his dirty uniform?' " asks a soldier in Edith Wharton's *The Marne*. " '*I* never have. I tell you, they're *white*. And they're fighting as only people can who feel that way about mothers and babies.' "[60] Surely it was not necessary for Cummings to stand before French machine guns in order for him to be horrified at the uses to which they were put.

Europe at the outbreak of the First World War was for most people in this country a thing of mystery or a joy forever; unlike World War II, when Americans (including novelists-to-be) were generally quite aware of the witch's brew seething beneath the surface of European culture and politics, attitudes ranged from vague disapproval of English diplomacy and French immorality,

[58] John Dos Passos, *1919* (New York, 1954), pp. 200–1. The scene is similar to the Caperetto retreat in *A Farewell to Arms*, in which troops shout "*a basso gli ufficiale! Andiamo a casa!*"
[59] John Aldridge, *After the Lost Generation* (New York, 1951), p. 5.
[60] Edith Wharton, *The Marne* (New York, 1918), p. 99.

to a naïve cultural and social romanticism. Among both the social and intellectual aristocracy in the United States, for example, Anglophilia was the rule rather than the exception. This was also true of the economic aristocracy, since the large financial houses (Morgan among others) did most of their business through London. And France, furthermore, was an aesthetic cause-unto-itself.[61] Queen of the arts and fine wine, her very name was a rallying cry for young Americans out of the liberal arts colleges, especially those—like Cummings—with artistic ambitions of their own. It was no accident that so many of the volunteers came from Ivy League universities.

Henry F. May remarks that World War I "shattered beyond repair . . . a picture that had been more deeply implanted in the American consciousness than most Americans realized . . . the picture of a United European culture."[62] It was a long way from *"La Belle France"* to the comment of Jean Le Nègre in *The Enormous Room "Les français sont des cochons"*[63]—or Cummings' own bitterness against "those unspeakable foundations upon which are builded with infinite care such at once ornate and comfortable structures as *La Gloire* and *Le Patriotisme*. . . ."[64]

There was, of course, more to shock American protagonists than disillusion with their allies. The spectatorial attitude so essential a quality in the postwar novel—the feeling of being a spectator at some heavy, unwieldy, often obscene and always death-orientated circus—had personal no less than abstract causes. Frederic Henry, for example, is himself under the sentence of death-

[61] Jerry Towers, in Larry Barretto's *Horses in the Sky* (New York, 1929), is thrilled simply by French place names and historical-aesthetic associations: "It was to some purpose that he had read the classics" (p. 5).
[62] Henry F. May, *The End of American Innocence* (New York, 1959), p. 362.
[63] Cummings, *The Enormous Room*, p. 272.
[64] *Ibid.*, p. 169. There is some ambiguity in the novelists' attitude toward Allies: while suffering their own disillusion, the writers make it a point to sneer at Americans prejudiced against Europeans. The attitude of Mister A in Cummings' book; the head nurse in *A Farewell to Arms* who hates Italians; the medical officer in *Through the Wheat* who refuses to treat "all kinds of people" (a *poilu*); the "Y" men in virtually all the novels—such bigots are not treated gently.

One might note that one of the bitterest statements of anti-Ally feeling is to be found in Archie Binns' *The Laurels Are Cut Down* (New York, 1937). The book's setting, the post-revolution Siberian expedition, makes it quite unique among the war novels, and the Cossack and White Russian "allies" here are very vulnerable indeed (see pp. 171, 175–76, 178).

through-absurdity, and refuses to remain quiescent under the sentence:

You had lost your cars and your men as a floorwalker loses the stock of his department in a fire. There was, however, no insurance. You were out of it now. You had no more obligation. If they shot floorwalkers after a fire in a department store . . . then certainly the floorwalkers would not be expected to return when the store opened again for business. They might seek other employment; if there was any other employment and the police did not get them.[65]

Other protagonists—Andrews, Methot, Harrison, Private Gordon (forced to butcher German prisoners), Zorn, Irwin—each in his own way suffers, and is broken or coarsened by a military environment which he never expected and which, in many ways, never expected him.

The American Army in 1917 was a civilian army forced into a professional mold that was already obsolete before the first troops left the United States. The testimony of writers like Ropp, Millis, Lanzo, and even Pershing himself, indicates that neither before nor since has a military organization been less ready to absorb so vast an influx of amateur soldiers—amateurs, moreover, who (along with the rest of the American population) had been primed with heavy doses of Wilsonian idealism, Francophilism, military romance, and a gigantic campaign of propaganda and opinion control.[66] Cummings' ironic remark on his own "Pilgrim's Progress" can be applied more widely; the American soldier, in a basic sense, was a "pilgrim" indeed.

We have already discussed the lack of preparation on the part of military leadership for the new war of attrition, trenches, and technology. This lack was later to be objectively analyzed by military experts and described by eye-witness accounts such as Alden Brooks's *As I Saw It* and Hervey Allen's *Toward the Flame*. Earlier commentators were bitter; Robert Herrick, for example, in 1920 reached the "inevitable conclusion" that "the military mind is ordinarily most incompetent . . . if mankind must have the sport of mass slaughter, the one thing to do at the outset of the war is

[65] Ernest Hemingway, *A Farewell to Arms* (New York, 1929), p. 248.
[66] Europe, again, had three years to adjust to military and political realities; by the time American troops arrived, there were few illusions left on the Continent.

to relegate all professional soldiers to subordinate administrative positions in the rear."[67] Allen was to be quieter than Herrick, but no less firm in his portrait of officers who had "played at war like men in the textbooks" while others died;[68] he offers, indeed, a reiteration of horrifying ignorance: "Each platoon was provided with its own rockets to signal artillery which, for the most part, none of us had the slightest idea how to use. No instructions were provided."[69] One is reminded of the American attack in *Through the Wheat*, where tanks literally guide German shells to their human targets, and direct advance results in wholesale—and unnecessary—slaughter:

A shell landed directly upon the moving front wave to the left of Hicks. An arm and a haversack foolishly rose in the air above the cloud of smoke. . . . Machine guns began. . . . More men fell. The front rank went on with huge gaps in it. On they stolidly marched.

"Close in there, Hicks!" somebody yelled, and Hicks asked whether the men were not being killed quickly enough, without grouping them together more closely. They advanced to a point where they were enfiladed by the enemy's machine guns. As the four lines had become two, so now the two lines became one. But on they marched, preserving a line that could have passed the reviewing stand on dress parade.[70]

It was not, however, in combat and organizational terms alone that the professional military establishment was unprepared for a civilian army. Like their European counterparts, American officers—commissioned and noncommissioned alike—regarded enlisted men as red-necks to be pounded into responsible soldiers only by "regular" discipline. Part of this country's historic schizophrenia toward war and armies (pacifism combined with militancy) was the conviction, often justified, that "joining up" was prima facie evidence of failure in responsible citizenship. Before World War I a man became a "regular" soldier—especially an infantry soldier—either because there was nothing else he could do, or because he had been involved in legal, economic, or social difficulties. Military life was a kennel in which a few gentlemen-professionals (officers) controlled the nation's watchdogs. Discipline was a leash.

Taken for granted so long as the kennel remained limited, the leash became intolerable when the civilian-soldier entered the

[67] Robert Herrick, "Telling the Truth about War," *Nation*, CX (June 26, 1920), 851.
[68] Allen, *Toward the Flame*, p. 124.
[69] *Ibid.*, p. 200.
[70] Boyd, *Through the Wheat*, p. 190.

closed circle of military life. Certainly American army discipline was not geared to a situation in which soldiering had become proof of enthusiasm rather than failure in citizenship. One must remember that the plight of the poor enlisted man was hardly mentioned, much less championed, before the war had begun; only when the rhetoric of the Great Crusade had settled did commentators like Herrick denounce "the military class" for claiming "the position of an autocrat with the wayward power of a God."[71] The bitterness against army life, in other words, so vital a theme in the World War I novel of protest, was at least to some extent evoked by a rigid army environment, by a mass military establishment, and by the idealism of the Crusade itself.

In 1921 Francis Hackett remarked of John Andrews (one of the central triptych in Dos Passos' *Three Soldiers*) that "he brought to the army certain large assumptions of the American sort about justice and freedom and equality and consent. . . . He was the type of crusader who discovered in the American machine a school of intolerance, brutality and self-seeking violating everything he had ever been taught of equality and freedom and consent and all the other shibboleths of democracy. So long as he kept faith in these shibboleths . . . he was a sick soul, with the "Y" men and the officers as the worst emetics of all."[72] Hackett's remark is significant because he refers not only to the intolerance and brutality which, again, belonged to the nature of things in the military kennel; he also notes the "self-seeking" so intrinsic to survival in a closed military society—a factor in military disillusion that the postwar novelists were to dramatize repeatedly. "War is as mean as poor-farm soup and as petty as an old-maid's gossip," says Private Luston in *Company K*;[73] the combination of wheedling, abasement, manipulation, informing, cheap cleverness, hypocrisy, and debased concentration on one's own appetites, all of which were part of a "regular sodjer's" equipment, later received almost universal testimony in the novels.

Sergeant Eadie the professional soldier no less than Mattock the opportunist is a master of intrigue and petty mechanism and reflects the philosophy of "take what you can get" basic to the military environment into which young Americans had been so rapidly

---

[71] "Telling the Truth about War," p. 851.
[72] Francis Hackett, quoted in "American Army Discipline as Spiritual Murder," *Literary Digest*, LXXI (November 12, 1921), 29.
[73] March, *Company K*, p. 141.

plunged. The contrast, indeed, between the "Warriors of Christ" rhetoric and the sordid reality of army politics was to offer a major dramatic resource for writers in defining the impact of war upon their protagonists. Mattock profits by his environment; Andrews (his fate finally and irrevocably sealed when he forces himself to play Uncle Tom) is alienated by it; Cummings deserts it; Irwin and Fuselli are reduced by it; Zorn is coarsened by it. Each in his own way dramatizes the result of an obsolete military environment quite aside from the impact of technological combat.

Compounding the difficulty was the very naïveté of the civilian soldier, his essentially provincial background noted both by Mr. May and by Alan Valentine (*1913: America Between Two Worlds* [1962]). Where the "regular" knew whoredom as a basic fact of military existence, for example, the Crusader—primed with the religiosity to be discussed later—was totally unprepared for it. In *Three Soldiers,* Dos Passos was able to see considerable irony in this situation: Fuselli, far from expecting whoredom, actually proposes marriage, contracting syphilis as a result of his "engagement." And punishment for Fuselli is precisely the same as for the five-hitch man—punishment, in other words, for a civilian soldier in a mass army sent to a European theater of operations, dealt out as though the offender were an old warhorse stationed at a backwater camp in Texas.

It was this lack of army flexibility that the novelists were to attack with particular vehemence. In one book it might be a man like Andrews arrested and held incommunicado for not having a school pass with him; in another, it might be a matter of "rest" camps where men were herded behind barbed wire like convicts and simply kept until the machine required their bodies; in another it might be military police arresting stragglers—or survivors—of front-line debacles; in still another it might be shell shock cases executed by their own officers. Such episodes must be read in view of the fact that the army itself too often persisted in regarding "sodjers" in the light of the Vera Cruz campaign. The continuation of such attitudes at the time of World War I may help explain Zorn's discovery, in *Soldiers March!*, of an unexpected military formula: men must be broken before they can be good soldiers; the army functions best when the individual is frightened of those above him and contemptuous of his subordinates.

It was a formula to which there were no objections after Vera Cruz, and to which there were violent objections, literary no less than historical, after World War I. The basic terms of the equation had changed; discipline accorded to watchdogs was not always efficacious when applied to white-collar workers, farm boys, musicians, teachers, small businessmen, young southerners with a local tradition of the masculine code (including the concept of the Intolerable Affront), or youngsters fresh out of a parental environment. Captain Powers, for example, in Faulkner's *Soldiers' Pay*, is killed by one of his own men; in *Three Soldiers*, Chrisfield (who kills an officer) cannot be secure in manhood until he acts to redeem it through violence, avenging insult by following a personal code; Dick Savage, discovering a pattern of pettiness, intellectual surveillance, and outright dishonesty, ultimately becomes what he most despises.

But traditional discipline was only one aspect of the kennel which caused difficulties in a civilian army. Watchdogs, after all, must be kept busy or they may get into mischief; when they cannot be kept busy they must be penned up or they may bite the little boy next door. The World War I novelists are unanimous in testifying to the demoralization produced by harshly ignominious fatigue duties and barbed-wire-and-mud "depots"—elements, again, whose theory of necessity belonged to stateside backwaters of army life, when the "sodjer" was considered, and was likely to be, a misfit cast up by a society in which he had no other place.

Hicks, for example, who is a good soldier and actually looks forward to combat, is disgusted by "working as a stevedore beside evil-odored blacks. . . . Soldiering with a shovel. A hell of a way to treat a white man."[74] The indignity of "military" labor, indeed, is often defined by the novelists in terms of racial allusion—a reflection of the stereotypes so prevalent at the time of the Great Crusade, when songs like "The Coon Conscript" (an early Edison recording) were nationally popular. Irwin, who like Fuselli and Zorn sees the army as a means of earning rank and status, is— along with his comrades in the engineers—nauseated "at being used as floor-moppers for syphilitic blacks";[75] Chrisfield (a farm protagonist who makes an interesting contrast to Miss Cather's good-natured hired hands), despite his complete readiness to do whatever shooting is necessary, complains: "This ain't no sort of life for a man to be treated lak he was a nigger";[76] and Andrews,

[74] Boyd, *Through the Wheat*, pp. 1–2.
[75] Paul, *Impromptu*, p. 111.
[76] John Dos Passos, *Three Soldiers* (New York, 1921), p. 139.

whose enlistment is a romantic military gesture, finds only "slavery" and ends—as he had begun—with another gesture, but this time "toward human freedom."[77] One might almost say that Andrews, having set out as a Foreign Legionnaire, finds his true calling as an abolitionist.[78]

The "slavery," of course, was accentuated by the very size of the Crusade itself; if the obsolete army environment was degrading to a civilian soldier, the sense of sheer mass—of being degraded by and for a machine—produced no less powerful an impact. One must remember that the military tradition, or rather the tradition of the civilian soldier in the United States, was still essentially a frontier tradition, what Archie Binns, in *The Laurels Are Cut Down* (1937), refers to as the "Winchester-on-the-wall" concept. Walter Millis remarks that the expectation of combat was still "we-uns against they-uns";[79] parallel to this was the consideration of soldiering—in general military terms, beyond that of combat alone—as a matter of personal action, personal status, personal identity. Americans were simply unprepared for new military necessities which reduced the soldier, as soldier, to "a cog in a great machine."[80] The very enthusiasm of the Great Crusade, moreover, with its home-town parades, commencement speeches, and personal stature suddenly heaped on young men, only deepened the shock when these same young men discovered that their lives, deaths, rewards, or punishments were not only arbitrary and often accidental, but also of no great concern to anyone but themselves.

The imagery of mass, of men no longer judged by their own good or evil, runs through the World War I novels accompanied by protest, as in Dos Passos' early novels; by a bitter, symbolic mockery, as in Cummings; by a benumbed understatement, as in *A Farewell to Arms* ("only 7,000 died of it in the army," Frederic Henry says of the cholera) and Harrison's *Generals Die in Bed;*

[77] *Ibid.*, p. 423.

[78] In Harrison's *Generals Die in Bed* total demoralization actually comes after, rather than during, combat; confinement in "rest" camps with military routine is a breaking factor by itself: "They take everything from us: our lives, our blood, our hearts. Even the few lousy hours of rest, they take those too. Ours is to give, theirs to take" (p. 49). And Andrews comments on the sudden plunge—after the rhetoric of Crusade—into futile and degrading "work": "He thought of Chrisfield and himself picking up cigarette butts and the tramp, tramp, tramp of feet on the drill field. Where was the connection? Was all this futile madness? They'd come from such various worlds, all these men sleeping about him, to be united in this" (p. 32).

[79] Millis, *Arms and Men*, p. 110.

[80] *Ibid.*, p. 157.

or by a realization of absolute futility, in which motive no less than action is helpless. Hence Corporal Rose in *Company K* becomes a "hero" by being able to spot a tomato crate on the high seas; Frederic Henry is offered a medal for being attacked by a stray shell; Hicks—after fulfilling every duty as a good soldier—is denounced for cowardice and tossed out of the hospital when he is suffering from shell shock; the men of the 181st, in Cobb's novel, after acquitting themselves loyally in battle after battle, must face death-by-firing-squad via a lottery; Dick Savage does his hardest and most useful medical service after being branded as a political undesirable by the rear echelon at Paris; Lieutenant Dill, in *Mattock*, becomes a war "authority," while Captain Johnny Hard is ruined. Praise and blame, cowardice and bravery, loyalty and treachery become jumbled together like the pile of German, Austrian, French, Belgian, and American corpses heaped indiscriminately in Boyd's novel: hence Frederic Henry's dictum that everyone is broken, no matter who—or what—he is.

If mass gave to individuals like the rear-echelon officer in *1919* both power and security, and to men like Claude a sense of almost sexual fulfillment, for the war novelists as a group there was the sense of a blind thing being led to a slaughter—what René Fulöp Miller in *The Night of Time* was later (1949) to develop as his lemming symbol. In *Three Soldiers* marching troops are "lead" and their feet are "pistons";[81] in *Impromptu* the tramping soldiers become "hideous processions of empty boots";[82] Colonel Dax, in *Paths of Glory*, measures death by kilometers; Richard Plume, in Stallings' novel, wonders bitterly at "the kilowat hours of pain" produced by the war. "The enormity, the relentlessness and the ironic impersonality of the chaos in which he was shuttled overwhelmed Irwin once again," Elliot Paul writes:

What malignant power was behind these grey, silent convoys, these night-faring troop trains, these wharves submerged with boxes, last hopes in red pantaloons, squareheads in field grey, railroad yards swarming with chanting Algerians? Wards full of quivering eyelids! Wards full of bare, brown buttocks. . . .

All at once it seemed the moving file of telegraph poles was a Gargantuan tape measure. . . . How many feet? How many yards? How many miles of soldiers? What did an individual amount to? They were being measured by the mile for slaughter.[83]

---

[81] Dos Passos, *Three Soldiers*, p. 135.
[82] Paul, *Impromptu*, p. 171.
[83] *Ibid.*, p. 137.

Zorn, with his first glimpse of returning front-line soldiers, begins to understand the machine which is to reshape his own personality; it is this machine, operating beyond motive, beyond reason, and beyond cause, which becomes for Irwin too the final absurdity:

The gun was detached, impersonal, obedient. Point it to the North and it shot into Germany, for the safety of the world. Wheel it in a semi-circle and it shot into France, for the Hun and the reign of terror. If the men who polished the gun wore olive caps like hickory nuts, the gun roared for the God of Hosts. If the cannon received its rations from the swarthy men with fezzes, it bellowed just as loud for Allah. . . .

The hills and woods were neutral too. The trunks offered themselves as hitching posts for all passersby. The foliage sheltered uniforms of any colour. . . .

The multiplication table was for everybody. All the artillery used the same figures, signs, tangents. . . .

The men had all the worst of it. The men who saluted and cut their hair by orders, who ate when they could and worked when they could not avoid it, who marched in endless columns through heat and dust or the night and rain. The men had customs, obligations, consciences. They had flags. They grouped the letters of their alphabets differently. If they faced north, they were heroes and soldiers. If they faced south, they were barbarians and swine. They could not work impersonally for whoever fed them and rubbed them down. They had ideals which made it necessary to cut their throats if they got into the wrong woods.[84]

The impact of "mud, smells, slops, vermin, insects,"[85] together with the debasement of "nigger" labor, kennel discipline, and the demoralizing anonymity of mass no less than technological warfare, was accentuated by the doses of propaganda which, as we have seen, preceded and followed America's official entrance into the war. It was the contrast between civilian rhetoric and military realities that provided a major target for the novelists, a target most memorably attacked by the "Unknown Soldier" episodes of March's *Company K* and Dos Passos' *1919*. The propaganda, furthermore, continued in the army itself and, according to the testimony of the novelists (in addition to scholars), was often presented with a remarkable lack of perspective, in the midst of precisely those aspects of military life that the amateur soldier was to find so demoralizing. Zorn's company, for example, is given a rhetorical pep talk about the Crusade for Democracy immediately before

[84] *Ibid.*, p. 173.
[85] *Ibid.*, p. 147.

being stuffed into cattle cars for transport ("Herded, jammed worse than cattle would be, cold, no provision for sleeping, no possible chance of lying down, no escape from sitting up . . .").[86] So too the moral and political rhetoric of the ubiquitous "Y" men created repugnance among troops returned to "rest" areas after combat; propaganda films and military speeches were hurled at men who were then marched off to mud-and-barbed-wire enclosures for days of heavy fatigue work.

The rhetoric of the Great Crusade, in other words, followed civilian soldiers to the army camp, followed them to France, followed them to the front line itself. While the American military machine was fumbling its way through a mass operation it never expected, while transport and supply difficulties created exhaustion among troops before they had even seen combat, the rhetoric continued. "That's what will survive you and me," Andrews says after a "Y" man finishes his performance. "By no stretch of his imagination could Irwin connect this conglomeration of mud, slops and salutes with Oliver Street," Elliot Paul's protagonist reflects after having his morale helped by a warriors-of-democracy, home-and-country speech. "Bull! Bull! Bull! Everything turned out to be bull if you tried to find out what the words really meant."[87]

If postwar novelists were to indict the professional army man for failing to realize that he was not dealing with veterans of the Vera Cruz campaign, they were almost preoccupied with the amateur officer, who had his own role to play in creating the impact of army life upon the draftee or volunteer. The amateur officer of the war books (Lieutenant Fairbrother in *Company K*, the "new officers" in Scanlon's *God Have Mercy On Us*), no less than the civilian soldiers under him, in addition to being inadequately trained, found "regular" military etiquette quite alien to his expectations or experience. One alternative was to retreat from responsibility altogether, retaining—as the young officer in Nason's *Sergeant Eadie* retained—little more than the ability to delegate authority. The other was to out-military the military in rear-echelon "rest" camps, on troop marches, and in the combat environment itself. Officer jokes, of course, were common coin in the Second World War as they had been in the First (one remembers Bill Mauldin's cartoon in which an officer, gazing on the glories of a country sunset, inquires of his companion if there is a view

[86] Fredenburgh, *Soldiers March!*, p. 47.
[87] Paul, *Impromptu*, p. 114.

for enlisted men). The difference between the officer and enlisted man, however, was far greater in World War I, and it created problems more complicated—and in some ways more pernicious— than the humiliation of individuals like Andrews; the analysis of such problems was to be the subject of detailed irony and continuing bitterness in the World War I literary protest.

Unlike his professional counterpart, the amateur officer was insecure in his exalted position; it was Johnny Hard rather than Captain Matlock (ex-floorwalker in a department store) who understood when rules were to be bent, when the eye of military authority was to be closed. Allen remarks that the American army tended to view war as a "business enterprise."[88] From the testimony of the war novels, his term is particularly applicable to civilian officers whose mannerisms were often those of an office supervisor in a roomful of recalcitrant typists. Not only did the businessmen-captains studiously apply all regulations, especially those pertaining to alcohol and sex, but—perhaps more important—they applied these regulations without fully realizing what the consequences for the enlisted man would actually be. In combat we have Captain Powers, in a "Shakespearean voice," ordering Hicks to "advance" upon a machine-gun post—or Lieutenant Fairbrother, who wraps himself with both dignity and rank and, despite the objections of his noncom, sends a group of men to their deaths by placing them in a totally vulnerable observation post. In rear areas, there is the maintenance of "discipline" by pompous dress inspections, insistence on all military protocol, and unreasonable "toughness" (Captain Matlock asserting his always doubtful authority by refusing passes). Appearance too was a vitally important matter for the civilian officer; in Scanlon's novel, for example, the fresh troops—never in combat—are selected for Paris leave: "The officers picked the men with the best-looking uniforms in order to make a showing in Paris. . . . We watched them ride away toward Paris. We fell in and hiked back toward the front."[89] And in *Impromptu* there is Captain Anderson, who in civilian life "practiced law in a very large and very respectable office":

The fact that he had been cheated out of prosecuting a court martial disappointed him, for he liked to write charges and declarations and affidavits. . . . From the first, he had taken his only prisoner very

[88] Allen, *Toward the Flame*, p. 183.
[89] Scanlon, *God Have Mercy On Us* (Boston, 1929), p. 114.

seriously. No other company in the regiment had a member in the guardhouse, and Captain Anderson felt a slight twinge of superiority as he passed Irwin, shoveling mud from the gutters, if there were any other commissioned officers present. The two armed guards, without ammunition, were always properly in evidence.[90]

The combination of pettiness, incompetence, and ferocity-born-of-ignorance was further compounded by the fact that the amateur officers were very aware of political purity (and impurity). For one thing they—again, like the amateur ranks under them—had been deeply affected by the rhetoric of the Crusade: Captain Matlock, for example, repeating the usual atrocity stories, orders the execution of German soldiers as a demonstration both of his patriotism and martial firmness; ironically enough it is Sergeant Pilton, a professional, who is disgusted by the action.[91] So too Dick Savage finds the most militant militarists among the rear-echelon patriots; it is they who are most shocked by his "cowardly" letters expressing doubts about the war and they who are most rhetorically extravagant in denouncing him for his lapse. And Cummings finds—in the "doughy" and highly moral Mister A.—a superior who not only cares for the moral and racial well-being of his charges ("stay away from those dirty Frenchmen"), but serves as political informer without the vaguest notion of the machinery he is setting in motion.

If the postwar novelists were to regard the civilian officers who carried the rhetoric of the Crusade into the army (indeed, into the combat environment itself) with particular loathing, they also remembered, with equal loathing, the role of these officers as political policemen. Historians, despite varying attitudes to the fact itself,

---

[90] Paul, *Impromptu*, p. 163.

[91] The men's reaction to the execution of German prisoners (ordered by Captain Matlock, the ex-floorwalker) is a cross-section of attitudes toward war itself: Sergeant Pelton, a regular army man, is disgusted but follows orders ("soldiers aren't supposed to think . . . if they could think they wouldn't be soldiers"). Corporal Foster, repeating propaganda, righteously butchers the prisoners and is mocked by Pelton for his enthusiasm. Private Drury refuses, risking court-martial. Private Gordon acts but turns completely bitter, seeing the world itself as a slaughterhouse. Private Inabinett steals "souvenirs" from the corpses, again outraging Pelton. Private Mundy pledges never to kill again and becomes a pacifist.

The matter of "souvenirs" is a recurrent theme of the novelists, who seem to have been impressed with American callousness toward the dead. "The German dead were lying there stretched out," Scanlon says in *God Have Mercy On Us*, "all pockets turned inside out, all buttons cut off, belts moved" (p. 332).

are unanimous in pointing out that ideological surveillance was an inevitable corollary of the Crusade's ideological basis, hence the national preoccupation, almost paranoia, regarding the evils of pacifism, socialism, anarchism, and what Wilson called "hyphenated Americanism"—all tossed into the same emotional hopper. "In the United States," Roland Bainton remarks, "the mood was a blend of hysterical nationalism and crusading idealism":

American churchmen of all faiths were never so united with each other and with the mind of the country. This was a holy war. Jesus was dressed in khaki and portrayed sighting down a gun barrel. The Germans were Huns. To kill them was to purge the world of monsters. Nor was such action incompatible with love, because their deaths would restrain them from crime and transplant them to a better land. The Lord God of Battles was rolling up the hosts of Armageddon to destroy the great beast of the abyss that the New Jerusalem might descend from the sky.[92]

The identification of nationalism with religion, of pacifism with blasphemy, had important results both in the development of Total Cause, and in the reaction against religion so marked in the postwar literature of protest. These developments are discussed elsewhere in this book. The concept of Jesus in khaki, however, had significant results within the military environment itself; given the view of the war as a total struggle for democracy and Christianity, the pattern of assent demanded a demonstration of faith over and above mere works, any mere fulfillment of soldierly duties alone. The search for heresy, in other words, was not limited to the home front. "Think American!" became a military no less than civilian imperative, and postwar novelists were to dramatize this aspect of military life as a major breaking factor of the war experience.

In this connection the work of Arthur Train, one of the most widely read novelists of patriotism, is of special interest. Train, of course, was part of the wartime literary environment against which the later novelists were to react so violently; he typified the various concepts of war-as-proving-ground, religious cause, and racial invigoration (the view of combat as a cure for decadence). In *Earthquake*, published in 1918, Train recapitulates the full national rhetoric; more relevant to our purpose here, however, is the fact that he sees the army not only as a means for socio-reli-

[92] Roland H. Bainton, *Christian Attitudes Toward War and Peace* (New York, 1960), p. 210.

gious assimilation, but also as a highly effective means of political decontamination. " 'I tell you when these fellows come out of the army,' " the narrator's son exclaims, " 'they will have a respect for the United States they'd never get in any other way. When Ikey and Abie go back to the East Side, if any greasy anarchist attempts to put anything over on them, Ikey and Abie will stand him up against the wall, and say . . . 'Uncle Sam's all right! Get out!' ' "[93]

The earliest and perhaps the most violent attack upon thought control in the American armed forces is Upton Sinclair's *Jimmie Higgins* (1919). While the novel is window dressing for Sinclair's own ideological position, it effectively dramatizes the dilemma of American socialism (indeed, of international socialism as a movement) during the war years. The enthusiasm with which the Socialist movements greeted the Russian revolution during the closing months of the war was accompanied by a sharp intensification of political-police activity in the American army after bolshevism was added to anarchism as an ultimate political evil. Beaten to a senseless pulp in an army prison compound as an ideological criminal (after serving bravely and well as a soldier), Jimmy takes his place, modestly and obscurely, along with Faulkner's Mahon and Boyd's Hicks as an antihero of total withdrawal.

Unlike Sinclair, however, whose literary anger on occasion reaches absolute fury, most war novelists view the political policeman and informer as still another element of absurdity.[94] Just as Martin Howe in *First Encounter* comes to see death itself—and the whole pompous international machinery of death—as a gigantic "circus," so Cummings, for example, reduces the ideological inspections of Mister A. and the French authorities to a subject of amusement, a comedy in which people suffer, of course, but one possessed of an irrationality so complete that only a sort of desperate laughter can do justice to it: hence Cummings' wild *non sequiturs*, puns, distorted syllogisms, and elaborate parodies (". . . the remarkable and demoralizing disclosure that President Poincaré had, the night before, been discovered in unequal hand to hand battle with a défaitistically-minded bed-bug" . . . "*Il n'y*

[93] Arthur Train, *Earthquake* (New York, 1918), p. 188.
[94] Ideological suppression at home receives much attention from the novelists, especially in books written from 1924 onward. Stallings as well as Binns attacks the organization of veterans in Red-hunt activities; Dos Passos, of course, in *1919* used his "newsreel" and "biography" devices, in addition to straight narrative, to demonstrate and protest ideological suppression as a whole.

a plus d'heures—les gouvernement français les defend!").[95] Hence too a whole series of absurd definitions for *La Ferté*—itself the basic symbol in Cummings' book for a world at war.

Although the war novels of protest, especially those of Dos Passos, Paul, and Binns, attack the ideological inspection which had extended from the home front to the army during the war (Eisenstein in *Three Soldiers* is court-martialed for "possible disloyal statements found in a letter addressed to friends at home"), the attack against the political informer reached in some ways its most effective statement in the work of James Stevens, whose *Mattock* is a novel of total satire—political, religious, and military. The alliance between Mattock himself and the flabby civilian officer Lieutenant Dill (who upon leaving the army makes a career of writing and lecturing on the Crusade to Conserve our Democratic Ideals) is portrayed with devastating detail; Stevens, for one thing, sustains his first-person dialect narrative remarkably well. Mattock's activities in discovering bolshevism, atheism, and various infringements of military regulations result in the demoralization of his company and the ruin of Captain Johnny Hard. The company's two sergeants make the final comment on this new war of ideological (as well as military) purity:

Jeezus, oh, Jezus! What a war, Novak! What a war, Novak! Chris', the crap that's pulled—the snivelin' bastards that do dirt and call it good because it's right or righteous—yeah, let's make the world safe for the democrats—let's sweep hell from God's fair earth—let's pull all the old crap we can think of for the Glory of God—one hell of a God, I'll say, when I pipe the birds that's always rootin' for him! . . . Yeah, she's a great war; and the old army, boy, how she's growed; and the old USA. Jeezus, amen, what a noble Chrischun country it's come to be! Let's go, Novak. Let's be good Americans from now on. No Bolshevism for us! From now on we play the grand, new patriotic, religious, upliftin' American game of snoop, spy, frame up and stool. Yea, bo! Gimme a cigarette."[96]

In commenting on an ideological situation in which facts have become drowned in rhetoric, truth made dependent upon political purpose, and words stripped of meaning, a protagonist in Binns' *The Laurels are Cut Down* reflects that "on closer inspection,

[95] Cummings, *The Enormous Room*, p. 122.
[96] Stevens, *Mattock*, pp. 236–37.

everything turns into something else."[97] So too Frederic Henry says, " 'I was blown up while we were eating cheese' "; Zorn, on morality, sees strength alone as the ultimate right and survival the only cause; soldiers in *Company K* are seen as "castrated sheep"; Henslow, in *Three Soldiers*, advises Andrews to "tie a rock on your scruples . . . this is the Golden Age";[98] Irwin, in *Impromptu*, sees the world as a "multiplication table" and men as the merest digits in a machine arithmetic of death; Martin Howe, oppressed with the "tumbrils" carrying battle fodder to the front, calls for a counter-crusade to sweep away "all the lies"; Captain Sancy, while picking men for punitive execution in *Paths of Glory*, remarks that "the world is an open graveyard, getting perpetual care from the survivors who are living off it";[99] Summers, in *1919*, sees the Crusade as "a goddamn whorehouse." A combination of horror, dehumanization, numbness, and absurdity is the heritage that World War I novelists brought back from their broken world of combat and military glory.

Of course the "lies" that Martin Howe, in *First Encounter*, sees as a "sticky juice overspreading the world, a living, growing fly-paper to catch and gum the wings of every human soul,"[100] were not washed away immediately with the signing of the armistice. Not enough had changed on the home front. Those same good men who at the beginning of the Crusade had joined to call for machine guns were now calling for normalcy. Business, for one thing, was to take place as usual (with some time out to hunt for union organizers and Bolsheviks), and the Unknown Soldier was to symbolize the military glory to which most Americans still assented as an ideal. In 1922, for example, Willa Cather could still silhouette her protagonist against the sky, with bullets rattling off his tin hat; as late as 1923 Miss Wharton could repeat every political and military cliché, every atrocity-inflated statement of the War to Preserve Civilization.

The earliest war novels of protest focused less on ideological debunking than on specific experiences of the broken world: there was urgent need to communicate the realities of technological com-

[97] Binns, *The Laurels Are Cut Down* (New York, 1937), p. 283.
[98] Dos Passos, *Three Soldiers*, p. 232.
[99] Cobb, *Paths of Glory*, p. 178.
[100] Dos Passos, *First Encounter*, p. 30.

bat and a mass military environment to a population still essentially unaware of them. And the racial propaganda, with its assumption of inherent Gallic and Anglo-Saxon nobilities, was also an early target: Dos Passos' *Three Soldiers* (1921), Cummings' *The Enormous Room* (1922), and Thomas Boyd's *Through the Wheat* (1923) are concerned primarily with the political nature of wartime allies, military life, and combat. After 1923, however, these areas of protest combine with a fuller statement of economic or political disillusion; along with the plight of the veteran rendered unfit for "normalcy" by physical or psychological wounds, there begins the detailed analysis of home-front ignorance, atrocity propaganda, political causes, economic duplicity, and ideological suppression. Stallings' *Plumes*, for example, published in 1924, demonstrates concern with economic factors which—no less than military realities—placed the Great Crusade in a frame of absurdity:

"I grant you that all war is a mistake, a brutal and vicious dance. . . . It was the tragedy of our lives that we had to be mutilated at the pleasure of dolts and fools. But when I went to France," Richard said eagerly, "there was a spirit America had never known before, a willingness to look at life in terms of humanity and not of imaginary geographic lines."
Gary frowned and narrowed his metallic gray eyes. "Don't be a fool, Plume. . . . Your phantom of humanistic purpose came when your government was spending one hundred and fifty million dollars a day. Any country can have a golden age if it will throw gold to the rabble. Of course there was no Democratic Party and no Republican Party for a year or so. Why should there have been? The money would go all around. No political rat lacked for cheese. . . . Yet you descant on international consciousness. I was here. I saw the thing. When the hundred and fifty millions a day became reduced and the political rats were driven from the house, the old devil's game began all over again."[101]

Historical revisionism, of course, began very early after World War I—a fact which may help explain much of the novelists' reaction to the Crusade. Certainly revisionist scholarship of the second war has been negligible in comparison; the overwhelming number of studies already published have served only to support rather than demolish the necessities of external cause, the evil of fascism itself. After the Armistice in 1918, however, a process of reversal began almost while the hallelujahs were still ringing

[101] Stallings, *Plumes*, p. 127.

from press and pulpit; major revisionist works like Harold Elmer Barnes' *The Genesis of the World War* and Harold Lasswell's *Propaganda Technique in the World War*, published in 1926 and 1927 respectively, were preceded by revelatory notes, books, and memoirs on atrocity stories, on political and economic purposes, on the causes of the war itself.

The growing World War I literary protest, in other words, was accompanied by a general revisionism which attacked all aspects of the Great Crusade, including the role played by business and religion, and this in turn was accompanied by increasing sophistication in the novels themselves. The rhetorical statement of horror and absurdity in *First Encounter* or *The Enormous Room* gives way to the ironies of *Impromptu* (1923), the postwar guilt of *Soldiers' Pay* (1926), the withdrawal of *A Farewell to Arms* (1929), or the broader canvas of *1919* (1932). And those novels which continue rhetorical protest—'*It's a Great War!*' in 1929, *Company K* in 1933, *Soldiers March!* in 1935—indicate a far deeper sophistication in economic and political matters: the realities of the Versailles Treaty, the role of financial interests, and the nature of ideological suppression (the Red hunt) receive increasing attention along with the immediate impact of the war experience itself.

If the soul of Hicks is numb because of combat horror, if the last gesture of Zorn indicates total repudiation of morality, if the bitterness of Dos Passos in *1919* is aimed at capitalist civilization itself, World War I impact and disillusion are perhaps best summed up by the remark of Private Webster's fiancée in *Company K*. Greeting her wounded man on his return from the war, Effie's reaction to his red badge of courage is swift. " 'If you touch me!' " she says, " 'I'll vomit.' "[102]

Believing

"**K**ill Germans!" thundered A. F. Winnington-Ingram, the Reverend Bishop of London. "Kill them, not for the sake of killing, but to save the world . . . kill the good as well as the bad . . . kill the young men as well as the old . . . kill those who have shown

---

[102] March, *Company K*, p. 156.

kindness to our wounded as well as those fiends who crucified the Canadian sergeant. . . . As I have said a thousand times, I look upon it as a war for purity, I look upon everybody who dies in it as a martyr."[103] The Bishop's call for *Ji'had*, for Holy War, was answered beyond even his sanguine expectations. Ten million corpses were produced in the combatant armies alone, and not since the days of the Crusades or Islamic expansion had slaughter been so blessed by men of God.

The association of religion and patriotism has been part of modern nationalism itself. "The nation is always endowed with the aura of the sacred," Reinhold Neibuhr remarks in *Moral Man in Immoral Society;* this is "one reason why religions, which claim universality, are so easily captured and tamed by national sentiment, religion and patriotism merging in the process."[104] There is also the tendency of religion to view idealistic cause in terms of complete antitheses. Religion, indeed, especially Protestant religion, exerts pressure "to obscure the shades and shadows of moral life, painting only the contrast between the white radiance of divine holiness and the darkness of the world."[105] This combination of nationalistic impulse and moral antithesis offers one explanation of why the European war was accompanied by so violent an explosion of religious rhetoric.

That Mr. Neibuhr's insight is limited, however, is demonstrated by the fact that the German churches—which shared the general characteristics he discusses—never came close to rivaling their counterparts among the Allies for violent declaration of Crusade and Holy War. Bainton, for example, points out that the attitude of the German churches toward the conflict was essentially one of political loyalty, of assent to the proposition that Germany's cause—as cause—was just.[106] Among the Allies, on the other hand, especially England and the United States, political cause was rapidly subordinated to Holy Cause; the enemy became the antichrist and the war became Armageddon, what Abrams calls a struggle of "light vs. darkness, virtue vs. sin, humanity vs. autocracy, civilization vs. chaos, and God vs. the devil."[107]

[103] Quoted by Bainton, *Christian Attitudes*, p. 207.
[104] Reinhold Neibuhr, *Moral Man in Immoral Society* (New York, 1948), p. 97.
[105] *Ibid.*, p. 69.
[106] See Bainton, *Christian Attitudes*, p. 207.
[107] Ray H. Abrams, *Preachers Present Arms* (New York, 1933), p. 55.

The atrocities reported by the enormous propaganda machine of the British (less than 15 per cent of which were actually committed anywhere by anyone, Reade notes), resulted in the portrait of a racially depraved, sexually perverted Teutonic Beast trailing clouds of brimstone across the fair cities of western Europe. Children disfigured and soldiers crucified; churches demolished and peasants put to the stake; civilians blinded and wounded soldiers castrated—the catalogue of depravity was endless. Most effective of all, perhaps, was the constant circulation of stories relating to sex perversions, sex abuses, and sex victimization that sent tremors of delicious horror up the spines of church ladies and Soldiers of Democracy alike. Certainly the scholars (Reade, Peterson, and Lasswell to name but three specialists in the study of war propaganda) are unanimous in testifying to the detail, the scope, and the effect of the atrocity warfare; Peterson goes so far as to brand the Bryce Report as "itself one of the worst atrocities of the war."[108] Small wonder, then, that a Raemaker cartoon could show a green beelzebub sprouting obscenely from a German pulpit, and that Eden Phillpotts, writing the caption, could attack "Teutonic Christianity" as blasphemous by its very existence.[109]

The atrocity story found especially fertile soil in the United States because of the aggressive pacifism, or pacifist militarism, so vital to American cultural development. Theodore Roosevelt's amazing mixture of humanitarianism and Darwinian faith (blood letting as a means of racial health) was typical of the long-standing American schizophrenia regarding military action we have already mentioned. For this reason Mark Twain, in "The War Prayer," had parodied the earlier sort of righteous blood lust which was to become far more common in World War I than in previous conflicts, and so universal a target among the postwar novelists:

O Lord our Father, our young patriots, idols of our hearts, go forth to battle—be Thou near them! With them, in spirit, we also go forth from the sweet peace of our beloved firesides to smite the foe. O Lord our God, help us to tear their soldiers to bloody shreds with our shells; help us to cover their smiling fields with the pale forms of their patriot dead; help us to drown the thunder of the guns with the shrieks of their wounded, writhing in pain; help us to lay waste their humble homes with a hurricane of fire; help us to wring the hearts of their unoffending widows with unavailing grief; help us to turn

---

[108] H. C. Peterson, *Propaganda for War* (Norman, Okla., 1939), p. 58.
[109] See Raemaker's *Collected Cartoons*, p. 97.

them out roofless with their little children to wander unfriended the wastes of their desolated land in rags and hunger and thirst, sports of the sun in flames of summer and the icy winds of winter, broken in spirit, worn with travail, imploring Thee for the refuge of the grave and denied it—for our sakes who adore Thee, Lord, blast their hopes, blight their lives, protract their bitter pilgrimage, make heavy their steps, water their way with tears, stain the white snow with the blood of their wounded feet! We ask it, Lord, in the spirit of Love, of Him who is the source of Love, and who is the ever-faithful refuge and friend of all that are sore beset and seek His aid with humble and contrite hearts. Amen.[110]

Once cause is given religious sanction, pacifism in America has always tended to vanish in the enthusiasm of Righteous Struggle. This tendency, under the impact of mass propaganda and atrocity campaigns, produced an explosion of religious violence; "the appeals to the citizens to wreak vengeance upon their enemies had only to be couched in holy phraseology to bring forth the desired responses from church people":

The Old Testament, with its war-god, Jahweh, the Holy Wars of the Israelites, the Imprecatory Psalms, and the Day of the Lord of Amos; the heathen in blindness vs. the Christian; the false vs. the true gospel; the Christian Crusades; the war hymns of the church; the example of Jesus driving out the money changers from the Temple and rebuking the Scribes and Pharisees; the sufferings of little innocent Serbia and Belgium, and the cross of Christ, the symbol of sacrifice for others and world redemption through the shedding of blood—these and a hundred other symbols were utilized to take advantage of the religiously motivated individuals, while the awful struggle was painted as the Battle of Armageddon or the Holiest War of all the ages. . . . The resulting success of the Allied governments, including our own, in their skillful handling of propaganda especially designed to appeal to the clergy and the church members, is proved in the remarkable support given the war by practically all the religious groups and ministers in the United States.[111]

The tradition of pacifism during peace and extreme belligerence during war had been characteristic of the American clergy;[112] if in World War I the belligerence began somewhat early, this was due to the effectiveness of propaganda and atrocity campaigns and emotional rallying points such as the *Lusitania*. The peace hopes of 1911–14, indeed, began fading from the moment the *Lusitania* headlines first appeared, when America's joy in Righteous Struggle

[110] "Europe and Elsewhere," *Portable Mark Twain* (New York, 1946), p. 582.
[111] Abrams, *Preachers Present Arms*, pp. xvii–xviii.
[112] Bainton, *Christian Attitudes*, p. 193.

102

came to the fore and clergymen like Rev. Frank Isley Paradise, rector of Grace Church, West Medford, Massachusetts, saw the role of the United States in biblical terms: "The God of Israel has anointed us to champion the struggle for world power. It will be the helping and healing power of Christian civilization."[113]

Although clergymen in general were not yet calling for immediate intervention, the sinking of the *Lusitania* produced a reaction of horror and indignation couched in the religious rhetoric that was to become a feature of the Great Crusade. "It is a colossal sin against God," ministers of major denominations and churches proclaimed from their pulpits; "barbarism and civilization clearly the issue"; "premeditated murder." The rhetoric gained impetus until by November of 1915 the *New York Times* reported Thanksgiving sermons in New York City to be overwhelmingly pro-arms, and in this respect "unlike Thanksgiving sermons that New York had ever heard before."[114] Rev. Charles Aubrey Eaton of the Madison Avenue Baptist church attacked Wilson's delay in "avenging" the *Lusitania;* it should have been done, he said, "if it took ten million men, if our cities were laid in the dust and we were set back a hundred years."[115] The American clergy were rallying to support the petition circulated by George Wharton Pepper—a petition signed by sixty-five prominent lay leaders and clergymen, including bishops, who pointed out that "sad is our lot if we have forgotten how to die in a holy cause."[116]

Once the United States entered the war, all the major religious denominations vied with each other in supporting the concept of Total Cause.[117] This was true not only of the fire-and-brimstone

---

[113] Quoted by Abrams, *Preachers Present Arms*, p. 27.

[114] *New York Times*, November 22, 1915.

[115] Quoted by Abrams, *Preachers Present Arms*, p. 28.

[116] *Ibid.*, p. 41. Abrams notes that while pacifist opinion continued, it was rapidly weakened under pressures from the Defense Societies, the Navy League, and the Security League.

[117] Once the war began, for example, the *Federal Council of Churches of Christ in America* assented with an enthusiasm made possible by a promise to "bring all that is done or planned in the nation's name to the test of the mind of Christ." Abrams points out that this process "was in reality never complicated. The government went ahead. . . . The churches . . . simply followed with a proper blessing" (p. 45). One might note that H. D. Lasswell, a highly respected student of war propaganda, is particularly ironic regarding the role of the churches. In *Propaganda Technique in the World War* (New York, 1927), Lasswell remarks that "the churches of practically every description can be relied upon to bless a popular war, and to see in it an opportunity for the triumph of whatever goodly design they choose to further. Some care,

103

Protestant sects, but also of those who, for various reasons, had resisted the Crusade; groups such as the Irish Catholics, German Lutherans, and Jews were under an added burden of proving their patriotism and avoiding the "hyphenated American" label. There were, of course, differences between the various denominations: "Those who came from the established churches of Europe," Bainton says, "talked in terms of 'inevitable necessity' (Lutheran), 'support of the constituted authority' (Catholic), and 'unfaltering allegiance to the government' (Episcopalian). The churches of the Calvinist tradition—the Congregationalists, the Unitarians, the Presbyterians, the Baptists, as well as the Methodists, looked upon the war as a crusade. . . . For them the soldier in such a cause was an imitator of Christ."[118]

The advent of a Holy War, certainly, offered great opportunities to religious leaders who had begun to view with alarm an increasingly materialist society. Provided with an antichrist, Abrams notes, religion and the religious life acquired new and exciting dimensions:

The clergy, who were honored with government positions, writing pamphlets, making speeches over the country, or four-minute ones between acts at theaters, positions as chaplains, social agents for commissions, or as secret agents, all had increased prestige, both real and imaginary.

The immensity of the cause, the outlet in strenuous denunciation of the foe, the revival of the idea of hellfire and brimstone (in this case the Germans being the sinners) gave the pulpit new life and vigor. The members of the clergy, as of other talkative professions, depend in large measure for a living upon their capacity to arouse an emotional response in the breasts of their clientele. When the public is warmed up to fight, the clerical who treats the matter coldly is committing suicide, just as is the writer or promoter. The clergy, in general, in their eagerness to depict sin and reform the world, are always prepared for a crusade against Satan and the powers of darkness. During the war, the Kaiser took the form of His Satanic Majesty—the incarnation of evil.[119]

Not only on the home front, however, did religious rhetoric set the tone of Holy War; since the soldier was an "imitator of Christ,"

---

of course, must be exercised to facilitate the transition from condemnation of wars in general, which is a traditional attitude on the part of Christian sects, to the praise of a particular war. This may be expedited by securing suitable interpretations of the war very early in the conflict by conspicuous clericals; the lesser lights twinkle after" (p. 73).

[118] Bainton, *Christian Attitudes*, p. 198.
[119] Abrams, *Preachers Present Arms*, p. 79.

Christian pastors felt obliged to remind young men of their proper role. Edwin Holt Hughes, a prominent Methodist Episcopal clergyman, pointed out that "God's son must be with our young men or there is not much hope for them. We are agents of God, and we are charged with the duty of keeping the sons of our houses in the war in the comradeship of the Son of God."[120] This duty provided a basic rationale for the YMCA's widespread activities— activities which were to be remembered with acerbity by the postwar novelists. Aside from the YMCA, however, religious rhetoric was issued to American soldiers almost along with their rations; before combat, after combat, sometimes even at the front line itself, Christ in khaki provided a unique element in the American military environment—unique because it was unparalleled in any of the combatant armies, including those of the Allies. Abrams points out that the pleas of sensitive clergymen like Rev. Daniel Polling, who insisted that the front lines were not the ideal setting for revivalist sermons, often went unheeded; one might say that the figure of "General" Booth immortalized by Vachel Lindsay had gone to war instead of to heaven and had done so with much the same enthusiasm. "I don't want to be disrespectful, Sir," says a soldier in John Whiting's *S.O.S.*, "but your Christ is just a Chief of Staff."[121]

The religious cynicism of the war novelists must be viewed within this frame of reference; the contrast between religious rhetoric and the realities of military life and combat were simply too great. In *The Modern Novel in America*, Frederick J. Hoffman notes the "frequent reaction against the 'holy abstractions' of Western Civilization, which in the midst of trench warfare seemed a culminating profanity against the dignity of man. The effect of all this was reductive and intellectually disenchanting. In the war literature of the 1920's, writers proudly displayed the irony of war facts contrasted with armchair heroics."[122] Such heroics, however, were often formulated in the pulpit rather than the armchair, and the reaction in the novels runs the gamut from deep anger to total mockery. " 'He ought to realize,' " Dick Savage says of a clergyman in *1919*, " 'that in urging young men to go into this cockeyed lunatic asylum of war he's doing everything he can to under-

[120] *Ibid.*, p. 59.
[121] John Whiting, *S.O.S.* (Indianapolis, 1928), p. 35.
[122] Frederick J. Hoffman, *The Modern Novel in America* (Chicago, 1951), pp. 91–92.

mine all the principles and ideals he most believes in.' "[123] In *Company K*, Private Wiltsee inspires his Sunday school class after the war with stories of how he had "saved" mortally wounded comrades by not permitting them to die until they had accepted Christ.[124] And in the same novel the men are authentically moved by a pastor who regales them with the rhetoric of the Great Crusade, only to suffer a reaction later, when Captain "Fish-mouth" Matlock has righteously ordered the butchering of German prisoners. " 'I stood there spraying bullets from side to side in accordance with instructions,' " Private Gordon remarks. " 'Everything I was taught to believe about mercy, justice and virtue is a lie. . . . But the biggest lie of all is "God is Love." That is really the most terrible lie that man ever thought of.' "[125] A further dimension of inanity is provided by the fact that it is Captain Matlock who literally forces the company to attend church, with "Pig Iron Riggin" checking every man off. " 'It looks as if they could leave a man alone on Sunday morning back of the line,' " one soldier says plaintively. And the others:

"If I have to listen again to that chaplain praying to God to spare all the American Galahads and destroy their ungodly enemies I'm going to get up and say: "Who was telling you? Where do you get all this inside information?" . . . If he does that again I'm going to ask him if he doesn't know that the Germans are praying too.—'Let's be logical about this thing.' I'm going to say; ' Let's pick out different Gods to pray to. It seems silly for both sides to be praying to the same one.' . . ."

"You're not going to say anything at all: You're going to do just what you're told, and you're going to pray and sing hymns and like it."[126]

The sense of absurdity reaches a memorable expression in the symbolic and almost surrealistic imagery of Cummings: a deserted altar amid "the mutterless tumbling of brutish shadows," a statue of Jesus ("a little wooden man hanging all by itself") about whose "stunted" loins "clung a ponderous and jocular fragment of drapery." A religious service is held at the prison (which itself repre-

---

[123] Dos Passos, *1919*, p. 216.
[124] H. C. Warren, a "Y" secretary whose letters are quoted by Abrams, is strongly reminiscent of Private Wiltsee. Like March's protagonist, Warren describes how he does "God's work" by entertaining soldiers with accounts of how he himself had been "saved," urging them to do the same.
[125] March, *Company K*, p. 86.
[126] *Ibid.*, p. 91.

sents a world at war), "it being obvious to *Monsieur le Directeur* that representatives of both sexes at *La Ferté Macé* were inherently of a strongly devotional nature":

> The priest was changed every week. His assistant . . . was always the same. It was his function to pick the priest up when he fell down after tripping upon his robe, to hand him things before he wanted them, to ring a huge bell, to interrupt the peculiarly divine portions of the service with a squeaking of his shoes, to gaze about from time to time upon the worshippers for purposes of intimidation, and finally—most important of all—to blow out the two big candles at the very earliest opportunity, in the interests (doubtless) of economy.[127]

The war novelists use various technical devices for developing their protest against the religious Crusade: rhetorical author-comment (Fredenburgh, Paul); equally rhetorical dialogue (Lazo, Whiting, Dos Passos, Stallings); total satire, in which the protagonist himself represents the Christian Soldier in all his fatuity (Stevens); and an antirhetorical dialogue—as in Harrison's *Generals Die in Bed*—strongly reminiscent of Hemingway in its strength and reticence. In Harrison's book, the narrator converses with a "kindly" old clergyman during a London leave:

> "Isn't the spirit of the men simply splendid? Sobered everyone up. West End nuts who never took a single thing seriously leading their men into machine-gun fire armed only with walking-sticks . . . but the best thing about the war, to my way of thinking, is that it has brought out the most heroic qualities in the common people, positively noble qualities . . ."
>
> > He goes on and on.
> > I feel it would be useless to tell him . . .
> > I offer to pay for the tea.[128]

An additional device is that of the scene or vignette, where action and background combine to produce the symbolism of protest. Martin Howe, for example (in an episode typical of Dos Passos' highly ornamental language in his early books), sees a calvary figure with crucifix propped "so that it tilted dark despairing arms against the sunset sky where the sun gleamed like a huge copper kettle lost in its own steam." After a few moments Martin notes that "where the crown of thorns had been about the forehead of Christ someone had wound barbed wire." Then he sees the faces of marching troops, "tortured and wooden," themselves Christ figures (or

[127] Cummings, *The Enormous Room*, p. 174.
[128] Harrison, *Generals Die in Bed*, pp. 171–72.

rather, Christ parodies) in their suffering. They march like specters, struggling under the weight of their equipment, floundering
in mud. Finally a straggler "suddenly began kicking at the prop
of the cross with his foot, and then dragged himself off after the
column. The cross fell forward with a dull splintering sound into
the mud of the road."[129]

A similar scenic protest is staged by March, in *Company K*.
Describing a bombardment, he first concentrates with ironic detail
on a "shell-shocked dog" who, with slavering mouth, chases himself
and howls:

At last little remained standing in the town except one wall of white
limestone. On this wall was a religious print, in a gilt frame, showing
a crown of thorns and a bleeding heart from which flames ascended;
while beside it, on a wooden peg, hung a peasant's shapeless coat.
I lay on my belly and stared at the wall. . . . The shells fell faster
and the frightened dog began to spin and chase his tail. The white
wall trembled and a few stones fell, and when I looked up again
the coat had slipped from its peg and lay in the dust like a sprawling
dead bat. . . . Then, suddenly, the shelling stopped, and the silence
that followed was terrible. The dog sniffed the air. He lifted his voice
and howled.

I got up, then, and put on my pack and a moment later Al joined
me. For a moment we looked at the white wall, still standing, and
at the sacred picture untouched in its place.

Al walked over to the wall and stood regarding it curiously: "Why
should that one wall remain?" he asked. "Why should it be
spared? . . ."

Then as he stood there adjusting his pack, and fumbling with the
rusty catch of his cartridge belt, there came a tearing sound, and
a sharp retort, and down fell the wall in a cloud of dust, smothering
the heart from which flames were ascending, and crushing him to
death with its weight.[130]

Hervey Allen, in *Report to Major Roberts* (a novella) combines
irony, rhetoric, and objective action in still another vignette, set
in the small French town of Crezancy:

A battalion of Americans and a regiment of Germans had left their
dead behind them. The place had been shelled into a shambles. Streets
of empty and desolate houses with collapsed roofs and fronts ripped
open, the contents gushing out of doorways like vomit out of a dead
man's mouth. . . . The large church in the town square stood with
one side cracked open, a large painting of Christ on the Cross looked
out over the shivered roofs and gazed at the gentle works of his fol-

[129] Dos Passos, *First Encounter*, pp. 89–90.
[130] March, *Company K*, p. 27.

lowers in the year 1918. In the courtyard of the town hall twelve abandoned horses, their eyes swollen shut with gas, milled about miserably and made bleating noises. Dick had them shot.[131]

Part of the reaction against religion, of course, was due to the nature of technological combat itself. Long discussions were held by home-front clergy as to whether Christ could possibly have been a pacifist and as to whether he would have used such weapons as the grenade, the machine gun, the bayonet, and the long-distance artillery piece. The YMCA had already reassured itself in the matter of hand-to-hand fighting—which was, after all, no more than wrestling with the devil—and so could distribute pamphlets advising soldiers how to eliminate the Disciples of Sin by attacking their testicles or removing their eyeballs.[132] But it was some time before the clergy could develop a sound rationale for the use of machine weapons. The difficulty was not insurmountable, however, and men like Albert C. Dieffenbach, editor of *The Christian Herald*, could draw a startling picture of Jesus as the Redeemer who "would take bayonet and grenade and bomb and rifle and do the work of deadliness. . . ."[133]

Once a rationale for the use of machine weapons had been developed, the next step was inevitable: the reiteration, in religious or spiritual terms, of combat as proving ground. Hence William L. Stidger, a Methodist minister, "Y" secretary in France, and author of *Soldier Silhouettes*, could see battle as a spiritual purge. "No boy goes through the hell of fire and suffering and wounds that he does not come out new born," he rejoiced. "The old man is gone from him and a new man is born in him. That is the great eternal compensation of war and suffering."[134] So too Dr. Ernest M. Stires of St. Thomas Church in New York proudly observed that after the war historians would record that "the very faces of the victorious soldiers were ennobled by the beauty of the ideals for which they fought."[135]

In commenting on this attitude Hervey Allen, whose nonfictional *Toward the Flame* parallels many of the major themes of the war novels, remarks first, that mass death involves a "loss of horror"; second, that there is "no escape" from the machine; and third,

---

[131] Hervey Allen, "Report to Major Roberts," *It Was Like This* (New York, 1940), p. 98.
[132] See Abrams, *Preachers Present Arms*, p. 67.
[133] *Ibid.*, p. 68.
[134] *Ibid.*, p. 60.
[135] *Ibid.*

that "one sees behind the scenes, the flowers and the grave-blinds, the opiate of words read from the good book and the prayers. . . . The sight of battlefields must always be a great blow to the lingering belief in personal immortality . . . the subject [spiritual values in combat] was never mentioned by anyone, contrary to the statements of religious enthusiasts."[136] What Allen said matter-of-factly, the novelists say dramatically or rhetorically: hence the "Unknown Soldier" episodes of Dos Passos or March, impassioned questions put by writers like Harrison ("How will we ever go back . . . and hear pallid preachers whimper of their puny little Gods who can only torment sinners with sulphur?"),[137] and the laconic conclusion of Ernest Hemingway, in "A Natural History of the Dead" (after a savage catalogue of battlefield sights and stenches): "few travelers would take a full breath of that early summer air and have any such thoughts as Mungo Park about those formed in His own image."[138]

The "Y" man, however, rather than the clergyman per se, was to become an object of universal disgust, even of hatred, among the novelists. Just as the military protest of the World War I writers must be seen in perspective, so the high pitch of their resentment against the YMCA must be viewed in terms of the role actually played by the YMCA at the time—a role which, fortunately, it has never quite managed to repeat.

For one thing, many "Y" activities aroused disgust. Men back from front-line combat found themselves shuffling forward in queues to buy cigarettes, candy, and coffee from "Y" secretaries at a cost which, in the particular circumstances, seemed outrageous. The reputation of the "Y" for profiteering was actually without foundation; the prices, however, were set according to stateside standards, so that the price tag on a cup of coffee might have secured *vin rouge* at the local bistro—if the bistro had not (as was likely) already been declared offbounds under the good offices of the YMCA.[139] The organization's role, at any rate, was not con-

[136] Allen, *Toward the Flame*, pp. 120–21.
[137] Harrison, *Generals Die in Bed*, p. 101.
[138] Ernest Hemingway, *The Fifth Column and the First 49 Stories* (New York, 1939), p. 542.
[139] The cost of YMCA items, however, is nevertheless something of a sore point in the novels. In *Company K*, for example, Private Hayes is willing to pay his ten dollars for a "Y" sweater—until he discovers, by means of a letter enclosed in the package, that the sweater was knitted by an old lady in a county home who did not receive a penny for her work.

ducive to respect. "The nature of their business," Hervey Allen remarks of "Y" secretaries, "selling gumdrops and cakes when the nature of civilization hung in the balance, was so petty that they were bound to be despised by the very men for whom they labored. All these things might have been issued as a part of the rations from the ration dumps or sold by accredited sutlers. . . . A religious organization that found its greatest field in purveying stationery, jelly and ginger-snaps behind the lines of battle merited the contempt which it so often received. As a matter of fact, there was little else it could do, and that in itself was a great comment."[140]

One might note that the "Y" secretaries saw their role as peddlers in a somewhat different light. H. C. Warren, for example, serving with the "Y" in France, sent one letter back to the United States in which he recalled the inspiring sight of American soldiers, steeped in devotion, "calling in Christ's name for cigarettes and chocolates."[141] This sort of pompous myopia—in which the merest slang becomes translated into an expression of religious faith—was a minor and persistent theme with the postwar novelists, who were irritated with the "Y" secretaries' personal asininity almost as much as by their religious verbiage.

But the "Y" did not limit itself to selling gumdrops, and for this reason novelists were to voice a somewhat more violent reaction than irritation. It was one thing to have the blood purge proclaimed at home, where clerical rhetoric added another dimension of excitement for troops who had only the vaguest notions of the realities awaiting them. It was quite another thing to have the Holy War proclaimed in France, where "Y" secretaries, fulfilling their role as propagandists, "exhibited the Bible as the greatest of all war books, and Jesus as the happy warrior going before into battle, thrusting his bayonet into the body of the Hun as an example to others."[142]

In addition to propaganda a function of the YMCA involved "saving the manhood of America that would otherwise be exposed to moral ruin when exposed to the temptation of life in the army," and erecting what Henry Sloan Coffin called "restraints that

[140] Allen, *Toward the Flame*, p. 181.
[141] Quoted by Abrams, *Preachers Present Arms*, p. 40.
[142] *Ibid.*, p. 175. One remembers Fuselli, in *Three Soldiers*, dwelling with fascination on a "Y" pamphlet replete with pictures and stories of "children with their arms cut off, of babies spitted on bayonets, of women strapped on tables and violated by soldier after soldier . . ." (p. 70).

checked brute lusts."[143] The lusts in question, of course, pertained to women and alcohol, neither of which was deemed appropriate for Christian Warriors; hence the court-martial offense for venereal mishap, and extremely heavy penalties for drinking. In *Company K*, for example, a "Y" secretary, complete with the usual tailor-made uniform, delicate laughter, simpering approach, and the aura of that peculiar mixture of effeminacy and "reg'lar feller" comradeship common to "Y" portraits in many other novels, decides to hold a dance for enlisted men:

"I'm sure you will agree that this is the strangest dance you ever attended. At first we wondered how to give a dance at all without members of the fair sex present. Some of the organization were in favor of inviting local girls, but I'm glad to say that idea was overruled: We felt it was not fair to you fine young men." The secretary's voice became grave. "I'm sure you know what I mean . . . fellows!" There was silence for a moment, and then the secretary shook his head and went on.
"Finally somebody had a happy thought and suggested that we invite boys from the various church homes and dress them in women's costumes, thus preserving the element of exercise, and at the same time eliminating the more objectionable features of the dance."[144]

The demoralization resulting from this enforced "morality" should not be underestimated, especially given the traditional attitudes of the professional army into which the civilian soldier was so suddenly plunged, and the fact that Allied armies had rather different policies. "For six days and nights we were fighting without sleep and without rest," Private Bordon tells us in *Company K:*

Since we were fighting under French orders, we drew supplies and food with them also. When the food arrived, there was red wine and a small ration of cognac for each of us. We were hungry, cold, and very tired, and the cognac warmed our blood and made the long night bearable.
But on the second day, when rations were delivered again, the wine and cognac were missing . . . the religious organizations in France had protested against rationing intoxicants to us: It was feared the news would get back to the United States, and that the Women's Christian Temperance Union and the Methodist Board of Temperance and Public Morals would hear of it and would not be pleased.[145]

---

[143] *Ibid.*, p. 172.
[144] March, *Company K*, p. 134.
[145] *Ibid.*, p. 33.

One other aspect of the Young Men's Christian Association must be mentioned in order to view the postwar protest in its own terms: in addition to doing everything in its power to ensure masculine purity, the "Y" also served as a subsidiary training organization for combat. Boxing programs, for example, were instituted because of what the International Committee of the YMCA remarked as "the very close relationship between boxing and bayonet movements";[146] pamphlets were distributed on the most effective means of hand-to-hand fighting. The ideal, ultimately, was a muscular and ascetic Soldier of Christ who neither drank nor womanized, but joyfully killed for the greater glory of God and Country and Mother. "The eye can easily be removed with the finger," revealed the Young Men's Christian Association; this sentence—together with religious rhetoric, the insistence on masculine virginity, the image of Jesus in khaki, the huge doses of mother, sister, and home (juxtaposed with delightfully detailed accounts of raped women)—can perhaps best symbolize the basis for the postwar protest. Certainly "Mr. Lark of Arkansas," YMCA secretary in Scanlon's *God Have Mercy On Us*, was to be remembered well as a type by the novelists: his oppressively neat uniform, his first-hand acquaintance with Jesus, and his ever-present ability to translate "morale" into religious and political hallelujahs, made him a natural target when the great hangover replaced the Great Crusade.

Loving

Before World War I the sexual emancipation of American women—and that of men—had not yet taken place. There were some startling developments in the years preceding the war: the female ankle, for example, still cotton-clad, peeped out from beneath skirts that no longer trailed the floor; foxtrots had been introduced among the more daring; and naturalist novels ("sex books," sniffed Arthur Train) were being championed by the avant-garde. But these were only beginnings. "The nineteenth century attitude toward sex," Mr. May points out, "so strange to Mr. Mencken

---

[146] Quoted by Abrams, *Preachers Present Arms*, p. 172.

and us, was still sacred to the overwhelming American majority";[147] the alternative to mother, sister, and home was, quite inevitably, the cesspool. In literature too the environment was nineteenth-century: naturalism itself had been reshaped by pre-existing Calvinist pressures within the United States, so that for novelists like Norris and Dreiser sex tended to represent a destructive rather than creative force. Unopposed by work, innocence, or will, sex could only be a moral threat rather than a personal fulfillment.[148] Young literary people, in other words, no less than other Americans, carried with them to France or Italy a marked naïveté in regard to sexual love.

Such naïveté was to have important results in the work of a man like Hemingway, for whom (under the additional impact of technological warfare) will and mastery become the very definition of *cojones:* love is permissible, as Edmund Wilson has remarked, only when its object is "amoebalike."[149] So too Dick Savage's spiritual ruin is foreshadowed not only by his affair with Edward's wife, but by his idleness (the "cook's tour") through much of his life overseas; his brief attempt at real work, in an episode reminiscent of Norris' Vandover, comes too late to save his soul from the monster of social organism, and he succumbs to the "buzz-saw." Claude, in Willa Cather's *One of Ours*, suffering from "dreams that would have frozen his young wife's blood with horror," finds in the action of war a legitimate assertion of thwarted erotic impulse. And finally Margaret, in Faulkner's *Soldiers' Pay*, redeems her three highly physical days with Captain Powers: acting as a mother figure for both Cadet Lowe and Mahon, she achieves final expiation—asexuality—by rejecting Gilligan.

As a breaking-factor in World War I literature, sex experience—like combat and military experience—must be seen in terms of initial expectation. Five elements emerge: first, the fact that Americans were becoming restive under the yoke of nineteenth-century attitudes, even if they were far from ready to discard them; second, the general American naïveté and sentimentality noted by Mr. May; third, the powerful religious rhetoric which imaged the American army as Soldiers of Christ whose purity

[147] May, *The End of American Innocence*, p. 340.
[148] See my article "Frank Norris and the Werewolf of Guilt," *Modern Language Quarterly*, XX (1959), 252–58.
[149] Edmund Wilson, "Hemingway: The Gauge of Morale," *Literature in America*, ed. Philip Rahv (New York, 1957), p. 388.

was their most powerful weapon; fourth, the ideal of ascetic muscularity always prevalent in American culture (from Deerslayer to the Rover Boys), raised to a semi-official Army policy by the YMCA and dramatized in the work of such writers as Arthur Guy Empey; and fifth, the huge doses of racial and cultural propaganda which—at the same time it idealized *La Belle France* and Classic Italy—defined lechery as one more bestial monopoly of the Hun. (Dorothy Canfield Fisher, for example, in *Home Fires in France* (1918), not only sentimentalized French culture as a sort of Gallic Methodism, but also portrayed Germans as monumentally lascivious, with sex appetites that would make a Hemingway hero turn green with envy.)

That sex attitudes were not quite so placid as their verbal surface is obvious from any study of prewar America, when certain tendencies among young people were already growing: a more personal independence (partially the result of a growing industrial society in which financial security could be achieved earlier by both sexes), a livelier curiosity, a fuller demand for experience. These tendencies were alarming to many of their elders, so alarming, indeed, that periodical writers and novelists like Train could view the war itself as a means not only of curing decadence and defeating materialism, but actually of strengthening moral behavior through Holy Cause. It is this attitude to which Dos Passos refers in *First Encounter*, when a young soldier—indignantly denying the possibility that the war has created immorality among the French—declares that "nothing is more purifying than sacrifice."[150]

Young people, however, authentically stirred by the ideals of the Great Crusade, were also aware of its opportunities and looked forward to a breaking-away that could not otherwise be achieved except with the harshest social penalities. Combined with a basic assent to what Mr. May calls "sacred" nineteenth-century moral imperatives, in other words, there was the expectation of some release from the imperatives themselves. " 'Any city of France is old in the ways of wickedness, a Sodom and Gomorrah that the most wicked city administration in the United States would not tolerate for an instant,' " Leonard Nason proclaims, breaking into the narrative of *Sergeant Eadie* to recapitulate his own memories of the war experience. His conclusion, however, best dramatized the unique mixture of moral purity and naïve erotic expec-

[150] Dos Passos, *First Encounter*, p. 22.

tation so characteristic of the Great Crusade, for after his violently Biblical interruption, Nason is almost charmingly subdued as he adds: " 'Americans . . . take kindly to the cities of France.' "[151]

The phallic impact of the war, of mass mobilization and a period of national hysteria, came to be a minor but persistent theme among postwar novelists.[152] "Boys hope innocently for the worst, full-blooded girls find it hard to sit still," Elliot Paul remarks in *Impromptu;* Margaret, in *Soldiers' Pay*, describes the pre-embarkation parties and elopements that gave to "shipping out" an aura of peculiarly erotic excitement (it is the falsity of the sentiment that Margaret later must expiate); and in *Company K* Jerry Blandford picks up a girl, a respectable girl, who not only agrees to spend the night with him for the Cause, but says—on the way to a hotel—" 'I don't care . . . I don't care who knows.' "[153] In one sense the "I Don't Care" girl, while beginning to emerge from her nineteenth-century cocoon during the prewar years, was able to make her full, radiant appearance only after the War for Purity had run its course. "Girl clerks," Stallings remarks in *Plumes*, bitterly commenting on the way wartime Washington greets the armistice,

having relinquished joyously a virginal condition which counted nothing in a single economic standard of the war years, were terrified at the prospect of a return to the mid-western double-standard. It had been a great war for these folks, a bursting of limited horizons, and they had not reckoned on its untimely end. A few of the girls sat upon the benches of the wide parks and swallowed bichloride. A few of the men killed themselves, but most of them returned to their dismal homes bravely, patiently to await there resumption of hostilities with any foreign nation whatsoever.[154]

But the restraints were there, as Mr. May indicates; if a few cracks had been appearing in the walls of the old morality even before the Crusade, the walls themselves were firm enough to make the rhetoric of righteousness an absolute necessity for new moral freedom to be justified. These restraints, indeed, may help account for the violence with which the American public responded to

[151] Nason, *Sergeant Eadie*, p. 110.
[152] A World War II novel—*Louisville Saturday* by Margaret Long (New York, 1950)—is an effective treatment of war's emotional impact on women. Miss Long's novel is the only full-length examination, in fiction, of this generally neglected subject.
[153] March, *Company K*, p. 9.
[154] Stallings, *Plumes*, p. 91.

atrocity stories—especially sex atrocities. Reade and Peterson graphically describe how stories of sex outrages rapidly became the chief staple of the Allied propaganda machines, and how Edith Cavell (much to the confusion of the German High Command for whom a spy was, quite simply, a spy) became a feminist martyr. "Why so much more sympathy for the women than for the men?" Jusserand demanded of Ambassador Lansing. His irritation, perhaps, can be understood more fully in light of the fact that the French executed nine female spies with complete impunity from American public opinion—which itself indicates how effective was the propaganda monopoly enjoyed by the Allies.[155]

American ladies, at any rate, who were shocked at new dress styles that exposed their ankles, could—with perfect respectability—dwell upon sex horrors narrated with ingenious variation of detail. There was rape, for a beginning; and multiple rape; and children forced to watch the rape; and burning oil poured over townspeople after the rape (a story repeated by Miss Fisher in *Home Fires in France*). Violence against such things becomes a moral imperative: hence the YMCA's ideal of the ascetic soldier, and—in fiction—men like Claude, who literally embrace battle and make love to war while "grimly disapproving" immoral proclivities among American troops.[156]

What Rev. George Parkin Atwater noted as the "thrilling ripple of machine-guns," in other words, was accompanied by an equally thrilling ripple of socially approved erotic excitement; and this excitement, precisely because of the restraints that were so much a part of American culture, was easily transmuted into violence. Certainly the postwar novelists were impressed—one might say oppressed—with the purgative violence exhibited by so many civilians, especially clergymen and ladies. Céline's American girl, with her insatiable appetite for blood, has her counterparts in most of the war novels produced by Americans. In *1919* there are "the long-faced Red-Cross women giving each other goose-flesh with stories of spitted Belgian babies and Canadian officers crucified and elderly nuns raped . . .";[157] in Stallings' *Plumes* Mrs. Bibb

[155] See Peterson, *Propaganda for War*, p. 62.
[156] Willa Cather, *One of Ours* (New York, 1922), p. 436. Miss Cather's men "walk out" with French girls as though they were teenagers on a Saturday night date. The idea that the American soldiers used whorehouses, or that French girls in garrison towns often charged for their services was, even as late as 1922, quite inadmissible.
[157] Dos Passos, *1919*, p. 103.

suffers some loss of reputation because "she had opposed Richard's being drafted from the first. Her words had no weight. 'She'd think different,' said Mrs. Kershaw, 'if she was one of those Belgian women and ravaged by every soldier in Germany.' The ravages weighed rather heavily on Mrs. Kershaw's mind."[158]

The violent attitudes of the men who wrote the novels of the twenties can perhaps be understood more clearly when one remembers that as late as 1923 Edith Wharton in *A Son at the Front* recapitulates—in all seriousness—precisely those beliefs so universally despised by the men who had been overseas. "As the months dragged on," Miss Wharton writes, intruding directly into her narrative, "a breath of lukewarmness had begun to blow through the world, damping men's souls, confusing plain issues, casting a doubt on the worth of everything. . . . No one seemed to feel any longer that life is something more than being alive; apparently the only people not tired of the thought of death were the young men still pouring out to it in their thousands."[159] The young men, however, were not only "tired" of the thought of death but were also tired of the Miss Whartons: the postwar literary protest gathered momentum from 1923 onward.

The sense of emotional explosion was not limited to the home front; soldiers too were exposed to large doses of religious and erotic excitement. No YMCA hut was without its atrocity literature; hence Fuselli, after a brief inspirational visit to the "Y," comes back with whirling memories of sex atrocities and horror pictures, and a warrior of democracy, after watching a propaganda film, exclaims: " 'I never raped a woman in my life, but by God, I'm going to. I'd give a lot to rape one of those goddamn German women.' "[160] And there is the most direct comment of all, voiced by Fuselli himself, for whom new horizons of excitement have opened up: " 'It's great to be a soldier. . . . Ye can do anything ye goddamn please.' "[161]

But "anything" could not be done—unless a man were prepared

[158] Stallings, *Plumes*, p. 56.
[159] Edith Wharton, *A Son at the Front* (New York, 1923), p. 372.
[160] Dos Passos, *Three Soldiers*, p. 27.
[161] *Ibid.*, p. 40. In *Company K* a wounded German asks Private Mooney for water: "I said: 'It was different when you were raping Red Cross nurses and cutting off the legs of children in Belgium, wasn't it? The shoe's on the other foot now.—Here's some of your own medicine.' Then I straightened out his head with my foot and pounded his face with the butt of my rifle until it was like jelly" (p. 116).

for the consequences, and severe consequences they were. Even in an atmosphere so explosively charged with violence and eroticism as the Crusade, nineteenth-century restraints were still very much in evidence; for this reason Cummings, in *The Enormous Room*, deals so extensively with the relationship between male and female prisoners. Rules are proclaimed under precisely those conditions guaranteed to make their violation inevitable, while the violation itself is punished with senseless cruelty. It is a symbolic statement of the Crusade morality aimed no less at Mister A. than at the petty administrators Cummings despises.

Unlike *La Ferté*, however, where restraints were simply external, those of the American "Enormous Room" were both external and internal; it is the moral assumptions of nineteenth-century Protestant America, indeed, even more than the mere stupidity of army regulations, which the postwar novelists would demonstrate as a major breaking factor of war experience. In *Mattock*, again, James Stevens used satire as his literary weapon: Mattock himself, who had already gotten a "Swamp Creek Girl" pregnant back home but had refused to marry her because "it would have broke Ma's heart," weeps over the "temptations" oppressing him. He is a "Christian Kansas young man" earnestly striving to maintain his purity: "I had never been in any of the dives and wineshops yet, and I had no idea going around them tonight. I'd just buy some souvenir handkerchiefs, probably, and maybe a pair of fancy-wrap leggins, then look around a bit and come back."[162]

Such is the ideal soldier's leave as it had been represented in the work of Temple Bailey, Edith Wharton, or Arthur Guy Empey; in Miss Cather's postwar *One of Ours*, soldiers go "mushroom picking" with French girls only when their moral fiber has been weakened by idleness—and do so, moreover, like Nebraska farm boys courting a neighbor's daughter. And Mary Lee's *'It's a Great War!,'* which reflects at least some of the war bitterness which by 1929 had filtered into popular literature, nevertheless continues the sanctified moral orientation: Anne, her heroine, wanders through wartime France like a suffering (and occasionally louse-bitten) Madonna who has just written a book of advice for teen-age girls. She is a "pal," of course, for soldiers, proud of the fact that American males "take up" sex only when their deeper desires for battle have been frustrated. " 'Most men take to military stuff like ducks to water,' " a lieutenant confides, adding—in proper *Deerslayer*

[162] Stevens, *Mattock*, p. 15.

119

fashion—that " 'what they don't like is what civilization does to war—organizes it, so that six men rot around in towns like this while one fights. The six can't get the fighting, so they revert to the male and female side of it. But don't think there's a man here who wouldn't rather be up front.' "[163] Anne herself, who ultimately is disillusioned not because of the war's cost in lives, but rather because of its failure-in-purity, discusses the moral crusade with a Frenchwoman:

"And your young American men—are they then so very cool toward women? Are they so very chivalrous in their designs toward them?"
"It depends on the woman," said Anne. "American men can usually live up to the standards women set them."[164]

Commenting on a friend's fall from moral grace, Anne reveals precisely those attitudes so universally resented among the novelists of protest: " 'But with Drennan!' " she says. " 'I rather think he'd have been an ordinary, serviceable husband if he'd stayed in the U.S.' "[165] It was too late: Drennan had seen a new world of experience, and so had the novelists themselves.

In the postwar novels, however, the break from nineteenth-century standards is never complete, never easy. Hemingway's work, of course, demonstrates the native-girl complex: the retreat from Glorious American Womanhood to the embrace of totally passive, erotic shadows. The protagonists of other writers are ultimately no less futile than Frederic Henry, but in different ways.

Fuselli in *Three Soldiers* and Private Wadsworth in *Company K* represent one form of the ironic reversal that our war novelists employ in so many areas of experience. Both men are ruined not because they defy nineteenth-century standards, but rather because they espouse them. Setting out on their bold journey determined to keep themselves pure (and, in Fuselli's case, to "get ahead"), their ultimate degradation comes about through those very sentimentalities which, by every proclamation of the Crusade, ought to have protected them. Wadsworth, indeed, maintains his male chastity against all the mockery and suspicion heaped upon it by his fellow soldiers; having exchanged a pledge with his fiancée "to remain pure for each other," he can suffer the mockery without damage. If he is unmoved by temptation, however, Wadsworth is helpless before sentiment, and when his comrades bribe a whore

[163] Mary Lee, *'It's a Great War!'* (New York and Boston, 1929), p. 91.
[164] *Ibid.*, p. 89.
[165] *Ibid.*, p. 108.

120

to personify "mother," "sister," "home," and "hardship"—all the sacred values and sacred martyrdoms to which Wadsworth assents—his seduction is inevitable. Like Haight in Norris' *Vandover and the Brute*, Wadsworth can function sexually only within an aura of delicately sentimental incest. The fact that he contracts syphilis with the best spiritual motives—providing comfort for his Sister in Christ—makes no difference: he ends his own Crusade as a convict in a labor battalion.

So too Fuselli, who assents to every aspect of the Crusade's rhetoric and quickly learns how to secure the approval of his military superiors by flattery and self-effacement, is literally ruined by his own goodness. From the time he first meets Yvonne knitting in her parlor, from the moment he meets her sister and brother, and actually has dinner before the family hearth, his fate is sealed. Possessed of a mother, sister, and brother, besides being able to knit, Yvonne must be a good girl, obviously no "hooker," and Fuselli determines to marry her.[166] Subsequently comes the shock of finding that his sergeant has also been enjoying Yvonne's favors, and the even greater shock of syphilis. The sergeant, of course, a professional soldier, escapes quite unscathed. Indeed, he takes precisely those precautions most offensive to Fuselli's moral code. The result is almost too obvious: Fuselli, convicted of sex, is sent to a labor battalion.

That the enlisted man would suffer in direct proportion to his own innocence was almost guaranteed by army regulations: venereal disease, again, was a court-martial offense, and the penalties for unsophisticated consumption of alcohol were almost as harsh. The enforcement of regulations, furthermore, was very erratic, especially regarding off-limit areas, with great discretion allowed to individual M.P. detachments. Even Mary Lee demonstrates some impatience: her protagonist becomes indignant (on the grounds that such regulations are insulting to American self-control) when the United States army, after the French had officially licensed prostitutes in the area, proclaims that "any American soldier seen on the street with women who are not in uniform will be arrested."[167] The novelists are particularly cynical with army regulations that tended to victimize those enlisted men who were least

---

[166] The discovery that bad girls can "look" good and that good girls can look bad is a frequent source of ironic comment in the novels. In *First Encounter*, for example, a soldier assumes a French girl is a whore because her hair is bobbed.

[167] Lee, *'It's a Great War!,'* p. 67.

educated in the ways of wickedness: it is the rascal ("Wild Dan" Cohen in *Three Soldiers*), the hypocrite (Mattock), the sophisticate (Henslowe in *Three Soldiers*), the professional soldier (Sergeant Eadie), or the amateur protected by rank who best survives.

In one sense ruination-by-morals is also typified by Irwin, protagonist of Elliot Paul's *Impromptu*, who sets out on the Crusade as an emotional adolescent. Irwin's military ideals are broken by machine and mass; his moral ideals are shattered by a sex environment to which he can react only with puerility. Significantly, it is only after a moral harangue that Irwin's sex education actually begins:

A "Y" man, not quite equal to his leather leggins, was speaking with earnest teeth:
"To win the war, we must have good feeling between the French people and ourselves. Set them an example. Show them what morals mean in a clean young nation across the water. If anyone tries to sell you dirty postal cards, look him straight in the face and see who drops his eyes first."[168]

Irwin's reaction is to go in immediate search of postal cards. But a shock awaits him: instead of the lecherous "he" of the "Y" man's speech, a greasy peddler quite unable to look a clean-cut American youth in the face, Irwin and a companion meet a French matron of distinguished, even motherly, appearance in a neat little shop. This apparition throws Irwin into a state of absolute panic, as though his grandmother had suddenly plucked a prophylactic from her sewing kit. The result is a mixture of guilt, fascination, and serio-comic reversal: "The stage-mother did not seem to be embarrassed. Irwin could not look her in the eyes. He blushed and was ashamed to select the ones he really wanted." And in the street, as the two men hurry back to their labor detail oppressed by the ease with which their moral surfaces have been upset, their guilt turns to outrage. " 'These Frogs,' " says Irwin's companion, the pornographic cards safely in his pocket, " 'ain't got no shame.' "[169]

[168] Paul, *Impromptu*, p. 115.
[169] Puerility also defines Irwin in his first visit to a whorehouse. Forced to soil his virtue under pressures which the army had officially ruled out of existence, Irwin suffers guilt, disgust, and fear of "catching something." To this is added the fear of being "found out" after "the captain lined them up and gave them a talk. Men who put themselves in danger of venereal disease were traitors; . . . the venereals ate the food and supplies that ought to go to men at the front. The captain had no pity for them and no sympathy with them. If it were not for danger of contagion, he would shove them into the front line trenches" (p. 125).

Just as sexual puerility foreshadows Irwin's future when he will withdraw completely to merest physical existence, so Zorn, in *Soldiers March!*, undergoes a sex experience that helps define what he is to become. Like Fuselli, Zorn begins the Crusade filled not only with moral and patriotic fervor but also with radiant visions of "getting ahead" in his military career—like an office boy working his way up the company ladder. In Zorn's case, however, the ironic reversal comes not from his failure to secure promotion, but rather from the fact that he achieves "success" only after every ideal he initially cherished is completely destroyed. Ultimately Zorn is rendered metallic by technological death and the military machine, and by impersonal sex as well: the young soldier who had been visited by mother in training camp (as though he were at a boy's vacation resort) is plunged with the briefest possible transition period, into a situation in which everything sacred is completely reduced by mechanism:

Zorn visited a near-by city and brothel there.
A sum of money was collected by Madam in advance.
A group of naked women appeared before the assembled soldiers.
Their bodies glistened in sweat as they whimpered or moaned in sexual orgy.
Zorn went outside and vomited into the gutter.[170]

As he leaves for a rear-echelon post at the end of the novel, Zorn's final, mocking gesture is indeed a vomiting-up of all moral and military idealism.

The spiritual coarsening of Zorn resembles the moral coarsening of officer protagonists, especially volunteers. For the latter, however, sex impact is less one of nausea than of absurdity, and Fred Summers' observation that "this ain't a war . . . it's a goddamn whorehouse" becomes simply one further comment on the general insanity of the crusade. Like Randolph in *First Encounter* (who is shocked because French women seem franker and more available than "drunken mulatto" women), Steve and Fred in *1919* do not particularly enjoy their first view of rear-echelon France; even Dick, in the same novel, who had been regarding himself as quite the man of the world because of his seduction of (or by) Mrs. Powers, is completely subdued:

As it got darker women leaned out towards them from behind all the trees, girls' hands clutched their arms, here and there a dirty

---

[170] Fredenburgh, *Soldiers March!*, p. 58.

word in English burst like a thrown egg. . . . The three of them walked arm in arm, a little scared and very aloof, their ears still ringing from the talk of the dangers of infection with syphilis and gonorrhea a medical officer had given the last day on the boat. They went back to the hotel early.[171]

They do not, however, "go back to the hotel early" for very long: with accommodation to a new world of mechanized sex, horror itself becomes comical: " 'It's a hoax, a goddamn hoax. . . . Sex is a slot-machine,' " Steve keeps repeating:

. . . and it seemed gigantically funny, so funny that they went into an early morning bar and tried to tell the man behind the counter about it, but he didn't understand and wrote out on a piece of paper the name of an establishment where they could faire rigajig, une maison, propre, convenable, et de haute moralité. Hooting with laughter, they found themselves reeling and stumbling as they climbed endless stairways.[172]

Ultimately there is the realization of final futility, the "*t . . d*" of *The Enormous Room*, the realization that death in wartime Europe has the comic overtones of a man suffering heart failure in a bordello.

The close relationship between the impact of sex reality and the disillusion with political, military, and religious rhetoric is indicated by the war novels as a group. An early "Camera-Eye" episode in *1919*, indeed, virtually recapitulates the various breaking factors already discussed:

washing those windows
K.P.
cleaning the sparkplugs with a pocket knife
A.W.O.L.
grinding the American Beauty roses to dust in that whore's bed (the foggy night flamed with proclamations of the League of the Rights of Man) the almond smell of high explosives sending singing eclats through the sweetish puking grandiloquence of the rotting dead
    tomorrow I hoped would be the first day of the first month of the first year[173]

Here is the sordid end of glorious military expectations, the "puking" result of inflated rhetoric, the whore's bed in symbolic mockery of Sacred American Love, and all three juxtaposed with

[171] Dos Passos, *1919*, p. 104.
[172] *Ibid.*, p. 208.
[173] *Ibid.*, pp. 8–9.

ironic reference to "the first day of the first month of the first year"—the bold journey itself.

Horror, dehumanization, numbness, absurdity, and education into political, cultural, and sexual realities: the brave new world had broken into fragments. Among these fragments, however, there were possibilities for survival either through mastering the "buzz-saw" or being absorbed within it. And, finally, there was the possibility of achieving a different sort of survival: an assertion of positive values within negation itself. In broad outlines, such were the alternative to be dramatized in postwar fiction.

III

HEROES

*This is a struggle between a cruel and
inhuman paganism . . . and the
teachings of Jesus Christ.*
—Arthur Train, *Earthquake*, 1918

*Eyes. Never miss an opportunity to destroy
the eyes of the enemy. In all hand holds use
the finger on the eyes. They are the most
delicate points of the body and easy to reach.
The eye can easily be removed
with the finger.*
—*Hand to Hand Fighting* (YMCA pamphlet)

*Our barbarian ancestors had to be brave or
perish, and it was the ones who had guts and
survived who fathered the race. . . . It's the
one noble thing about war, that.*
—Mary Lee, *'It's a Great War!,'* 1929

*"They say that if you can prove you did
any heroic act you can get the silver.
Otherwise it must be the bronze. Tell me
exactly what happened. Did you
do any heroic act?"
"No," I said. "I was blown up while
we were eating cheese."*
—Ernest Hemingway, *A Farewell to Arms*, 1929

The War Lover: Claude (Willa Cather)

Despite her inability to deal with army and combat realities far removed from her own experience, Willa Cather in *One of Ours* created a study of erotic war motivation unequaled until John Hersey's *The War Lover* appeared in 1959. Less clinical than Hersey, far less sophisticated in the use of military and psychological science, Miss Cather intuits what the later writer deliberately describes. Indeed, her book, beneath its sentimentality and intrusive rhetoric, can be seen as a case history of a man for whom the idea of death is the only possible aphrodisiac.

The World War I novels as a group, certainly, must be understood in terms of the nineteenth-century environment from which the Great Crusade developed. This is especially true of *One of Ours*, a novel whose protagonist goes to war as to an assignation. The definition of Claude Wheeler as a man is to be found less in his martyrdom as a soldier than in the midwestern farm life, the feminist codes, and the sterile marriage which make war a personal rather than a political necessity for him. Still searching for his own virility, Claude finds it with a phantom: the goddess who walks not in beauty alone, but in blood. She, ultimately, is the only wife he can embrace. And all the political rhetoric, the ideology of the Crusade itself, becomes a veneer applied to a deeper and far more urgent need than any external cause. "The sound of the guns had from the first been pleasant to him, had given him a feeling of confidence and safety," Claude reflects a moment before sleeping when—at last—he is in the war:

What they said was that men could still die for an idea. . . . Ideals were not archaic things, beautiful and impotent; they were the real sources of power among men. . . . He would give his own adventure for no man's. On the edge of sleep it seemed to glimmer, like the clear column of the fountain, like the new-moon—alluring, half-averted, the bright face of danger.[1]

Here is the definition of war "lover" indeed: stimulation by violence; dutiful application of "ideals" to sanction violence; and—when the rational edifice of consciousness is most relaxed—the translation of violence into erotic fulfillment.

[1] Willa Cather, *One of Ours* (New York, 1922), p. 420. Subsequent references to *One of Ours* will be indicated parenthetically in text.

Just as Hersey's protagonist, however, must be admired before he is revealed, so Claude apparently lacks nothing in the way of moral and physical virtues. There is his manly good health (always a point of fascination for Miss Cather, for whom "red" and "perspiring" seem essentials of masculine beauty), his love for his mother and obedience to his father, his decency, his promptness to defend helpless or insulted womanhood. Blessed with an instinctive "love of order," he regards unmastered sexual emotion as both disordered and dishonest, so that the talk of hired hands, instead of "corrupting" him, gives him a "sharp disgust for sensuality," a renewed "pride in candour." Certainly there is nothing unclean, nothing twisted about Claude. He is a good boy, a pure adolescent, an efficient farmer, a faithful husband, a generous friend, a brave soldier, an effective officer. And also like Buzz Marrow in Hersey's book, these qualities—so laudable in themselves—become for Claude an overture for death, the queen of all virtues. For if goodness surrounds Claude like a halo of midwestern sentiment, it is violence—the image of destructive power—that accompanies his every move.

Even as a boy Claude is defined by violence; the imagery of suppression, struggle, and explosion runs through Miss Cather's narrative like a trail of gunpowder on a velvet cushion. His youthful "look" is a "quick, blue flash"—a spiritual detonation that must turn inward upon itself because his environment lacks permissible targets. Ultimately he can respond fully to things or people only by means of action, thrust, imposition of will. He learns the mysteries of his own body, for example, by "imposing physical tests and penances upon himself"; he deliberately scalds himself to "conquer" fire; he walks coatless in winter to "triumph" over cold; as a young farmer he rapes rather than cultivates his property ("He flung himself upon the land and planted it with what was fermenting in him, glad to be so tired at night that he could not think. . . . He buried a great deal of discontent in its dark furrows" p. 78.). A storm calls up in him a virtual epiphany:

It was a storm that died down at last—but what a pity not to do anything with it! A waste of power—for it was a kind of power; he sprang to his feet and stood frowning against the ruddy light, so deep in his struggling thoughts. . . .
The stranger scrutinized Claude with interest. He saw a young man standing bareheaded . . . his fists clenched in an attitude of arrested action. (p. 119)

What the stranger sees is the basic reality of Claude himself, a frustrated violence ("storm," "power," "sprang," "frowning," "struggling," "fists," "clenched," "arrested," "action") destined to find its final release—indeed, to take its pleasure—only in the act of death.

" 'There must be something splendid about life,' " Claude reflects in one of his frequent moments of despair, but his desire to find this something springs neither from intellectual ambition nor aesthetic sensitivity. Conditioned by an environment in which "it was beneath his dignity to explain himself," an environment where action is its own justification, Claude's attitude toward intellectuality parallels that of Hersey's Marrow, for whom men of paper (whether navigators or school teachers) are almost physically repugnant. It is less Brother Weldon's religion, for example, than his "pear-shaped head and thin, rippled hair," his "purring" voice and white necktie, that arouse Claude's disgust. Even during his brief stay at college Claude finds "no friends or instructors whom he can regard with admiration"; surrounded by a form of authority that envelopes rather than strikes, his chief reaction is one of suspicion: he suffers as one "terribly afraid of being fooled."

Triumph is the ultimate splendor for Claude, the vision of life as a target to be struck or substance to be subdued, and his personal heroes are neither talking at universities, laboring on farms, nor raising families. "There must be something more!" he says to a friend, who—in contrast to Claude—achieves a happy marriage and later goes to war reluctantly. Claude's ideal, indeed, is not flesh but bronze: the "statue of Kit Carson on horseback" in the village square. "But there was no more west, in that sense, any more," Claude reflects; "there was still South America; perhaps he could find something below the Isthmus. Here the sky was like a lid shut down over the face of the world" (p. 118). The lid, unfortunately, remains shut even after Claude falls in love. Motivated by pressures he cannot admit even to himself, he marries a woman whose façade of submission covers a will stronger than his own. One might say that in her refusal to become her husband's "South America" Enid becomes his Waterloo—until Claude's manhood is redeemed by the golden chance of war itself.

Marriage to Enid, however, is no very important matter for Claude until the loathesomely bookish Brother Weldon provides serious competition. The competition, the resistance, even more than the girl engages Claude's attention, and the courtship takes on something of the nature of a military campaign: "He hadn't seen Weldon do anything but retreat before her eager questions. He, an 'atheist,' would have given her stronger reinforcement" (p. 132). Enid herself, furthermore, unlike the vibrant and somewhat more fleshly Gladys, is ethereal, delicate, and—apparently—gentle: "The pallor of her skin, the submissive inclination of her forehead, and her dark, unchanging eyes, made one think of something 'early Christian'" (p. 127). Even her deep religious faith is, for Claude, a stimulant: "Women ought to be religious," he proclaims; "faith was the natural fragrance of their minds."

Enid's delicacy, however, proves to be unbreakable toughness, while her faith is a force of will, determination, and self; indeed, the "fragrance" of her mind rolls over the defenseless Claude like a soft and unexpected cloud of poison no less deadly for being insubstantial, and in this atmosphere Claude virtually finds himself choking. But his wound is far more serious than infected lungs. Even when the radiance of war finally clears the air of Enid and all she represents, Claude never again turns to a woman for erotic fulfillment.

Claude defines Enid—or wishes to define her—as a love *object*, a thing malleable, there to be conquered, warmed by his heat rather than its own. It is essentially the same need which drives Marrow, in Hersey's book, to pursue Daphne. But Marrow becomes impotent when Daphne offers her body to him: passivity in the love-object, a basic condition for his virility, has been upset. Like Marrow, Claude is aroused only by passivity. He dreams of making love to Enid "while she was still and unconscious like a child"; he pictures her slowly becoming "warm," feeling "what he was feeling"; she is a "statue" warmed only by his will (p. 145). After his marriage, when Enid puts him ignominiously out of their train compartment, Claude suffers "a storm of anger, disappointment, and humiliation." He feels "unmanned," and yet he does nothing because there is nothing he can do (p. 198). Unable to master Enid's will, faced with a sudden and totally unexpected realization that her being is not his own, Claude suffers an emotional and sexual shock; just as Marrow must take to his airship for the sake of his virility, so Claude dreams of "danger," follows the wonderful new war in Europe with increasing attention to atrocities and casualty reports, and looks forward to his own impending salvation through violence.

Enid herself perceives that as a result of their marriage Claude has become "a big machine with the springs broken inside"; he has been "cowed" by his delicate new wife. With his pride shattered, with gossamer threads binding him at every turn, Claude suffers and dreams—but tries "not to think . . . when he could, he avoided thinking" (p. 208). The farm is helpful in this respect, for back-breaking labor alone permits him to sleep "like the heroes of old"; only work controls the emotional pressures building up within him. The very desperation of his labor, however, eliminates the farm as a resource, for with prosperity such narcotic action is no longer possible. The European war comes as a release—indeed, as an emotional necessity—and Claude's excitement rises with each atrocity, each report of new destructive weapons. As he reacts to rumors of the surrender of Paris, for example, Claude is strongly reminiscent of Marrow in Hersey's novel, who lovingly peruses photographs of bombing attacks. " 'I should think they'd burn it first, the way the Russians did Moscow,' " Claude says. " 'They can do better than that now, they can dynamite it' " (p. 169).

Juxtaposed with Claude's growing desperation, in other words, there are increasing references to the war—to righteous indignation, the thrill of vicarious violence. Society, of course, approves of violence only for unselfish reasons (Belgium, the *Lusitania*, Edith Cavell) and to this idealization Claude readily agrees, even sacrificing his German-American friends in the process. For his motives involve no thought of personal gain; all he desires from violence is violence itself.

Vicarious violence, however, is at best only a stopgap, especially when Enid goes off to Africa as a missionary, in a final assertion of will. Left to his own resources, weakened by leisure, Claude faces the precipice: "he felt unmarried and free; free to smoke as much as he liked, and to read and dream. Some of his dreams would have frozen his young wife's blood with horror" (p. 212). The very furniture of his home becomes distasteful: it is "rubbish, junk" that "exposed and condemned all the dreary, weary, ever-repeated actions by which life is continued from day to day. . . . He wondered how he was to go on through the years ahead of him unless he could get rid of this sick feeling in his soul" (p. 213). Even without Enid, Claude's freedom is limited to his dreams: the religiosity of his mother binds him just as the spirituality of his wife unmanned him.

Claude's relationship with his mother is ambiguous. " 'It's almost like being a bride, keeping house for you, Claude,' " she remarks when his father goes away on a business trip (p. 78). Watching a snowfall (which Claude, according to his own emotional necessities, sees as beautifully "submissive") he and his mother "clung together in the pale, clear square of the west window, as the two natures in one person sometimes meet and cling in a fated hour" (p. 87); after his marriage Mrs. Wheeler informs her son that " 'your father talks a great deal more at home than formerly, and sometimes I think he is trying to take your place' " (p. 242). And when Claude finally enlists, seizing upon the Crusade as his last chance for manhood, there is a remarkable scene indeed:

She rose, reaching toward him as he came up to her and caught her in his arms. She was smiling her little, curious intimate smile, with half-closed eyes.

"Well, is it goodby?" she murmured. She passed her hands over his shoulders, down his strong back and the close-fitting sides of his coat. . . . Her chin came just to his breast pocket, and she rubbed it against the heavy cloth. Claude stood looking down at her without speaking a word. Suddenly his arms tightened and he almost crushed her.

"Mother!" he whispered as he kissed her. He ran downstairs out of the house without looking back. (p. 263)

Small wonder that even in France Claude remembers what he never fully escapes. Admiring cathedral glass in Rouen, for example, "he felt distinctly that [the light] went through him and farther still . . . as if his mother were looking over his shoulder" (p. 343).

From the moment Claude sets out on the Crusade he experiences a complete sense of well-being: the training camp is splendid, his men are fine, and he feels blessed with "purpose." On board the troopship he becomes fully alive. Danger from submarines provides the initial stimulation, and when a soldier voices alarm over the possibility of death at sea, Claude becomes almost radiant: " 'We don't worry about that,' " he says. " 'If the Germans should sink a few ships it would be unfortunate, certainly—but it wouldn't cut any figure in the long run' " (pp. 256–57). Claude's lack of dread will later make a sharp contrast between him and Victor, the airman. Victor's orders—service over the Verdun line—mean almost certain death, and Victor himself makes no effort to hide his bitterness and gloom at so dangerous an assignment. Claude, on the other hand, reacts like a man just given a stimulant: "the very sound of the name was grim, like the hollow roll of drums. . . . He felt more 'over' than he had done before, and a little crackle of excitement went all through him" (pp. 331–32).

On board ship, meanwhile, there are better things available than mere dreams of blood. An epidemic of pneumonia breaks out and Claude, working with dead or dying men, rejoices in a "sense of ever-widening personal freedom." His enthusiasm, indeed, is finally noticed by the doctor, who comments upon so incongruous a radiance. "It was quite true," Claude admits silently. "The doctor had caught him. He was enjoying himself all the while and didn't want to be safe anywhere":

life had never seemed so tempting as it did here and now. . . . He had them [his dying friends] on his mind and did all he could for them, but it seemed to him just now that he took a sort of satisfaction in that, too. . . . He awoke every morning with that sense of freedom and going forward, as if the world were growing bigger each day and he were growing with it. Other fellows were sick and dying, and that was terrible,—but he and the boat went on, always on.

Something was released that had been struggling for a long while, he told himself . . . the miracle had happened . . . their golden chance. . . . The feeling of purpose, of fateful purpose, was strong in his breast (pp. 311–12).

From the time he arrives in France until the very moment of his own death Claude defends the war, quickens to violence and signs of violence, and resents any delay or interference with the purge by blood. Arguing with Gerhardt, who sees the war as a tragedy, Claude accuses his friend of being unable to understand " 'the hard molds and crusts the big guns had broken open' " (p. 375); at the same time, however, he "grimly disapproves" of the sex adventures of the men under his command, viewing such adventures as intolerable distractions from the "legitimate business" of killing and being killed.

Before his first combat Claude's only emotion is one of delighted expectation: "they were bound for the big show, and on every hand were reassuring signs: long lines of gaunt, dead trees charred and torn, big holes gashed out of fields and hillsides." Claude marches along "wearing a stoical countenance, afraid of betraying his satisfaction in the men, the weather, the country" (p. 358). And combat itself provides no disillusion: David may be bitter because the war has no true reasons to justify such slaughter, but Claude simply admires the French landscape, joyfully convinced that "the period of happy youth . . . which he had never experienced, was being made up to him now" (p. 410). Listening to French women discuss the fate of various relatives and friends ruined or dead because of the war, Claude draws the remarkable conclusion that for them "the war was life, and everything that went into it. To be alive, to be conscious and to have one's faculties, was to be in the war" (p. 416).

During a scene in a French and German graveyard, Sergeant Hicks, who had embarked on his own Crusade with high morale, suffers a vision of futility and waste. " 'Who put 'em here, and what's the good of it?' " he asks. Claude, however, is too busy admiring the noble sacrifice of the Unknown Soldier to be depressed. " 'Search me,' " he murmurs "absently," thinking that *Soldat Inconnu, Mort pour la France* was "a very good epitaph. . . . Most of the boys who fell in this war were unknown, even to themselves. They were too young. . . . The name that stood was *La France*. . . . It was a pleasant name to say over in one's mind, where one could make it as passionately nasal as one pleased and never blush" (p. 394).

After each confrontation of death, each stimulation by violence, Claude experiences a sense of peace. Following a bloody engagement in which his men are butchered, for example, he simply admires—once again—"this beautiful land, this beautiful people." His well-being is total; far from suffering under the impact of machine death, Claude enjoys an almost post-orgasmic relaxation. Certainly we feel that Claude, after he witnesses the protruding viscera and mutilated genitals of one of his own men, will remember the episode as one of those experiences he "wouldn't have missed for the world." And welcoming his own death-against-the-sunset, Claude at last achieves his own virility: "unconquerable" now is the "big machine" whose springs had been broken by Ideal Woman, by Home, by Society, and by life itself.

One of Ours is unique among the postwar novels in that technological combat reinforces rather than destroys the expectations of its protagonist. Miss Cather, of course, knew very little about the war she was describing; her picture postcard trenches, her pretty villages, her "mushroom-picking expeditions" had little to do with the impact of actual war experience. For this reason Ernest Hemingway, in "Torrents of Spring," could sneer at "this American Willa Cather who wrote a book . . . where all the last part . . . was taken from the action of *The Birth of a Nation*." Miss Cather's book, however, is valuable not so much as a treatment of war, but rather as an examination of particular psychological needs which helped fashion the bold journey into war. That technological combat shattered rather than fulfilled is something Miss Cather could not be expected to grasp in 1922, when the nature and impact of such combat was only vaguely understood by most Americans. The war lover, indeed, was unlikely to find fulfillment in the first great war of the machine, when combat threatened rather than redeemed manhood. But this is not the concern of *One of Ours;* as a study of erotic frustration and virility-through-violence, a violence made possible by a cosmetic surface of idealism and abstraction, the novel at least helps us to understand the environment from which the bold journey began. For the world of war itself, we must turn to other writers.

Scar Tissue: Zorn (*Theodore Fredenburgh*)

On the very first page of Theodore Fredenburgh's *Soldiers March!* the recruiting officer asks, " 'You are quite enthusiastic about going to war, aren't you?' " " 'Yes Sir,' " young Eddie Zorn replies. " 'It seems to me the duty of every man to fight for his country in a crisis—to—to die if necessary.' "[2] The brightness is unfeigned, for war comes to Zorn as both opportunity and reward: the world could not have done any better if it had celebrated the end of his adolescence with a display of fireworks.

We first meet Zorn as a "lad of twenty; fresh-faced, and with a clear, direct eye." Setting out on his bold journey to "play the man" and be "successful," he enters the army as though it were a local bank in which—by firm loyalty and diligent application—he can "work his way up." Civilian virtues, in other words, brought sincerely to a military environment, must receive not only their just reward but glory as well. "He'd worked hard day and night," Zorn reflects after receiving his first promotion in army camp. "This was the life; master the jobs and rank showered upon one. His mind leaped ahead. Sergeant—First Sergeant. 'First Sergeant,' he sighed." Caught up in dreams of military adventure and per-

---

[2] Theodore Fredenburgh, *Soldiers March!* (New York, 1930), p. 156. Subsequent references to *Soldiers March!* will be indicated parenthetically in text.

sonal advancement, Zorn is almost the direct antithesis of a World War II antihero like Saul Bellow's Dangling Man, who despises the very thought of "climbing on the backs of the dead."[3]

Zorn, however, has no wish to climb on any backs, dead or living—and this in one sense defines both his development and tragedy. Expecting glory or, at the very worst, a noble death-against-the-sunset, looking forward to power without corruption, Zorn finds that neither is possible in the machine he must serve. Youthful radiance becomes spiritual scar tissue, and his moral and military values are doomed; they cannot survive precisely because Zorn himself does. Survival, indeed, becomes the ultimate value, what Tomlinson calls "Dagon" or "might makes right";[4] like General Cummings in Norman Mailer's *The Naked and the Dead*, for whom fear and hate are the only realities, Zorn becomes a hero of metal. " 'A futurist must be disgusted at nothing except weakness and stupidity,' " proclaims Sardinaglia, the disillusioned Italian officer in *1919*. " 'A futurist must be strong and disgusted at nothing . . . that's why I admire the Germans and American millionaires.' "[5] And this preview of European fascism is indeed the "future" of Zorn himself, beaten into an efficient part of a monolith whose existence he had never expected.

When his mother visits Zorn at training camp and reassures herself that "this harmless looking adventure" offers no real threat to her son, Zorn is still radiant; it is only five weeks later, on board a troop transport, that he feels complete and terrifying anonymity. In an experience reminiscent of Irwin's in *Impromptu*, Zorn confronts the senseless violence and equally senseless passivity of the sea. Beneath the sea there is the submarine, "a spider suddenly silent, awaiting its prey, expelling its venom when the time was ripe." And there is a vision of "struggling figures spewed forth," their deaths both ludicrous and pathetic. "Somewhere in Zorn's consciousness," we are told, "a doubt stirred. Patriotism— the flag, bands, ideals of service—here at sea meant only iron and blood" (pp. 12–13).

The image of nature reduced to a machine and of a machine transformed to a force of nature is expanded with each step in Zorn's development. In his first view of returning front-line troops, for example, "the dead monotony of their faces fascinated him":

[3] Saul Bellow, *The Dangling Man* (New York, 1944), p. 64.
[4] H. M. Tomlinson, "War Books," *Yale Review*, XIX (1930), 450.
[5] John Dos Passos, *1919* (New York, 1954), p. 220.

What had happened to rob their eyes of light? What had branded their faces with this imbecilic immobility?

Subconsciously, Zorn felt the creeping fingers of an unseen, unmeasured force fastening upon him. Human values, individual values, that had been evident to him all his life, became by some hidden process extinct. The loading at the boat in New York. The rest-camp, and the animal-like herding of counted bodies of men in wire enclosures.

Looking at the human wreckage before him, Zorn felt the calculating coldness of the war machine. Men—any man—could stand a certain strain. Some more; some less. The machine decided when the breaking-point had been reached. The machine, all-minded and all-seeing, its tentacles reaching far and wide, observed, weighed, decided always in its own favor. . . . The machine cared only for its own existence. Broken blades were repaired that they might cut again. Dull ones, such as these before Zorn, reconditioned and resharpened, were returned to take up their work until permanently discarded. (pp. 44–45)

The mixed metaphor here—the "machine" with "tentacles"—reflects a growing subordination of horror to assent: horror because the machine is inhuman, and assent because it represents nature itself. To oppose it becomes purposeless suicide. The machine, in other words, is the world; and Zorn quickly perceives that while this machine world consumes flesh, it uses rather than consumes steel. The conclusion is obvious:

He was in it; a part, a tiny part, of a great cold system. It had no sympathy for human pain. It pursued its own ends exclusively. Let the individual take care of himself. If he could not stand the strain let him break—the system would discard him quickly enough, its only regret the loss of a rifle, perhaps not even that, since the passing of a weak link purged the whole of a defect. The rules were made by the system. He must adhere to them, or be eliminated . . . he must appear to acquiesce and find a way to retain himself in spite of the system. He must expect nothing but hardship and steel himself. . . . In time, he would harden to it. Let others do the same. . . .

"The fellows that make the grade have got to be as hard as the conditions they live under. Understand? I'm going to be as hard as I need to be and I am going to play this game the way it's played." . . .

"My people always told me to give the other fellow a chance. The only chance in this racket is the one you grab for yourself. . . . We're in a damned different situation now. Old rules don't work." (p. 49)

" 'Old rules don't work,' " Zorn says—and this becomes true for more than battle alone. Combat, indeed, is simply the machine in its final and most immediately destructive phase; long before combat, during months of filth, sickness, lack of medicine, and inadequate shelter, when men are "herded, jammed worse than cattle," survival becomes a matter of accomodating oneself to an entire system whose basic commandment is self-preservation at all costs. " 'Our worst enemies are the lice, some of our officers, and death,' " Harrison remarks in *General Die in Bed;* his observation will be more clearly understood if one remembers that only death, and not the military monolith as a whole, was mechanized in World War I. Supply and transport were far less developed than machine fire power, and the result was widespread demoralization and noncombatant casualities. For this reason Zorn, before he so much as sees combat, perfects his philosophy of survival:

He watched the company slogging toward the barracks. He seemed to see them at a great distance. Mechanical figures moving away. Puppets. He felt alien to them all. Grim satisfaction possessed him. Soldiers? Then let them toe the soldier's mark. Let them survive if they can, and if they can't let them die. That's the system. . . . Survive if you can, it said, and turned to other matters. Well, he'd survive, barring a hunk of steel in his body. Let others stand clear of his path or be trampled. (p. 133)

The entire process is one of coarsening: the "generosity" and "selflessness" so traditionally the result of shared hardship are nowhere to be found. " 'You take a fellow that's been through what we have and he's damned glad to help a guy out,' " says a soldier in Thomas H. Kelly's *What Outfit Buddy?* " 'This old war's teachin' a few guys there's others in the world besides themselves.' "[6] Such lessons, however, are obsolete for Zorn and for most other protagonists as well. " 'I tell you war is a business, like everything else, and if you get anywhere in it you've got to adjust yourself to its peculiarities and play your cards the way they fall,' " Donohoe remarks in *Company K*.[7] And this is the only "teaching" Zorn ever receives from the Great Crusade—an education also defined by Harrison in *Generals Die in Bed:* " 'We know what soldiering means,' " the protagonist says. " 'It means saving your own skin and getting a bellyful as often as possible . . . that and nothing else. *Camaraderie—esprit de corps—* these are words for journalists to use, not for us. Here in the line they do not exist. We fight among ourselves.' "[8]

Zorn, however, comes to see "fighting among ourselves" as a necessary—even desirable—condition for military survival. Hate

[6] Thomas H. Kelly, *What Outfit Buddy?* (New York, 1920), pp. 142–43.
[7] William March, *Company K* (New York, 1957), p. 14.
[8] Charles Yale Harrison, *Generals Die in Bed* (New York, 1930), p. 91.

is the weapon for mud, filth, and forced marches, just as numbness, luck, and caution are the defenses against technological combat. In the same way that the "futurist" Italian officer in *1919* points to European authoritarianism, Zorn's survival-through-strength points to the military fascism of General Cummings in Mailer's World War II novel. " 'They hate me so thoroughly,' " Zorn boasts of the men under his command; " 'they march until they fall off their horses' " (p. 137).

In a military machine whose anonymity is equaled only by its intrinsic absurdity (the "pot-bellied generals" asking foolish questions, the mass sex taken surreptitiously by men as though they were misusing public toilets, the machine death of artillery, poison gas, and invisible enemies), hate and strength not only protect a man but—together with total opportunism—they come to define him. And Zorn, at last bound for officers' training camp and the "success" he dreamed of, is no longer the "fresh-faced" boy who entertained his mother at an army camp. "His mouth full of hard-tack and corned beef," Zorn makes his final gesture of derision on the last page of the novel. He has not been broken. But he has been transformed. As is the case with Dick Savage in *1919*, the individual survives the shattering of a moral world.

Success Story: Richard Savage (*John Dos Passos*)

Maxwell Geismar describes the early Dos Passos hero as suffering from "failure of nerve." He lacks, says Mr. Geismar, any real purpose in life, and the energy "not merely to fulfill such purpose, but to conceive one. . . . The Hemingway hero is a man to whom things happen, but the early Dos Passos hero is in effect a man to whom very little can happen," a man who "no longer rebels against his society so much as he ignores it. The revolt against the communal forms of his time becomes a movement of indifference."[9]

"Failure of nerve," however, pertains less accurately to early protagonists like John Andrews than to Richard Savage in *1919*. Andrews, indeed, using his indifference and futility as forms of

[9] Maxwell Geismar, *Writers in Crisis* (Boston, 1942), p. 100.

assertion, commits himself to a gesture, a negative act, while Richard eliminates both assertion and act and ultimately becomes what he most despises. It is Eleanor Stoddard and Ward Moorehouse rather than the military police who "take" Richard, and the result is not social alienation, but absorption: if Andrews maintains his individuality through failure and futility, Richard gives up his identity to indifference and success.

" 'Don't monkey with the buzz-saw,' " Richard is told after his opinions have made him a military undesirable:

"Your opinions . . . don't matter. The American people is out to get the Kaiser. We are bending every nerve and energy towards that end; anybody who gets in the way of the great machine the energy and devotion of a hundred million patriots is building towards the stainless purpose of saving civilization from the Hun will be mashed like a fly."[10]

And it is the buzz-saw, the machine which ultimately determines Richard's fate no less than Zorn's or Andrews'. Unlike Fredenburgh's novel, however, or the more personal drama of *Three Soldiers*, individual choice in *1919* no longer depends upon the individual, and for this reason the chief protagonist of the book is the "buzz-saw" itself; people are "flies" caught up in an environment they cannot control.

Certainly the theme of impotence which Martin Howe introduces in *First Encounter*—the vision of "good" men writhing helpless under the "sticky juice" of lies—becomes in Dos Passos' later novel a total reality, not so much a force to be struggled against or deliberately met on its own terms (the solution of Zorn), but rather a monolith whose operations continue no matter what the pattern of individual resistance might be. "The war," Charles G. Walcutt remarks, "had generated bigness—centralized power—which combined with public exhaustion to make people believe they were less than ever in control of their fates."[11] It is this concept of mechanism, of Dagon, which provided so basic an impetus to the development of the *roman-fleuve* and Dos Passos' own collectivist techniques. No longer is the individual himself the focus of attention: the cross-sectional triptych employed by Dos Passos in *Three Soldiers* as a simple development of Unamism gives way

[10] Dos Passos, *1919*, p. 224. Subsequent references to *1919* will be indicated parenthetically in text.
[11] Charles C. Walcutt, "Fear Motifs in the Literature Between the Wars," *South Atlantic Quarterly*, XLVI (1947), 227.

142

to the monolith; the drama of the individual has been replaced by analysis of the machine.

Richard Savage, in other words, by no means plays the central role in *1919* that Zorn does in *Soldiers March!* or Claude does in *One of Ours*; as a protagonist, indeed, he cannot be fully understood apart from the various devices of the novel—the camera eye episodes, the biographies, the newsreels, and the other characterizations which overlap his own reality or help define it. He does, however, represent a particular type of war hero, or rather, war result: the individual who finally neither opposes nor triumphs, but vanishes. If Zorn beats the machine at its own game, Richard refuses even this effort; like Randolph in *'It's a Great War!*,' he sees the game itself as absurd and simply drifts into personal invisibility which, in *1919*, takes the shape of Ward Moorehouse's drawing room.

Absurdity shapes Richard just as thwarted eroticism shapes Claude and brutality turns Zorn into scar tissue; this absurdity, furthermore, has no resource beyond itself. In *The Enormous Room* Cummings finds his "delectable mountains" through art; in *Plumes* there is the firm, clear area of the laboratory; in *A Farewell to Arms* a love relationship provides a new cause and dimension of manhood; in *Three Soldiers* there is the gesture of renunciation, and Andrews makes his final exit accompanied by the drifting pages of his music. For Richard, however, there is only absurdity: work is futile (he is technically a deserter when he does his few weeks of productive labor with battle casualties); love is a "slot-machine," and art is irrelevant. The result, simply, is a breaking off of all rhetoric—even the rhetoric of anger. Writing to Mrs. Powers, for example, he succeeds only in demolishing his own protest:

"I don't believe in Christianity any more and can't argue from that standpoint, but you do, or at least Edwin does, and he ought to realize that in urging young men to go into this cockeyed lunatic asylum of war he's doing everything he can to undermine all the principles and ideals he most believes in . . . it's not on the level, it's a dirty goldbrick game put over by governments and politicians for their own selfish interests, it's crooked from A to Z. If it wasn't for the censorship I could tell you things that would make you vomit."

Then he'd suddenly snap out of his argumentative mood and all the phrases about liberty and civilization steaming out of his head would seem damn silly too, and he'd light up the gasoline burner and make a rum punch. (p. 216)

And one symptom of the "lunatic asylum" is the fact that this letter—the futility of which Richard himself understands, and the anger of which he himself disowns—is precisely the reason for his discharge as a political undesirable.

Reversal without recourse is the meaning of war experience for Richard; expectation is destroyed with nothing to take up the emotional slack. " 'Fellers this war's the most gigantic cockeyed graft of the century, and me for it and the Red Cross nurses,' " proclaims Fred Summers (p. 204); and the theme of hysterical inanity is developed throughout the Richard Savage episodes of *1919*. Love becomes a giggle of sex; battle becomes drunken and desperate soldiers being carted off for butchery; admiration for Our Glorious Allies becomes awareness of corruption (or the spectacle of pre-Fascist officers developing a worship of strength to counteract the corruption); adventure becomes a "cook's tour" of desultory pleasure-taking in the midst of poverty and death. And when Richard discovers that the American virgin he seduced has become pregnant, there can be no question of marriage; the "American beauty" has long since been ground to dust in the whore's bed, and Richard cannot act according to codes which the entire world seems committed to shatter: this would be the greatest absurdity of all.

When a *Saturday Evening Post* correspondent envies Richard and Steve their "good looks and idealism," Steve remarks that "he ought to be goddamn glad that he was forty years old and able to write about the war instead of fighting in it" (p. 210). The correspondent points out—reasonably enough—that they aren't fighting either, but this reply calls forth no guilt whatever. Steve, indeed, defiantly refers to both Richard and himself as *embusqués*. The difference between the correspondent and the young men, however, is that the former persists in taking seriously, even pompously, what the latter refuse to take at all: the correspondent has seen nothing, while the young men have seen and learned too much. They have ridden the "tumbrils" emotionally if not physically, and have fornicated on the dung-heap; for them the role of *embusqué* is the only rational one possible. But even as Steve and Fred Summers determine to use the monolith for their own purposes (" 'all bets is off,' " says the cognac-drinking sailor), they maintain at least the pride of mockery; if they cannot oppose the monolith, if opposition itself is absurd, they can at least disown it by means of their spectatorial role.

For Richard Savage, however, the spectatorial role is intolerable.

Once his own education in absurdity is complete, once he is forced to confront absolute futility (the death of Sister) in personal no less than ideological terms, he can salvage his identity only through action. First there is his desperate attempt to secure front-line duty; then, when the buzz-saw deprives him even of this chance for redemption, no choice remains. He must take whatever role is assigned to him, ultimately becoming a performer in precisely that circus of horror which Steve and Fred most despise. As a bright young man in Ward Moorehouse's orbit, neatly packaged for success, stamped with Eleanor Goddard's approval, Richard Savage's last act of the novel (the final scene, indeed, of the book itself) is to "put down" his friend and with that act—less an act than a protective reflex—his own experience and his own identity. Richard, like Zorn, has survived: Zorn through the assertion of will, Richard through its elimination.

Babbitt in Khaki: Mattock (*James Stevens*)

Whereas Richard Savage and Zorn are heroes shaped by the machine, Mattock is the machine itself, feeding and thriving on the religious-moral-political-military necessities of war. A moral chameleon for whom survival is the only imperative, Mattock wears religion and patriotism like a false skin, and the final horror is not merely that this skin provides a cover of greasy rhetoric for appetite, fear, and lechery, but rather that Mattock himself is unaware that it does. Richard struggles and Zorn suffers; if the machine ultimately degrades each man's finer nature, it does so only after a process of dramatic opposition. For Mattock, on the other hand, there is no opposition precisely because he is a definition rather than product of the Crusade, and as such is less a conscious hypocrite than a moral vacuum; the fact that he speaks with his own voice is perhaps the most effective dramatic device in *Mattock*. With this first-person narrative, certainly, James Stevens is able to recreate rather than demolish his target, and the result is a remarkably well-sustained parody of all aspects of the Great Adventure.

A "Christian Kansas young man," a master of religious simpering or suffering (as he struggles against or succumbs to temptation), Mattock echoes the inevitable "Y" man of other war protest novels, but with this difference: he is the "Y" man seen from the inside. Although the end result is the same, Stevens' method of monologue-parody gives us the process in addition to the final portrait, and we are able to follow the hand-me-down verbalisms, the essential cowardice, the instinctive opportunism of a mind essentially without any morality of its own. The triumph of this mind, a triumph made possible by the very nature of the Crusade itself, emerges as the central fact of the book; when rhetoric replaces reality, the master of rhetoric survives the extinction of the real human being. Even Johnny Hard, the professional soldier, must be crushed by a war which is also a Crusade.

For Mattock, reality is essentially verbal; thus he can define (or virtually recreate) the nature of all behavior according to the strategic needs of the moment. Lechery becomes love and treachery becomes patriotism; cowardice becomes bravery and avarice becomes thrift; nothing exists apart from the rhetoric surrounding it. As a result, action has no meaning whatever until the social verbalisms have been applied, and so Mattock is able to transmute his own weaknesses into proof of spiritual strength. If, as the result of a comedy-of-errors brawl, for example, he finds himself with a totally unearned reputation as "fighting fool," this for Mattock is enough; the reputation itself convinces him of its validity. Each step in his development occurs because the words, sentimentalities and slogans so basic to his role as Young Christian American Soldier can be taken up to define his actions: if he deserts a pregnant girl, it is only to avoid "breaking his mother's heart"; if he informs on his fellow soldiers, it is because of "patriotism"; if he helps ruin Johnny Hard, it is only to "make his way in the world" and avoid "coming to an early end." Words, indeed, serve Mattock better than any alchemist's stone, changing his heart's desire into religious or patriotic gold.

Evil, however, is also a matter of verbalisms, and for this reason Mattock is able to assent wholly to the concept of ideological criminal. Seeing all "goodness" in terms of verbal labels socially applied, he also perceives that any pattern of action which insists upon its own terminology is dangerous. A man who writes poetry is a Bolshevik; Jews who ask questions and don't "talk American" are potential Bolsheviks at the very least; Johnny Hard scorns the patriotic syrup of Lieutenant Dill and so must be crushed.

146

Of all his fellow soldiers, indeed, only one group remains for Mattock natural allies rather than potential victims:

There wasn't a foreign name among the Tennesseans, they were every last one of them patriotic, and I knowed from the start I wouldn't have any Bolshevism to report on these replacements. I doubted if they had ever heard of it. They didn't know where England was, and they probably had no idea at all about Russia. And I would have no more looked for a Socialist among them than I would a Roman. They were just real Americans of the old stock.[12]

"Resigned" to being deprived of front-line duty; praying for his salvation under the "burden" of his sin with Odette; busily engaged in ferreting out "bolshevism" among those made vulnerable by literacy, religion, or honesty, Mattock finds only one bitterness in his military experience: nobody (aside from Lieutenant Dill) likes him. And Mattock wants to be "well-liked," wants to "get along" even with those who must, unfortunately, be destroyed. Basic to Mattock's character, indeed, is a desperate desire to avoid unpleasantness and an equally desperate desire to be regarded as a "regular fellow"; throughout the novel he whines under the realization, composed equally of self-pity and bewilderment, that his fellow soldiers distrust him for some inexplicable reasons of their own. "They wouldn't let me join in the harmonizing, though I had the finest kind of bass voice," he complains, and as the narrative continues this feeling of being alienated, of being "left out of things," becomes almost strong enough to make him regret his various patriotic and religious endeavors.

After the war, however, he enjoys a "conversion," marries a preacher's daughter, and comes to understand that a certain amount of resentment from inferior souls is only to be expected by "a young Christian American like me." As a result of his conversion his service as an informer takes on a new and spiritual light. "Boosting" his home town, the virtues of Patriotism, Racial Purity, Political Conservatism, and Powerful Friends—all synonymous with True Americanism—Mattock fulfills his final role: that of Veteran Crusader. If there remain some unpleasant memories of having been "disliked" for his police activities, he takes comfort from the spiritual glories of earnest citizenship:

"I am humble and meek under the divine will. I bear a cross because in my time of sin I was ashamed and sorrowful over good works.

---

[12] James Stevens, *Mattock* (New York, 1927), p. 207. Subsequent references to *Mattock* will be indicated parenthetically in text.

147

That is the truth I have figured out. For now in my righteousness
I am ashamed only of the sin, but proud of the good works. And
it is when I am suffering the hardest oppression from the cross I
bear that my soul is most inspired to eternally fight the good fight
against law-breakers, Reds, Romans, and Foreigners." (p. 320)

As Private Bartow in *Company K* remarks when he finds, much
to his own surprise, that after a military career of fraud and boot-
licking he is hailed as a returning hero: "You've got to use your
brains if you expect to survive."[13] Just so does Mattock live out
his war.

The Subterraneans: Irwin and Fuselli
(Elliot Paul, John Dos Passos)

Embarking on a troopship for his bold journey into meaning, Willa Cather's hero notes that "the whole superstructure was
coated with brown uniforms; they clung to the boat davits, the
winches, the railings and ventilators, like bees in a swarm."[14] The
same war machine that produces an image of sweetness for Claude
creates for Irwin, protagonist of Elliot Paul's *Impromptu*, an image
of "hideous processions of empty boots." And it is this combination
of unreality and horror which ultimately defines Irwin as a Subterranean: the individual emasculated by the very forces to which
he assents.

Impromptu is less a novel of war protest than a study of ironic
process within mass, technological war; like Dreiser in *An American Tragedy* Elliot Paul uses his protagonist to define rather than
oppose a system represented by the protagonist himself. Irwin,
like Clyde in Dreiser's book, is a logical extension of precisely
those values which must break him down. Betrayed by his own
expectations and appetites, the tragedy of Irwin (a subtragedy
of pathos) lies in the fact that neither his expectations nor his
appetites are self-willed. Irwin's fate, in other words, is set up
by a vast system which first spawns and then eats its own children.

"Success" is always close to Irwin in terms of sensual gratification and of personal identity which he can develop only as the
result of social or external definition. Too close to be ignored, such

[13] March, *Company K*, p. 143.
[14] Cather, *One of Ours*, p. 273.

148

success is at the same time too distant to be achieved, at least without the violation of those moralities (or sentiments of morality) Irwin himself embraces as the creature of his social system. He desires with all his heart the "good life," the extra meat, medicine, and whores available to officers. He yearns toward the possibilities of adventure and romance just outside the barbed-wire work depots or slavish labor assignments which become his world as an enlisted man. This world is bounded by "mud, smells, slops, vermin, insects," and just beyond there is success and exotic beauty, within sight and almost—but not quite—within reach. "Ever since the midnight start from Camp Devens," Irwin reflects, "it had been like this":

He had been dirty and miserable and discontented within reach of beautiful and strange experiences. On the boat, he had wallowed in a dungeon of indigo light and evil smells, with good sea air and miles of leaping blue water seven decks above. At Brest, he had been imprisoned in a walled camp of drizzle, tarboard and hospital antiseptic, forbidden to explore the first foreign city. On the train, aching and cramped limbs, and the sweaty presence of crowded, surly comrades had soiled the romance of travel. Now, sentries kept him confined in the only dirty and manure-soaked spot, with fragrant miles of beauty all around him.[15]

Irwin, however, is incapable of acting without qualms in order to ensure "success"; always there is the pause which first depresses and then degrades his self-image. He requires, in short, the sentiments of the system along with its fruits, and in his progress through a mass military environment can achieve only his own debasement.

Like Fuselli in Dos Passos' *Three Soldiers,* Irwin does not renounce the system. Neither, however, does he use it for his own purposes. The result is ineptness, which the system may use but will not forgive. Unable to triumph in the machine by becoming a part of it, Irwin is likewise unable to oppose the machine by an act of repudiation which would redeem his own manhood; he is left floundering in a half-world of unrealized desires, puerile retreats, and vaguely defined fears, a world toward which he can react only as a slave toward his master. While John Andrews is the aesthetic rebel against such slavery, Irwin is its personification. A creature of futility, "blind with hate for everyone," he

[15] Elliot Paul, *Impromptu* (New York, 1923), p. 156. Subsequent references to *Impromptu* will be indicated parenthetically in text.

survives only by means of a subterranean scheming aimed solely at the gratification of whatever appetites remain to him in the sewer of rear-echelon boredom.

Irwin's downward progress, again, is ironic because he never opposes the system as such. What he resents, what he hates, and what he ultimately disappears beneath is a mass irrationality, a blind power distributing rewards and punishments to no purpose whatever. Like the rat in the laboratory experiment, Irwin is conditioned to recognize all the proper signals for the sweet things in life. When somebody—or something—changes the signals, when the conditioning itself produces shocks rather than rewards, he is driven into succeeding states of fury, madness, and comatose indifference. "Irwin's senses were being deadened." Elliot Paul writes:

No longer did he fight the noise out of his ears, nor lie paralyzed with fear in an air raid. Blood spots on blankets he picked up from the fields did not make him shudder. His shirt did not provoke him to scratch. He seldom spoke, and while shoveling, took no load at all, merely going through the motions. He took it as a matter of course when a strange officer bellowed abuse into his face because his leather jerkin was outside his blouse. Like a vessel with the engine dead, he moved only by the momentum that remained from his last conscious efforts, indifferent that he would soon come to nothing. . . . (p. 195)

And when Irwin learns of the death of Dutch—a good man, a brave fighter, and his closest friend—the reaction is one of neither surprise nor protest:

Klein was speaking. "Have you heard . . . ."
  "Heard what?"
("Hold up your cup. How in hell . . . .")
  ("Aw go chase yourself.")
"Heard what?"
  "About Dutch?" A blank. "Dutch is dead." A mess kit of slum was leering up at Irwin. The potato was rotten. He was being pushed out of the way.
  "How do you get that way? Give me another spud," he snarled; he was walking away, balancing his coffee cup and mess kit, stumbling into mudholes, avoiding the turds.
  "Dutch is dead," Klein repeated timidly.
  "Aw shut up. I heard you," and Irwin hid the dirty spoon in the hot stew. As he ate he mumbled to himself. "Yeh. He's dead. They took him away in a Dodge. Everybody's dead . . . the whole damn country's dead."

He slammed the mess kit to the ground, clenching his fist and turning on Klein. "You're not dead, are you? You're fast and as lively as hell, aren't you?" Then he wilted sullenly to a box, drooling and wiping out his cup. (pp. 195–196)

Finally nothing is left. Under the succeeding impact of degrading military "work," impersonal sex, meaningless combat (in which chance alone determines survival), mass indifference, unthinking brutality, and —later—of a home front that prostituted his fiancée as the war front has prostituted him, Irwin finds his true vocation: he becomes a peacetime "sodjer." The inept and unfulfilled dreams of lust, success, and violence are over. And the final portrait of Irwin, which is also the last scene of the novel, is a study of spiritual vacuum, a tool of flesh cared for and despised by the very machine it serves:

On the sunny side of the sea-wall, prone in warm sand, a soldier in olive drab is sleeping with his mouth open. His shoes are polished. The hair is clipped from the back of his neck. His fingers twitch in his sleep.
A corporal, walking the top of the wall, steps down to kick the soldier's feet.
"Get up you lazy bugger, and salute the colours."
Yawning and grumbling, Irwin Atwood, private lcl, US Coast Artillery, struggles to his feet, brushing the sand from his blouse.
"Damn the colours," he mumbles. "Stew again tonight."

A spiritual vacuum, of course, is no fit subject for either the rhetoric or the dramatization of tragedy, and for this reason Elliot Paul's attitude toward his protagonist is no less ironic than are his attitudes toward home front patriotism and military values. Absurdity permeates the entire novel and the prose itself becomes an extended sneer; clergymen, military officers, brave soldiers (who are brave precisely because of their stupidity), intellectual Jews, crusading idealists, Innocent American Women, and finally Irwin himself, with his combination of whining and emotional puerility, are objects of a knowing but hopeless derision.

Even in his demolition of major targets—the "Y" men or technological slaughter—Paul never goes beyond irony. Always there is withdrawal from indignation, a return to detachment achieved by means of devices reminiscent of Dos Passos in *1919*. Objective "public events," for example, interspersed among and giving ironic dimension to narrative events, fulfill much the same function as Dos Passos' "newsreel." And there are short, asterisked chapters as well as sentences composed of single nouns or phrases ("Sugar, twenty-two cents a pound. Spies. Treachery. Visiting Heroes. Hands, speeches, flags, departing villains.") which contribute to detachment, irony, and a sense of fragmentation. The very structure of the book, despite its musical pretensions ("a novel in four movements," says the subtitle) is cinematic: physical descriptions make a camera cycle (pan, close-up, fade, and pan) to provide transitions between multiple and shifting points of view. The final effect is an impersonal tragi-comedy where men suffer without purpose and "succeed" without reason; a tragi-comedy, indeed, in which they are reduced to "crickets" by a vast intermeshing of forces beyond their control.

The fate of Irwin in Elliot Paul's novel is paralleled by the development, or debasement, of Fuselli in John Dos Passos' *Three Soldiers*. Like Irwin, Fuselli survives only by withdrawing to a level of mere physical existence; he becomes an underground creature whose sole protection is invisibility. Hopeless, loveless, angerless, and (for the first time in his sentiment-ridden life) morality-less, Fuselli finds his ultimate fate as a shuffling panhandler in the back alleys of the military machine.

" 'I don't give a damn,' " Fuselli remarks in his final appearance of the novel; " 'what's the use?' " Both fear and ambition have long since been replaced by lethargy, and when Andrews expresses some shock at Fuselli's permanent labor assignment—a life bound quite literally by horizons of garbage—the only reaction is a shrug: there are "good eats," regular hours, and equally regular opportunities for drunken sex. To Andrews' own revelation of a plush university assignment, moreover, Fuselli is indifferent. " 'I'm glad I'm not goin' to school anymore,' " he remarks, dismissing the world outside as no more comprehensible than his own infection with syphilis. For this reason Andrews must react to the human shell before him in terms of embarrassment rather than indignation; in Fuselli he sees not the suffering of manhood, but rather its total cessation. For Fuselli, standing "with his hands in his pockets and his legs crossed, leaning against the wall behind the door of the barracks," has returned to the street corner days of his city adolescence.[16] Only as an adolescent could he, like Irwin,

[16] John Dos Passos, *Three Soldiers* (New York, 1921), p. 203. Subsequent references to *Three Soldiers* will be indicated parenthetically in text.

152

come to terms with a world of abstract and terrifying power.

Fuselli's debasement, however, is in some ways more dramatic than Irwin's precisely because his initial, or potential, manliness is emphasized rather than depreciated by the author. Whereas Elliot Paul is at considerable pains to demonstrate the moral vacuum of Irwin even as a boy, Dos Passos introduces Fuselli as a young, extremely naïve, but promising soldier, not lacking a certain sympathy for others, whose determination to "get in right" at first seems only natural in view of his personal and physical sturdiness. " 'Keep neat-like and smilin' and you'll get on all right,' " he advises a discouraged companion. " 'And if they start to ride yer, show fight. Ye've got to be hard-boiled to git on in the army' " (p. 14). A city boy, far more accustomed to personal anonymity than are small-town protagonists like Irwin or aesthetes like Andrews, Fuselli swaggers into the military machine. If ultimately he shuffles out, it is because all expectations—moral no less than military—are slowly reversed under the unrelenting pressure of irrational force.

This process of reversal drives Fuselli underground as a subterranean for whom cause and effect have been disconnected in a world without proper labels; it begins from the moment he embarks on his "ocean voyage." Looking forward to travel no less than promotion and success in the proving ground of combat, Fuselli finds himself herded like a steer and guarded like a criminal. His initial reaction is one of fury and defiance; "toughness" and "fight," after all, are essential qualities in the mystique of the soldier to which Fuselli so enthusiastically subscribes. It is precisely these qualities, however, that the machine must destroy without mercy; Fuselli, indeed, discovers that personal effacement, calculated "friendship," and caution are crowning virtues for an enlisted man who wishes to "make good." And it is on board ship that fear replaces pride and "whining" replaces defiance; "I mustn't get in wrong. I mustn't get in wrong" becomes a thematic counterpoint to Fuselli's ultimate fate.

As a product of a semi-slum urban environment, however, Fuselli holds something of an advantage, at least initially, over men whose backgrounds have set up clearly defined levels of social or personal status. It is for this reason that Meadville, a "westerner," watching Fuselli's anxiety to please his superiors, comments that nothing more is to be expected from " 'you guys who live in the city. . . . Ye're just made to be sheep' " (p. 45). It is also for this reason that, unlike Chrisfield, who redeems his manhood by murdering an officer (an act made imperative by a deeply inbred code of the Intolerable Affront), Fuselli limits his own protest to mere nightmares of proud insubordination, nightmares that, in his waking hours, he finds no difficulty in shaking off "as a dog shakes off water" (p. 18).

The "dog" image introduced by Dos Passos is in truth the definition of Fuselli as he works his way—or crawls his way—into the promised land of a corporalship. He ingratiates himself with his sergeant and lieutenant by efficiency as a laborer, willingness as a servant, humility as a messenger boy, and tail-wagging geniality as a companion; he flourishes on precisely those levels openly despised by individuals like Meadville or "Wild Dan" Cohen, who maintain inviolable areas of manhood and so commit the ultimate sin of "getting in wrong." Fuselli, in short, can achieve even his temporary success only through a reversal of expectations: the personal effacement and forced humility he had endured as a small-time civilian clerk and had desperately hoped to escape are those very qualities he must perfect as a soldier. Both his truculence and swagger vanish under a new and unforeseen set of "military" necessities, and by the time Fuselli receives his corporalship he has become an emotional clerk once again—suspicious of others, fearful of his superiors, and enjoying violence only in his dreams.

This reversal, however, is at least to some extent conscious; it represents a series of compromises made for an ultimate "good," promotion in rank. Fuselli shakes off every impulse toward self-assertion, and while the process is accompanied by a growing sense of insecurity, fear, and personal isolation, he can maintain his equilibrium by reviewing his hopes: as a corporal, certainly, he would be redeemed through status. It is the moral reversal represented by Yvonne rather than the military reversal alone which ultimately reduces Fuselli to the shell we meet at the end of *Three Soldiers:* with Yvonne, indeed, he makes no compromise at all. Acting in strict accordance with moral sentiments he knows to be "pure," Fuselli is ruined by innocence rather than by calculation or selfishness, and this provides the final irony of his debasement.

The machine, in other words, makes no allowance for honorable intentions, and it is precisely the morality of Fuselli's intentions that proves to be his undoing. Unlike the sergeant, for whom backstairs fornication is simply one more fact of military existence, Fuselli reacts to Yvonne in terms of the sentimental labels which for him embody morality itself. To be sure, Fuselli at the beginning of the novel boasts of his experience with "coozies"—experience which, necessarily verbalized, becomes a merit badge of manhood. Along with the boasting, however, there is the heavily sentimental memory of his "good" girl, his "true" love who had sent him off to war with tears, chocolates, and protestations of purity. But Yvonne does not seem to fit into this neat antithesis of good and bad; the signs, again, are confusing. She knits, and she has a mother; she cooks, and she has a sister and brother; she runs a neat little shop, talks pleasantly, smiles a great deal, and has never bobbed her hair. The result is inevitable: since Fuselli's concept of the Great Crusade (unlike his dream of military glory) has not yet undergone the great reversal, he proposes marriage, is cuckolded-before-the-fact by his own sergeant, suffers a silent and futile rage, and is punished for the court-martial offense of venereal infection.

Just as expectations of military power had led only to self-efface-ment, fear, and humility, so his insistence on moral "right" leads only to the garbage dump. And it is here that Fuselli, like Irwin, simply gives up: the fly speck of individuality, the "insect" used so often by World War I novelists as an image of hapless manhood, finds the dung heap at last, and is content.

We have already seen that the concept of war as a purgation for weakness—as a method of guaranteeing a healthy national stock through "survival of the fittest"—was swept away by the realities of technological combat and a mass military environment. Certainly the World War I novelists of protest were to dramatize this process as a major concern of their work; military "success," for them, and survival as well, all too often came as the result of coarsening, cynicism, hypocrisy, or complete failure of will. The "good soldier," indeed, was precisely the one least likely to survive—unless he took up the posture of Zorn with his dehuman-ized worship of strength and authority. Running parallel to the theme of alienation and expatriation, in other words, is the theme of accommodation: Private Bartow in *Company K*, the professional veterans in *Plumes*, Randolph in *'It's a Great War!,'* and a host of others. Certainly the representative individuals analyzed here— Claude, Zorn, Richard Savage, Mattock, Irwin, and Fuselli—are types which have, unfortunately, become associated with religio-patriotic veterans groups organized after World War I. The substitution of violence for thwarted erotic impulse; the insistence upon authoritarian patterns of loyalty and action; the lemming morality taking its strength only from group identity; the definition of patriotism as religious belief or political conservatism; the giving up of self to the monolith of organization—these are historical realities dramatized rather than invented by the novelists. If their antiheroes were to become expatriates or psychological cripples under the impact of a broken world, one might say that their heroes were to become good Legionnaires, or Babbitt himself, for the same reason.

IV

*"Gee . . . this war's a lucky thing for me.
I might have been in the R. C. Vicker
Company's store for five years and never
got a raise. An' here in the army I got a
chance to do almost anything."*
—JOHN DOS PASSOS, *Three Soldiers*, 1921

*"I tell you when these fellows come out of
the army they will have a respect for the
United States they'll never get in
any other way."*
—ARTHUR TRAIN, *Earthquake*, 1918

*"We know what soldiering means. It means
saving your own skin and getting a bellyful
as often as possible."*
—CHARLES YALE HARRISON, *Generals Die in Bed*, 1930

*The war will drive away all the fakes and
fortune-hunters, and will introduce our
daughters into the best society for us—the
society of men who are going to save and
then govern the country.*
—ARTHUR TRAIN, *Earthquake*, 1918

B eyond the subterranean survival of Irwin and Fuselli (who exist within the machine at the cost of manhood), and pointing to the negative action of antiheroes such as Andrews, Cummings, and Frederic Henry (who redeem their manhood by opposing or deserting the machine), there is an area where protagonists simply exist as spiritual sleepwalkers. No longer an overture for worship of strength, withdrawal through weakness, revolt for aesthetic cause, or value in personal relationship, numbness becomes its own ultimate—a limbo in which men like Mahon in *Soldiers' Pay* vanish beyond "an imminent nothingness more profound than any yet." And in Faulkner's novel this totality of neither/nor serves not so much to define Mahon as to comment upon a world which labored mightily only to produce him, a vacuum so impotent that all life forces—those of protest and affirmation alike—are dissipated as though substance had never existed in the deceptive framework of its flesh.

Perhaps one might say that Faulkner's novel is an account of the world which produced the war which produced Mahon; certainly *Soldiers' Pay* differs sharply from Thomas Boyd's *Through the Wheat* despite the fact that the protagonists of both novels are brought to a point of final numbness. Less interested than Boyd in the actual process of the military machine, less concerned with the impact of technological combat and mass absurdity, Faulkner offers a narrative whose very personae symbolize the culture which made the absurdity possible. Margaret Powers, Reverend Mahon, Cadet Lowe, Cecily, James Dough, Donald Farr, Joe Gilligan, even young Robert Saunders (" 'I just want to see his scar.' ") are placed concentrically around the magnetized vacuum, the empty shell of Mahon that sets them in motion and identifies their humanity, their failure, or their guilt.

Reverend Mahon, for example, a voice of the nineteenth century, is thoroughly charming, totally good, and completely inept. In his very first appearance we see him gracefully exchanging witticisms with Januarius Jones, who in his role as a flabby Pan is a parody of physical joy and cultural accomplishment. The Reverend, however, fails to understand the creature of debased appetite grimacing before him; seeing only the familiar surface of a new reality, he

159

betrays the one as he remains unaware of the other. The failure to distinguish between surface and substance defines his pathos, for in a sense Januarius Jones, Cecily, and Margaret Powers are the Reverend's "children" no less than the spiritual nothingness that returns to him wrapped in the skin of his son. A value structure based upon sentimentality, feminine delicacy, the glory of manhood through battle, rhetoric, and faithful love, degenerates into the anti-values of lechery, selfishness, and impotence. And through it all the Reverend Mahon wanders confused in a world which his generation all too clearly has made, his very optimism the result of ignorance and his faith reduced to futility.

If Reverend Mahon is blind to the reality of Jones and nonplussed by the total vacuum of his son, he is also unaware of the true nature of Cecily, and this too defines the measure of his failure. For behind her lacework-and-light façade Cecily is a predecessor of those Faulknerian women for whom the meaning of "new freedom" is a combination of sex appetite and personal degradation. The degradation, indeed, plays no small part in creating the appetite, and in Cecily there is a hint, an aura of that corruption which so often accompanies sex in Faulkner's later work. For this reason even the cautious Januarius Jones, who sees behind the façade (and who, indeed, is a counterpart of Cecily behind his own), can approach her in perfect safety. Joe Gilligan defines the sterility and essential lack of emotion behind Cecily's public sentimentalities: " 'I tell you I seen that letter: all the old bunk about knights of the air and the romance of battle, that even the fat crying ones outgrow as soon as the excitement is over and uniforms and being wounded ain't only not stylish no more, but it is downright troublesome.' "[1] But Jones understands her even more completely: Cecily can be reached—and mastered—not by love, but by crudity; she is attracted rather than repelled by the implication of perversion or violence. All emotion, however, is for Cecily a threat rather than fulfillment, and under the pressure of Jones's knowledge she offers her body to Donald Farr (" 'Oh well, it had to be sometime I guess . . .' ") with little meaning or emotional truth; her surrender is a protective gesture just as her betrothal to Mahon at the time of his bold journey into war

[1] William Faulkner, *Soldiers' Pay* (New York, 1951), p. 35. The first edition of the novel appeared in 1926. Subsequent references to *Soldiers' Pay* will be indicated parenthetically in text.

had been a sentimental gesture. Both acts are parodies, one of sexual and the other of heroic emotion.

Even involvement, however, becomes corrupt when shaped only by rhetoric, and in this respect Margaret Powers represents still another element of impotence, of futility, so basic a theme in *Soldiers' Pay*. If Cecily must offer her body but not her self, Margaret is able to offer her self but not her body. Remembering that she had assented to rhetoric, even encouraged it to secure justification for her physical adventure with Captain Powers (who "died believing" in the rhetoric itself), caught in a pressure of expiation, Margaret can function only as a mother figure with Cadet Lowe or as a sacrificial testimony with Mahon—never as a woman. Her good sense and frankness, her "clean, muscular grasp," her "firm, sexless embrace"—these are qualities of the Nursing Nun rather than those of the actual or potential lover; and Margaret is, indeed, a spiritual nurse not only for Mahon, but for herself. Just as marriage is the only act which can permit the tortured hulk of Mahon to die peacefully, so renunciation is the only cure for Margaret's disease of guilt. Gilligan, to be sure, offers her both love and forgiveness. For Mrs. Captain Richard Powers, however, desperately attempting to rebuild her own moral image, forgiveness must be earned rather than accepted. Expiation is the only currency at her disposal, and Gilligan himself assents to the justice of this moral bargain even while attempting to reason it away; the expiation, after all, is precisely what sets Margaret apart from the New Woman so incomprehensible to the returning veterans.

Despite their disillusion with the Great Crusade, men like Gilligan and Sergeant James Dough belong to a prewar world that believed in Ideal American Womanhood and so are unable to cope with the frank sensuality and careless freedom surrounding young people for whom the war served chiefly as a means to achieve social and sexual emancipation. Having seen the horror behind the rhetoric of military glory, such men nevertheless maintain a moral code rendered obsolete during their absence. Their very position is anomalous: they are at once more and less sophisticated than the young people who never left home. Gilligan, for example, certainly "younger" in matters of sensuality than the shallow youngsters he despises, is discomfited by the female even while he respects Womanhood: "Whenever he was among flowers," Faulkner tells us, "he always felt as if he had entered a room full of women; he was always conscious of his walk, feeling as though he trod on sand. So he believed he did not like flowers" (p. 74). Gilligan's relationship with Margaret reflects just such ambiguity; his love, indeed, is based on precisely those moral qualities which make love's consummation impossible.

Still another element of futility is provided by the fact that Captain Powers died no death of a betrayed Hero believing in a Cause; he died—his face blown off by one of his own men during a nonexistent gas attack—believing in nothing at all. Margaret's need for moral sacrifice, in other words, a sacrifice which must abort her love for Gilligan, is no less absurd than the rhetoric which made possible her brief idyll with Powers. And so the cycle of futility revolves: guilt creating impotence cured by sacrifice based on absurdity; desire based on moral strength defined by sacrifice preventing consummation. So concentric, indeed, is the narrative structure that Faulkner can actually break into his plot progression with a series of dramatic asides, each serving to recapitulate the set relationship of various individuals to Mahon himself. And the very definition of Margaret, like the definition of others surrounding the central vacuum of Mahon, is rendered through thematic or incremental repetition (strongly reminiscent of *As I Lay Dying*), a device in which each character is identified by the quality of his particular futility.

It is, again, a cycle of impotence, of negation, at the center of which is the figure of Mahon. In youth a vibrant aesthete, "thin faced, with the serenity of a wild thing, the passionate serene alertness of a faun," he is now buried within a different sort of serenity. And from the living tomb of Mahon's flesh comes the parody of affirmation: a monosyllabic "yes" serving only to mock the impotence which he represents, and the futility of an entire world surrounding him.

Looking at the man who is to be the symbol of her own guilt and the vehicle for its expiation, Margaret Powers notes the horror beneath Mahon's neatly pressed uniform, his splendid decorations, and punch-drunk acquiescence. " 'The man that was wounded is dead,' " she remarks. " 'He doesn't seem to care where he is or what he does' " (p. 113). Mahon's death-in-life marks him as a counterpart to William Hicks in *Through the Wheat*. Both men are psychological corpses, complements in vacuum: both are set apart not only from the World War I heroes of survival, but from the antiheroes of negative action as well.

As he advances toward the enemy for the last time, Hicks recapitulates the process of total withdrawal and spiritual death. Disgust becomes scar tissue ("a dead man is a dead man"), fear becomes self-preservation, survival becomes indifference ("it's all damn foolishness"), and indifference becomes complete alienation on all levels of consciousness. Nothing remains: neither hope, self-preservation, nor personality itself; there is only a blind stumbling-by-rote, a dim and half perceived memory of something—somewhere—left undone. Like Mahon returning for his impotent marriage to achieve a physical release from a world in which he has no further part, Hicks sleepwalks toward the German lines for his forgotten but now useless gun, and returns as nothing more than a phantom: "He raised his chin a little. The action seemed to draw his feet from the earth. No longer did anything matter, neither the bayonets, the bullets, the barbed wire, the dead, nor the living. The soul of Hicks was numb."[2] Hicks, indeed, at the moment of his final appearance in Boyd's novel, becomes Mahon himself as we first meet him in Faulkner's. But Mahon must be accepted merely as a catalyst for the drama of interlocking futility surrounding him. As the narrative center of *Through the Wheat*, on the other hand, Hicks develops through successive stages of expectation, hope, disillusion, impact, lethargy, and withdrawal; rather than functioning as a given quantity of nonexistence, he becomes the drama itself.

Essential to this drama is the fact that unlike the subterraneans (Irwin and Fuselli) or the rhetorical antiheroes (Andrews or Cummings), Hicks is far from inept as a soldier. He does, to be sure, bitterly resent "the grinning weakness which men call authority"—but this is only to be expected from a civilian plunged into a professional military establishment for which he was unprepared. The point is that Hicks does cope with the military machine; while despising the flabby incompetents, both professional and amateur, who (as Hervey Allen put it) "play at war," he learns to respect those who know what they are about. Resisting the pressures toward dehumanization on one hand, and the equally powerful pressures toward escapism, calculation, or self-pity on the other, Hicks learns to be an efficient soldier, and survives to understand that

[2] Thomas Boyd, *Through the Wheat* (New York, 1923), p. 266. Subsequent references to *Through the Wheat* will be indicated parenthetically in text.

his learning makes no difference at all, either to himself or to the machine to which he is committed. Just as the machine reduces Irwin and Fuselli according to their weakness, so it consumes Mahon and Hicks according to their strength.

Courage, cowardice, knowledge, determination, experience— nothing matters; the difference between a good officer and a bad one is that the former gets blown up while cursing rear-echelon idiocy and the latter meets the same fate while charging invisible machine guns with a saber. Sergeant Harriman, the professional soldier, ultimately shoots himself under the demoralization produced by machine death; Hicks, exhausted and gassed, is accused of cowardice; apathy replaces horror, and combat creates a numb sense of absolute fatality rather than exhilaration. Finally neither the stench, the piles of corpses, the lice, nor attrition have any effect at all. His company almost destroyed by repeated battles in which futility and passivity take the greatest toll of manhood, Hicks sees war itself as the vague memory of some unnamed discomfort. Stumbling forward in search of his forgotten gun at the end of the novel, wandering like a punch-drunk in some gymnasium of death, Hicks is no more concerned with death than he is with life; he has, indeed, become invulnerable to both.

While the ultimate numbness of his protagonist points both to *Soldiers' Pay* and *A Farewell to Arms*, the literary style of Thomas Boyd is far more closely related to the aesthetic rhetoric of Dos Passos and Cummings. Deliberately choosing a protagonist of average education and social background, making him, moreover, a willing fighter and a fairly efficient soldier, Boyd nevertheless betrays his own literary frame of reference with an intrusively ornate manner. Aesthetic allusions, heavily metaphoric passages, and a certain delicacy of observation create a peculiar distance between the actual narrative and the center of consciousness (Hicks) through which the reader is to perceive experience.

Boyd describes a dead German, for example, as having "a face like a battered sunflower in the evening" (p. 107); during a barrage "the spiteful crack of the 75's turned the funeral music into a scherzo" (p. 92); while Hicks sleeps miserably in a field, "the dampness seemed like a heavily draped ghost that wanted to kiss Hicks' entire body" (p. 24); dawn comes up "like a fifty year old virgin . . . showing its hard, cold face" (p. 43); nightfall too arrives with a flourish of metaphor: "Dusk, like soft blue smoke, fell with the dying spring air and settled upon the Northern French village. In the uncertain light one and two storey buildings set along the crooked street showed crisply, bearing a resemblance to false teeth in an ash-old face" (p. 1). Certainly the narrative itself belies both the character of Hicks and his progressive alienation; so great is the gulf between protagonist and author that Boyd's frequent attempts at modified interior-monologue seem almost schizophrenic. This is not the case in even Dos Passos' heavily rhetorical novels like *First Encounter*, since his style is consistent with the particular sensibility (Martin Howe's) he is rendering; nor, for that matter, is it true in the case of Cummings, where sheer linguistic virtuosity compensates for any limitation of perspective.

As a dramatization of total withdrawal, Hicks is closely related not only to Mahon, but, in a limited sense, to Frederic Henry as well. Thomas Boyd, furthermore, as author, reveals himself as cut from the same aesthetic mold as antiheroes such as Martin Howe, John Andrews, Cummings, and Methot (in *Company K*). And this is one of the chief interests of the book. Quite aside from its detailed account of military impact, *Through the Wheat* affords a point at which two major World War I literary reactions intersect: rhetorical indictment on one hand, and benumbed negation on the other.

V

*Who are a million, a trillion, a nonmillion
young men? All are standing. I am standing.
We are wedged in and over and under each
other. Sardines. Knew a man once who was
arrested for stealing sardines. I, sardine,
look at 3 sardines, at 3 million sardines, at
a carful of sardines. How did I get here?*
—E. E. CUMMINGS, *The Enormous Room*, 1922

*By the light of the burning ammunition I saw
a man's legs lying by the road, buttocks up.
The whole upper part of the body had been
taken off by a shell, and the two naked legs
looked exactly like a giant frog's.*
—HERVEY ALLEN, *Toward the Flame*, 1934

167

"It has the raucous indirectness of a song-and-dance act in cheap vaudeville, the willingness to go the limit in expression and emotion of a Negro dancing." So John Dos Passos, reviewing *The Enormous Room* in 1922, hailed Cummings' boisterously bitter war novel as a major testimony of the Great Crusade. "It is the sort of thing that knocks literature into a cocked hat," he announced to readers of the *Dial;* "it is nearer the conventions of speech than those of books. . . . One thinks of Defoe because of the unashamed directness with which every twitch of the individual's fibers, stung or caressed by the world flowing outside, is noted down. . . . Here's a book that has been conceived unashamedly and directly, without thought of . . . fitting into any one of the neatly labelled pigeonholes of novel, play, essay, history or travelbook, a book that exists because the author was so moved, excited and amused by a certain slice of his existence. . . ."[1]

The matter of "pigeonholing" *The Enormous Room* is still a subject for debate, since the book is one of those mavericks of literature in which the author becomes his own subject; under Cummings' blithe disregard for literary proprieties, indeed, prose becomes poetry, suffering becomes comedy, and form itself seems not so much denied as ignored. A new generation of readers, coming to *The Enormous Room* with the experimentation of the twenties already behind them, may not be unduly startled by the pyrotechnic displays of metaphor, mockery, and surrealist posturing. But in 1922 the book was unique.

Although his contemporaries occupied themselves with war protest, Cummings in a very basic sense focused upon war parody; in his book the rhetoric of indignation becomes the drama of absurdity. Differing from protagonists such as Martin Howe or John Andrews, who serve as evangelists of individualism (and who, like most evangelists, are often too serious to be taken seriously), Cummings refuses the pulpit altogether. Perceiving that the machine gets along quite well without his assent, perceiving also that the indignant man must be a Don Quixote in a world of metal, Cummings simply tosses his lance away, puts bells on his toes and a feather in his hat, and balances absurdities (including self-ab-

[1] John Dos Passos, "Off the Shoals," *Dial*, LXXIII (July, 1922), 97–102.

surdities) on all the points of his narrative. He is the antihero in motley, a Dostoevskian underground man trailing rags and tatters of metaphor wherever he goes and enjoying his own performance without the slightest quiver of decent shame.

The enjoyment, however, is of a very particular sort. While Cummings plays the jester, the juggler, his readers become aware of the fact that those objects leaping from his fingers are human faces—human skulls—and the result is horror, a carnival in a graveyard; it is the carnival rather than the graveyard which patriots and military historians are most likely to resent. Cummings protests nothing, or mocks himself when he begins to protest anything, and this is what makes his book so remarkable (and outrageous) a performance. He refuses to suffer. He settles in the dung heap of *La Ferté* and proceeds to pluck roses, golden skulls, the "Delectable Mountains" of human personality from the filth.

Human personality is at once the subject of Cummings' book and the clue to his performance. All description, all symbolic commentary upon the larger situation (*La Ferté*, the war itself) refers back to the individual, and the individual, in turn, defines the larger situation. "Doesn't *The Enormous Room* really concern war?" asks the anonymous interviewer in the preface to the 1932 edition. "It actually uses war," Cummings replies,

to explore an inconceivable vastness which is so unbelievably far away that it appears microscopic.

When you wrote this book, you were looking through war at something very big and very far away?

When this book wrote itself, I was observing a negligible portion of something incredibly more distant than any sun; something more unimaginably huge than the most prodigious of all universes—

Namely?

The individual.[2]

The individuals of *The Enormous Room*, however, the "Delectable Mountains," are not always elevated; nor, for that matter, are they necessarily delectable. Here Cummings offers still another departure from the sentiments of aesthetic rebellion, in which victims and villains are defined less by the irreducible thumb prints of their own personalities than by the morality role they must play (or suffer) within the juggernaut of war. Cummings' people

[2] E. E. Cummings, *The Enormous Room* (New York, 1934), p. vii–viii. Subsequent references to *The Enormous Room* will be indicated parenthetically in text.

have no role but their own existence. They exist: that is enough. That, indeed, is their miracle, and it accounts for the almost unholy zest with which Cummings defines prisoners and officials alike. The Silent Man, the Schoolmaster, Judas, the Bum, Zulu, Orange Cap, One-Eyed David, *Le Directeur*, Lena, Count Bragard—they make up a poetry of individuality, and they are complete as well as precise (unlike Hemingway's subordinate characters, who are precise but never complete). Indeed, they often seem more real than Cummings himself.

"The *planton*," Cummings remarks of one of *La Ferté's* guards, in a characteristic mixture of mockery, horror, and sympathy, ". . . was a solemn youth with wise eyes situated very far apart in a mealy expressionless ellipse of a face, to the lower end of which clung a piece of down, exactly like a feather sticking to an egg. The rest of him was fairly normal with the exception of his hands, which were not mates; the left being considerably larger, and made of wood" (p. 81). After a few moments of relaxation with the *poilu* guarding him on a train, Cummings defines both personality and situation with a brief, savage stroke: "Suddenly," he tells us, "t-d [tin-derby] woke up, straightened and buckled his personality" (p. 12). An early "interview" features ". . . eyes which sat at a desk. Two belonged to a lawyerish person in civilian clothes, with a bored expression, plus a moustache of dreamy proportions with which the owner constantly imitated a gentleman ringing for a drink. Two appertained to a splendid old dotard (a face all ski-jumps and toboggan-slides), on whose protruding chest the rosette of the Legion pompously squatted . . ." (p. 13). For contrast, there is the schoolmaster, who "used to teach school in Alsace-Lorraine. . . . In speaking to you his kind face is peacefully reduced to triangles. . . . [He is] led about by his celluloid collar, gently worried about himself, delicately worried about the world. . . . There are two holes where cheeks might have been. Lessons hide in his wrinkles. Bells ding in the oldness of eyes . . . he is altogether incapable of anger, wholly timid and tintinnabulous . . . a notorious seditionist" (pp. 118–19). And finally there is Jean le Nègre, criminally vibrant and irresponsibly alive:

—Boy, Kid, Nigger with the strutting muscles—take me up into your mind once or twice before I die (you know why: just because the eyes of me and you will be full of dirt some day). Quickly take me up into the bright child of your mind, before we both go suddenly all loose and silly (you know how it will feel). Take me up (carefully; as if I were a toy) and play carefully with me, once or twice, before I and you go suddenly all limp and foolish. Once or twice before you go into great Jack roses and ivory—(once or twice Boy before we together go wonderfully down into the Big Dirt laughing, bumped with the last darkness). (p. 293)

Always there is the manipulation of language itself, the alternation of jazz rhythms, funeral dirges, fish-wife screams, sexual leers, tonal shrugs, whispering rituals of religion rendered obscene by the reality surrounding them, or the heavy, brass echo of Patriotism which Cummings first imitates and then demolishes. It is the method of parody rather than argument.[3] But parodies are almost intolerable when the context is serious, when the physical and metaphysical stakes are high. Prepared to cope with an indictment, we are faced with a rictus, a demonstration not only that comedy may exist within tragedy, but that tragedy itself may be comic. The result is exasperating. Each time Cummings leads up to a point of anger, or pathos, or disgust, he simply refuses to take any responsibility for it; he kicks over the traces; he vanishes behind impossible laughter and leaves us with bits of broken puns, onomatopoetic jokes, or verbal anticlimax. "A mouldily mouldering molish voice, suggesting putrefying tracts and orifices, answers with cob-webbish patience," he tells us, first preparing and then ruining what should have been a moment of despair. "I contemplate the bowl," he says, "which contemplates me. A glaze of greenish grease seals the mystery of its contents. I induce two fingers to penetrate the seal. They bring me up a flat sliver of *choux* and a large, hard, thoughtful, solemn, uncooked bean" (pp. 26–27).

La Ferté itself, moreover, as the controlling symbol of the book, is no less a mixture of tragedy and foolishness than the individuals so helplessly stumbling about within its walls. A multinational, multilingual struggle for survival in a locked chamber, a babble

---

[3] "The lively satisfaction which we might be suspected of having derived from the accomplishment of a task so important in the saving of civilization from the clutches of Prussian tyranny," Cummings writes, "was in some degree inhibited, unhappily, by a complete absence of cordial relations between the man whom fate had placed over us and ourselves" (p. 3). This sort of verbal imitation is frequent throughout *The Enormous Room* and is very effective when Cummings juxtaposes it with more direct language. For example: "When we asked him [Mexique] once what he thought about the war, he replied, 'I t'ink lotta bullshit,' which, upon copious reflection, I decided absolutely expressed my own point of view" (p. 181).

of ludicrous horror, the "enormous room" becomes the war and the war becomes the "enormous room" whose inhabitants—or victims—are cut off from all meaning, so that motion defeats itself, space and time are annihilated, and human communication is reduced to the merest noise:

All about me there rose a sea of the most extraordinary sound . . . the hitherto empty and minute room became suddenly enormous: weird cries, oaths, laughter, pulling it sideways and backward, extending it to inconceivable depth and width, telescoping it to frightful nearness. From all directions, by . . . voices in eleven languages (I counted as I lay Dutch, Belgian, Spanish, Turkish, Arabian, Polish, Russian, Swedish, German, French—and English) at distances varying from seventy feet to a few inches, for twenty minutes I was ferociously bombarded. (p. 60)

Throughout the book Cummings expands and proliferates this sort of image until the room becomes a perfect vehicle for symbolic expression, a vehicle, in other words, where meaning operates through and beyond specific experience. All external differences vanish under the filth, degradation, slime, and comedy of irrational power; the "room" is a stage for the drama of humanity itself. " 'The finest people are here,' " Count B. says casually; and his remark, in the symbolic context, takes on a terrible significance indeed.

"Through the bars I looked into that little and dirty lane whereby I had entered," Cummings remarks, "in which a sentinel, gun on shoulder, and with a huge revolver strapped at his hip, monotonously moved" (p. 37). " 'This filth . . . this herding of men like cattle—they treat us no better than pigs here. The fellows drop their dung in the very room where they sleep,' " complains Count B. (p. 72). A train becomes "the ghastly miniature roar of an insane toy"; regulations are introduced and enforced despite the fact that they are impossible to obey, until punishment exists for its own sake in a cycle of built-in pain ("Having acquainted me with the various *défendus* which limited the activities of a man . . . my friends proceeded to enliven the otherwise somewhat tedious morning by shattering one after another all rules and regulations" [p. 81]). The most hapless of victims suddenly takes on the dimensions of a toy Dybbuk, a child-monster of vengeance: "O *gouvernement français*, I think it was not very clever of You to put this terrible doll in La Ferté; I should have left him in Belgium with his little doll-wife if I had been You; for when Governments are found dead there is always a little doll on top of them, pulling and tweaking with his little hands to get back the microscopic knife which sticks firmly in the quiet meat of their hearts" (p. 142). And finally, as I have previously noted, there is the ultimate horror of mutual cannibalism:

> The shrinking light which my guide held had become suddenly minute; it was beating, senseless and futile, with shrill fists upon a thick enormous moisture of gloom. To the left and right through lean oblongs of stained glass burst dirty burglars of moonlight. The clammy, stupid distance uttered dimly an uncanny conflict—the mutterless tumbling of brutish shadows. A crowding ooze battled with my lungs. My nostrils fought against the monstrous atmospheric slime which hugged a sweet unpleasant odour. Staring ahead, I gradually disinterred the pale carrion of the darkness—an altar, guarded with the ugliness of unlit candles, on which stood inexorably the efficient implements for eating God. (pp. 58–59)

And yet it was not necessary for Cummings to be in *La Ferté* at all; one might say that he volunteered for the "enormous room" just as he had first volunteered for ambulance service and then—ineffectually—volunteered for combat. Cummings, indeed, almost goes free in his preliminary hearing, but convicts himself because he refuses to say that he hates Germans. He says, instead, that he loves France. This is not enough, for—as one of the interrogators points out— " 'it is impossible to love Frenchmen without hating Germans.' " From here on Cummings encounters all the official stupidity, the "Prussian" pomposity, the flatulent phrase-mongering which (mistakenly) he thought to escape by associating himself with *La Belle France*. Basic is a conception of the purely verbal nature of reality itself; faced with this absurdity, Cummings quite properly takes pride in what has been called a "dereliction" from military duty. Pride seems indecent in a deserter, unless one remembers that a good deal depends upon what a man is rejecting. Neither Andrews nor Frederic Henry feels his manhood until he deserts; pride in negative action, given the dung heap to be negated, is a major characteristic of the World War I antihero. Hence Cummings' mocking sympathy—mocking, but still sympathy—for those men "cursed with a talent for thinking during the warlike moments recently passed; during that is to say an epoch when the g. and g. [great and good] nations demanded of their respective peoples the exact antithesis to thinking; said antithesis being vulgarly called Belief" (p. 139). The very fact that "belief" rendered "thinking" politically indecent and morally obscene explains Cummings' zestful acceptance of *La Ferté:* the only alternative to the "enormous room" was French officialdom, Mister A., or the abattoir.

For Andrews war becomes a crime against the individual and an aesthetic outrage; he is basically a very serious man. For Frederic Henry war becomes a threat to existence, virility, and love; he, too, (as Rinaldi perceives) is very serious, almost pompous. But for Cummings war is a giggling, undignified, and haphazard perversion in which nothing is worth the protest of rhetoric, a bad little slaughterhouse where there are funny little trains, amusing little victims, delightfully grotesque heroes who are also villains, and a mutual butchery almost miraculous in its complete irrationality. There is nothing to do but laugh at it, and this Cummings does, using every linguistic weapon at his disposal. But there is mockery in his laughter. The poet has become a rictus which, in turn, demonstrates the very horror the poet so proudly denies.

The Aesthetic Rebellion: John Andrews (John Dos Passos)

Unprepared by either his eastern education or Virginia family background for the military machine he had embraced as a volunteer, John Andrews giggles, "What the hell do we care now? . . . This is the damndest fool business ever.'" Andrews, however, the focus of sensibility in *Three Soldiers* despite the novel's unamistic pretensions, cares very much indeed.[4] That he does care is precisely what sets him apart from Cummings' retreat (as

---

[4] Unamism in French literature between the wars was a form of the novel in which social masses, or several protagonists, were manipulated to achieve a panorama or broad-scope movement rather than a chronological narrative focusing upon a single hero. The method of *Three Soldiers* (in which the narrative shifts between Chrisfield, Fuselli, and Andrews) is a limited attempt at the form. As Chrisfield says, "You're from the Coast, this feller's from New York, and Ah'm from ole Indiana, right in the middle" (John Dos Passos, *Three Soldiers* [New York, 1921], p. 26; subsequent references to *Three Soldiers* will be indicated parenthetically in text). In his later work, of course, Dos Passos built the unamistic framework into his collectivist technique. Other World War I novels—*Company K* in particular—attempted to achieve the cross-sectional effect so basic a development in the literature of World War II.

character) into a world of art or Frederic Henry's appeal to love, the analgesic for shattered virility, as an alternative to war.

Neither art nor love is a final solution for Andrews, who is deeply involved not in the withdrawal from noble action, but in its assertion. Viewing love as a sign of self-indulgence rather than of strength, he must give up love in order to prove his own will; viewing art as the ultimate value, he must sacrifice art in order to achieve the supreme gesture unmotivated by self-interest, a gesture, indeed, which by virtue of its own totality may redeem manhood by proving the existence of choice. In this respect Andrews is entirely consistent. There is far more to his drama than military protest alone.

Andrews had set out on the Crusade in order to achieve meaning through sacrifice; he objects to the "slavery" of army life largely because it exists quite independently of his own consent. There can be no self-abnegation, after all, without freedom to choose, and for this reason Andrews' actions at the end of the novel are entirely in character. Refusing to clear up his legal difficulties— which, as Genevieve tells him, are far from insurmountable—and deliberately destroying "The Queen of Sheba," he succeeds in playing his almost biblical role to the hilt. " 'I,' " he announces to the nonplussed Genevieve (who fails to understand the sacrifice necessities involved), " 'have made a gesture, feeble as it is, toward human freedom.' " Haloed by the drifting pages of his music, scorning the milk and honey of that very school assignment he had groveled to secure, returning to the wilderness of the prison stockade comforted only by his sense of righteousness, Andrews becomes what he had always desired: the central protagonist in a modest crucifixion.

Andrews cannot be characterized, as Maxwell Geismar suggests, merely as an individual who suffers from "failure of nerve" or "vague aspirations and the failure to fulfill them."[5] Granted that Andrews resembles Martin Howe (later described by Dos Passos himself as "a bookish young man of 22 who had emerged half-baked from Harvard"),[6] and granted also that Andrews, again like Howe, often behaves as though "he hates everything about the war principally because it interferes with his aesthetic appreciation of

[5] Maxwell Geismar, *Writers in Crisis* (Boston, 1942), p. 95.
[6] See Dos Passos' introduction to the Philosophical Library edition (1945) of *First Encounter*.

Europe,"[7] the fact remains that Andrews differs from his predecessor by virtue of his resources for negative action. Where Howe is completely the spectator (" 'I must see,' " he declares to the rather startled French officer; " 'I want to be initiated in all the circles of Hell' "), Andrews searches for and ultimately finds a way to redeem the inferno itself.

Their own self-images help to define their separate roles. Martin Howe sees himself as a sort of Dante, whereas Andrews sees himself as a vehicle for symbolic sacrifice. As such Andrews may be viewed as a development from rather than a parallel to the "half-baked" twenty-two-year-old of *First Encounter*. If Andrews' method of renunciatory action does appear somewhat too precious, too "arty" and melodramatic, this may well be a comment upon our own moral environment rather than his. Contemporary readers, after all, are likely to lose patience with any protagonist who is overly self-dramatic, while the willful destruction of his own music would probably strike us as inept rather than tragic. ("I cannot regard it [the war] as a wrong against myself," says Saul Bellow's reluctant warrior-to-be, the World War II Dangling Man.)[8] For Andrews himself, however, and for the literary audience of the twenties, such a gesture of renunciation could be both deeply courageous and authentically moving precisely because of the aesthetic sacrifice involved.

Andrews, at any rate, who enlists because of a need for sacrificial gesture ("he had not been driven into the army by force of public opinion, he had not been carried away by any wave of blind confidence in the phrases of bought propagandists" [p. 208]), discovers in the war of mass and machine an environment which makes any such gesture impossible. Out of such an ironic reversal comes his role as antihero: that is, the hero of negative action. Just as Fuselli, hoping to escape from the office, finds himself sentenced to perpetual clerkdom, so Andrews finds himself without any chance to carry through the motives for his enlistment. Having renounced civilian life as both vulgar and mechanical, he discovers vulgarity and mechanism as the basis for the Crusade. From the moment he enters the recruiting office, with its aura of imbecile routine, sterile mechanism, and dehumanization ("legs were all being made the same length on the drillfield"), he must continue his search—a

---

[7] George Snell, *The Shapers of American Fiction* (New York, 1947), p. 249.
[8] Saul Bellow, *The Dangling Man* (New York, 1944), p. 84.

search that cannot be realized while he is retrieving cigarette butts or Uncle-Tomming an indifferent officer for permission to attend school.

But neither can this search be realized through any simple escape from humiliation and brutality. Certainly Andrews cannot follow the advice offered by Henslowe (" 'Have a good time . . . the hell with 'em' " [p. 230].) even after he has made good his physical salvation, finding his own "joy" as a composer in khaki:

He was free now of the imaginings of his desire, to loll all day at cafe tables watching the tables move in changing patterns before him, to fill his mind and body with a reverberation of all the rhythms of men and women moving in the frieze of life before his eyes; no more like wooden automatons knowing only the motions of the drill manual, but supple and varied, full of force and tragedy. (p. 289)

It is not enough. His rebirth while recovering at the hospital proves deceptive after all, for it is not "freedom" that John Andrews wants, not the chance to escape from being a "slave among slaves," but rather the opportunity to perform an act of nobility. "Half by accident he had managed to free himself from the treadmill," he reflects, and then makes the ultimate self-indictment: that he had not "made a gesture, however feeble, however forlorn, for the sake of other people's freedom. . . . He had not lived up to the name of John Brown" (p. 431). And this failure is, indeed, more terrible to him than all the "slavery" he so vehemently protests against throughout the novel. Refusing to humble himself to achieve a "freedom" he cannot claim as his own, Andrews destroys his music, awaits the military police, and submits to degradation once again, but this time with full knowledge of what is in store for him. The terms of his original gesture toward individuality and renunciation have been met at last; Andrews defeats the machine by an act of negation—a sentimental act, perhaps, but an act nevertheless.

Malcolm Cowley has described the early Dos Passos as "a late romantic, an individualist, an aesthete moving about the world in a portable ivory tower."[9] The observation is useful providing we remember that John Andrews represents an authentic historical type, a sensibility which in the United States provided one extremely fruitful ground for the Great Crusade because pride in gesture was simply one more manifestation of the naïveté which

---

[9] Malcolm Cowley, "John Dos Passos: The Poet and the World," *New Republic*, LXX (April 27, 1932), 303.

enabled the Crusade to take shape. Unlike the gesture of Methot the poet in *Company K,* however (another aesthetic rebel who seeks his own death because of "alienation"), the gesture of Andrews is diluted because protest and emotion alike come framed in a filigree of baroque verbiage. It is not Andrews' insistence upon gesture, his indignation, or his fierce pride in individuality that seem gratuitous, but rather the fact that the prose surrounding Andrews is so completely over-ripe, so undigested within the narrative itself.

Although the author of a tripartite novel must vary his narrative tone according to the particular point of view involved (and Dos Passos manages quite well to shift between such disparate figures as Fuselli and Andrews),[10] the difficulty is simply that Andrews all but vanishes beneath the weight of adjectives, literary and musical allusions, color poems, chiaroscuro "moments," and enameled surfaces which often have little to do with the experience to be rendered. In this respect Dos Passos carried the tendency already noted in the work of Thomas Boyd to an extreme and sometimes overwhelming conclusion. "There were tiny green frogs in one of the putty-colored puddles by the wayside," he tells us, and proceeds—in the middle of a forced march, one might say—to add that "John Andrews fell out of the slowly advancing column a moment to look at them . . . that way he could see their tiny jeweled eyes, topaz-colored" (p. 193). Or there is the episode when "the pink and yellow and violet shades of the flowers seemed to intensify the misty straw color and azured grey of the wintry sun and the shadows of the streets" (p. 284). Narrative too often becomes a veritable spectrum of scenic absorption, something more suitable for a nineteenth-century kaleidoscope than for a novel of technological warfare.[11] Both Howe and Andrews move almost

[10] Even as early as *Three Soldiers* Dos Passos is by no means unable to produce dialogue with the ring of truth, and—when he gets far enough away from Andrews—does use understatement. When a young soldier is found in his bunk, for example:

"He ain't fainted . . . the kid's dead," said the other man. "Give me a hand."

The sergeant helped lift the body on the bed again.

"Well, I'll be goddamned," said the sergeant.

The eyes had opened. They covered the head with a blanket. (p. 123)

[11] Both Andrews and Martin Howe have continual resource to color adjectives, and the result is sometimes ludicrous. In *First Encounter:* "The indigo dome of the afternoon sky was full of the snoring of motors" (p. 64). Andrews also contributes quite a spectrum: "frail sunlight," "parti-colored grapes," "ochre-colored," "amber clouds," "pearly lavender mist," etc.

without warning from shouted protests to subdued, parti-colored appreciations of landscapes, old churches, young girls, paintings, and whatever else is sufficiently picturesque to offer a chance for cultural name dropping.

Andrews' relationship with Genevieve, for example, remains an unfortunate combination of adolescent sensuality, Jamesian *tableaux* (the "moment" at *Porto Maillot*), and guidebook allusion: "When he caught her he threw his arms about her recklessly and kissed her panting mouth . . ." (p. 323). "Her eyes [were] very large, a pale brown, as large as the eyes of women in those paintings of Artemisias and Berenikes found in the tombs of the Fayum" (p. 316). Or, again, just when we are prepared to share Andrews' indignation and anger, he retreats into Flaubert, "reading the gorgeously modulated sentences voraciously, as if the book were a drug in which he could drink forgetfulness of himself" (p. 208). Within the same point of view, Dos Passos attempts to sound both a clarion trumpet of individualist rebellion and a violin elegy in a country churchyard; the result is a weakening of protest and a diminishing of sensibility.

Dos Passos' problem, of course, was resolved in *1919*, where the various elements are separated into "Camera Eye" (aesthetic rebellion), "Newsreel" (social landscape), and "Biography" (political protest), and the straightforward narrative progression of Dick Savage, Joe, and the other protagonists. Only in his later work could Dos Passos translate his own duality—aesthetic sensibility and the politics of individualism—into a narrative system of counterpoint in which the various parts remain separate but offer thematic support to the work as a whole. The difference, however, is one of technique rather than of philosophical or moral orientation; far less separates the Dos Passos of *Three Soldiers* from the Dos Passos of *1919* than is commonly supposed. Themes and images from the early work appear in the later: there are the "tumbrils," the "lies," the repulsive "Y" men, the semi-hysterical laughter, the political indignation, the breakup of a moral world, and—perhaps most important—the faith in protest itself as a means of revelation and corrective action.

Neither the anger nor the gestures were superficial. Within hopelessness, indeed, there remained both hope and faith, a pride in action and feverish excitement created by the revelatory impact of the war itself. "If you hit the right words Democracy will understand, even the bankers and clergymen," proclaims "Camera Eye" in *1919*;[12] commenting on the Russian Revolution, Aubrey in *Three Soldiers* sees a different sort of promise, a wonderful new world of travel and sex ("Damnation to the good old times. . . . Here's to the good old new roughhousy circus parades,")[13] while both John Andrews and Cummings see their respective acts (aesthetic renunciation and aesthetic assertion) as serious moral imperatives. It is this sense of purpose, hope, action, and zest which is so uniquely a part of the World War I antiheroic posture. And it is the absence of this sense, the absence of meaningful negative possibilities, which provided a major impetus—and justification—for the neoconservative movement after World War II.[14]

Death and Cojones: Frederic Henry
(Ernest Hemingway)

"B yronic," says Alfred Kazin of Frederic Henry and *A Farewell to Arms,* and the view of Hemingway's protagonist as a neo-Romantic lover has long been with us. George Snell dismisses the love story of *A Farewell to Arms* as "not only trite but so sentimentalized as to be almost preposterous"; Edmund Wilson speaks of Hemingway's "amoeba like" women; E. B. Burgum refers to "colorless banality"; Francis Hackett sneers at Catherine as a "divine lollipop"; Isaac Rosenfeld notes "the perpetual adolescence of the emotions to cover a fear, and subsequent hatred, of adolescent love"; while Carl Van Doren more optimistically sees a romantic emancipation from the old duality of flesh vs. spirit ("if both were fused the mind might draw strength from the body and hold its head up in self-respect and joy").[15] Whether for praise or blame,

[12] John Dos Passos, *1919* (New York, 1954), p. 110. The first edition of *1919* appeared in 1932.
[13] John Dos Passos, *Three Soldiers* (New York, 1921), p. 237.
[14] Dos Passos, in his 1945 introduction to *First Encounter,* remarks: "War and aggression in the early years of this century appeared to us like stinking slums in a city that was otherwise beautiful and good to live in, blemishes that skill and courage could remove. To the young men of today, these things are inherent deformities of mankind. If you have a clubfoot you learn to live with your clubfoot." In Merle Miller's World War II novel, *That Winter* (New York, 1948), Peter dramatizes Dos Passos' observation. "The purpose," he remarks, of war, politics, and life in general "is purposelessness" (p. 12).
[15] Alfred Kazin, *On Native Grounds* (New York, 1942), p. 330; Snell, *The Shapers of American Fiction,* p. 158; Edmund Wilson, "Hemingway: The

most of Hemingway's commentators have agreed that "romance" of one sort or another defines his protagonists in general and Frederic Henry in particular.

What this "romance" represents, however, remains obscure; the word itself is one of those quicksilver epithets often handled and seldom fixed. Perhaps the best clue to the basic "romance" of Frederic Henry is to be found not in criticism, but in the remarks of Rinaldi in *A Farewell to Arms*—Rinaldi, who refuses to take Frederic Henry's value-through-love seriously, who deflates his sudden solemnity, and who dances a jig of verbal mockery around the very bedside of the New Redemption: " 'I know, you are the fine Anglo-Saxon boy,' Rinaldi says. 'I know, I will wait till I see the Anglo-Saxon brushing away harlotry with a toothbrush. . . . All my life I encounter sacred objects, but very few with you. I suppose you must have them too.' "[16] For Rinaldi is not impressed with the new-found passion of his friend. He is disappointed. And the reason for his disappointment is the fact that he sees Frederic Henry as dependent upon that very crutch of Protestant sexuality from which he had assumed this American to be exempt.

Hemingway's protagonist, indeed, with his sense of manhood shattered by technological rape (" 'I was blown up while we were eating cheese' "), turns toward his "lovely cool goddess" because there is nothing else. Deprived of that initiative so essential to Hemingway's concept of virility, unable to ritualize his role in the war so as to act rather than be acted upon, threatened with the horror of male passivity, Frederic Henry is reduced to the "worship" Rinaldi so ironically defines. Action and violence, once simple, have become complex, and would master Frederic Henry rather than be mastered by him. For this reason Catherine does indeed become "sacred"; only through her mirror-surface, her re-

---

Gauge of Morale," *Literature in America*, ed. Philip Rahv (New York, 1957), p. 388; E. B. Burgum, *The Novel and the World's Dilemma* (New York, 1947), p. 185; Francis Hackett, "Hemingway: A Farewell to Arms," *Saturday Review of Literature*, XXXII (August 6, 1949), 32; Isaac Rosenfeld, "A Farewell to Ernest Hemingway," *Kenyon Review*, XIII (1951), 144; Carl Van Doren, "Post-War: The Literary Twenties," *Harper's*, CLXXIII (1936), 279.

One might also note Robert Penn Warren's parallel between Hemingway and Wordsworth in his introduction to the Scribner edition (1949) of Hemingway's *A Farewell to Arms*.

[16] Ernest Hemingway, *A Farewell to Arms* (New York, 1929), pp. 179, 181.

nunciation of self, can Henry once again take comfort from the reflection of his own face.

Only a love-object, in other words, an erotic shadow shaped by passivity, can return to Frederic Henry the initiative essential to his manhood. Catherine offers to become " 'whatever you want' "—and this is what the war, what voluntary violence itself, should have been and was not. From the moment that violence and action intrude upon Frederic Henry's will, from the moment that they cease to exist merely by virtue of his consent (as they do exist in Hemingway's later work by virtue of the bullfighter's consent, or the hunter's, or the fisherman's), his relationship with Catherine becomes far more vital than a "chess-game" of idle fornication; its urgency and inviolability are shaped by a pursuit of an absolute psychic need. For Frederic Henry does not require romance from Catherine, but medication, and in this respect he is less the Byronic lover than patient. Catherine, who is simply there at his disposal, permits him his masculine role: action determined and made necessary by nothing beyond its own will. And when this last cure also proves illusory, when Catherine asserts her own individuality by the very act of dying, there is nothing left of manhood at all. Frederic Henry takes his final walk into the rain as a sort of Jake Barnes, who in *The Sun Also Rises* stares blankly at the mirror of his own impotence. The hyena of passivity—always a nightmare for Hemingway—reduces Frederic Henry to a spiritual *castrado*.

Essential to this emasculation is the inability to handle any quality of *otherness* except in terms of ritualization. The other— whether animate or inanimate—is tolerable only insofar as it can be manipulated, controlled as one controls the trout line, the bullfight, the hunt, or the female—who achieves her own "truth" and "purity" by becoming an object. Since any experience that is an extension of self holds no terror, only those experiences that are extensions of self may be absorbed (or mastered). Even death, providing it can be arranged and patterned, may serve as an exercise in virility; only when death refuses to be patterned, when action—impersonal if not antipersonal—becomes its own perpetuator, does flight into other areas of experience become an undignified and involuntary imperative. There is no question of *cojones*, of will, among those soldiers groveling and "choking through the whole attack" in "Champs d'Honneur" (written while the war experience was still all too fresh in Hemingway's mind). What

Frederick J. Hoffman sees as the "violation" or "traumatic shock" of technological war is a vital aspect not only in the relationship between Frederic Henry and Catherine, but in the literary career of Hemingway himself.[17]

Unpatterned, unritualized, and other, the war intrudes upon Frederic Henry and therefore is bad; Catherine never intrudes, never seizes the initiative, and so is "good." It is such "purity" that Rinaldi, the ubiquitous and clever diagnostician, so thoroughly distrusts; " 'You never know if the girl will really like it,' " he churlishly remarks. Catherine has become too completely an object; her very desire is "pure" for Frederic Henry because it creates narcissism (" 'I want what you want . . . there isn't any me any more, just what you want' ").[18] The total effect, indeed, is something more; it is autoerotic. For only the autoerotic image, love without the other, can be counted upon not to change, not to escape into complexity, not to threaten, and not to break into the controlled act by thrusting forward a pattern of its own.

All depends upon the mystique of ritual, even art itself; for this reason Hemingway's language conveys that peculiar sense of caution, wariness, and deliberation which so belies its own realistic surface. Although there is no doubt that a reaction against the rhetoric of the Crusade powerfully affected Hemingway's style, Harry Levin's reference to his "verbal skepticism" explains the particular quality of that style only partially.[19] It is not skepticism that underlies ritual, but fear—fear of the unknown or unmanageable. In the bull ring men can defeat death even while dying because they surround it with form: the initiative, in a very real sense, remains theirs. As a bulwark against passivity, ritual—whether in the temple, the bedroom, the arena, or the battlefield—has been one of humanity's basic psychological needs, and it is in this sense that Hemingway so carefully, indeed so compulsively arranges and limits experience.[20] Technological warfare eliminated the battlefield as a resource for ritual, while flabby rhetoric and political oppor-

[17] Frederick J. Hoffman, *The Twenties* (New York, 1949), pp. 57, 68.
[18] Hemingway, *A Farewell to Arms*, p. 113.
[19] Harry Levin, "Observations on the Style of Ernest Hemingway," *Kenyon Review*, XIII (1951), 592.
[20] An incisive comment upon Hemingway as an artist is the general question put by Andre Malraux: "How can one make the best of one's life . . . ? By converting as wide a range of experience as possible into conscious thought." Quoted by Philip Rahv, "The Cult of Experience in American Writing," *Literature in America*, p. 552.

tunism eliminated the temple. Only love remained, but very briefly and very deceptively: Catherine, after all, shattered Frederic Henry's ritual by dying quite without his consent. And after love too has been "spoiled" there is only the arena, a resource for Hemingway throughout his subsequent career.

Ritualized language and prescribed limitation of experience to be rendered or even talked about may produce honest and precise writing. Despite all the insistence on precision and virility, however, there is in Hemingway's work an almost maidenish fear of the full spectrum of potentialities within experience. This is particularly true of love, and it is with reference to love as an alternative to meaningful action, unmistakable choice, or virile death that Hemingway's dietetic art can become so inadequate that it may seem a parody of its own virtues. While action and ritual can be rendered by his type of art, person or process cannot; for this reason Catherine (as Rinaldi understands) becomes a leaf of lettuce nibbled by a man on a mountain top where the only sound he hears is the sound of his own teeth. There is no flavor here, and little flesh either. Frederic Henry's lettuce-woman may leave him always hungry, no matter how much he takes of her, but this insatiability is due less to a virile appetite than to a lack of substance-to-be-consumed. It is a measure of the book's essential Puritanism (rather than romance) that autoeroticism becomes the "clean," the "pure," the "true," and the desperate analgesic for reduced manhood. A world of violence has rejected all the rituals of love and violence alike, and the result is total defeat. Even the "mountains" are spoiled for Frederic Henry because (unlike Cummings, who uses an identical symbol to represent diversity), he attempts, but fails, to shape the universe according to his own image.

The loss of initiative represented by technological violence and the attempt to regain this initiative through the bedroom or the arena are basic elements in *A Farewell to Arms* and Hemingway's later work. The war itself, certainly, represents a break in the continuum from natural violence in the northwoods to ritualized violence in the bull ring; it is the one area where death cannot be mastered through the assertion of will, the ritual of *cojones*, and for this reason it threatens rather than fulfills what Alfred Kazin calls "the individual's fierce unassailable pride in his pride"—virility itself.[21] For pride is impossible when no choice

[21] Kazin, *On Native Grounds*, p. 330.

is offered, when the initiative is stolen, and Hemingway tends to avoid rather than confront any experience where initiative becomes external. Confrontation, indeed, is a theme of Hemingway's work only in a special and very limited sense: his protagonists attempt to confront death in terms of ritual or they refuse to confront it at all.[22]

This dependence upon ritual, and consequent horror when the impossibility of ritualizing reduces the individual to passivity, indicates that Hemingway's preoccupation with death is something far removed from existential confrontation. That so many critics have indeed read Hemingway in existential terms is due to a double failure of perception: first, the failure to perceive that technological violence in World War I deprived death of any "moment of truth" whatsoever; and, second, that a World War I protagonist like Frederic Henry, " 'blown up while we were eating cheese,' " becomes a refugee from precisely that form of obliteration, of *nada,* he no longer can master.[23]

Critics like Philip Young, John Atkins, Edmund Wilson, Alfred Kazin, and others have read a consistency into Hemingway's attitude toward violence, and this is perhaps one reason why a commentator like John Killinger, writing as recently as 1960, could actually define Nick Adams and Frederic Henry as existential heroes. But the post-World War II existential demand for total involvement despite absurdity (indeed, within absurdity) can no more be equated with Hemingway's ritual escape than Nick's hunting or fishing in the northwoods can be equated with the industrialized slaughter of World War I. Nick went to war as though he

---

[22] See Melvin Blackman, "Hemingway: The Matador and the Crucified," *Hemingway and his Critics,* ed. Carlos Baker (New York, 1961). Mr. Blackman notes two categories of formal response: the matador, representing "a great force held in check, releasing itself proudly in a controlled yet violent administration of death"; and the crucified, "taking of pain even unto death with all of one's courage and endurance so that it becomes a thing of poignancy and nobility" (p. 245). Either one or the other is necessary; where neither is possible there is no confrontation at all.

[23] Hemingway's own World War I wound, the circumstances of which resemble in so many ways Frederic Henry's (the brave man whose bravery is discounted by a stray shell), is described by Charles A. Fenton: ". . . at midnight on July 8, near the tiny village of Fossalta, two weeks before his nineteenth birthday and seven days after his first admission to the trenches, he was struck by the exploding fragments of a trench mortar which landed a few feet from him. He was handing out chocolate to the Italian soldiers" (*The Apprenticeship of Ernest Hemingway* [New York, 1954], pp. 65–66).

were casting for trout; he found another genre of experience (or antiexperience) altogether.

Hemingway's ritual of death, possible only outside rather than within modern war, is escape rather than confrontation; when the ritual is not possible, there is no confrontation at all.[24] Like the Hemingway love relationship (which, when it is "good," is always between a man and his shadow and so avoids the threat—and the reality—of the other), Hemingway's ritual is both formal and abstract, and so represents a retreat from rather than acceptance of existential absurdity. This is the real meaning of the World War I experience (death without ritual), and it explains why Hemingway afterward was successful only in those areas where ritual became possible: the bullfight, the safari, the fishing trip. For post-World War II existentialism, however, ritual for its own sake is no more acceptable a formula—precisely because it is a formula—than art for the sake of art; the illusions of ritual do not truly confront and defeat death any more than a cocktail party confronts and defeats human isolation.

Too many critics have failed to realize, or remember, the enormous difference for Hemingway between World War I death and the death which either preceded it (death in the woods) or followed it (ritual death in the bull ring). Mr. Killinger, indeed, in *Hemingway and the Dead Gods*, sees no difference at all: "In the blinding flash of a shell, in the icy-burning impact of a bullet, in the dangerous vicinity of a wounded lion, in the contact of a bull's horn, in that ill-defined twilight between life and imminent death where time and place are irrelevant questions, man faces his freedom."[25] But Frederic Henry knows better. There was neither "choice" nor "freedom" for him, no reason for medals or even talk; he was "eating cheese"; he was totally—almost obscenely—*done to;* he was, as Frederick Hoffman remarks, "violated"; his experience was emasculatory because passive and therefore feminine. "Soldiers never do die well," Hemingway tells us in "Champs d'Honneur," and his entire career as a writer was in a vital sense a search for those areas where a man can at least maintain the illusion of making love to death rather than being violated by it. The question is one of manhood itself, of initiative, and on this question

[24] Maxwell Geismar perhaps overstates the escapist element in Hemingway's work, but notes the presence of fear as a motivating force. See *Writers in Crisis*, pp. 62–63.
[25] John Killinger, *Hemingway and the Dead Gods* (Lexington, Ky., 1960), p. 18.

the war experience is simply ruled out because it becomes unmanageable. There is nothing one can do with technological warfare but make a "separate peace" against it. And this is precisely Frederic Henry's sole course of action. For when nobody follows the rules, a man is under no obligation to play the game; indeed, when the game threatens to play the man, there is no alternative but flight. As the drunken sailor in *1919* says, " 'All bets is off.' "

The very fact that flight is possible, however, points up the difference between Hemingway and existentialism. Despite all his talk about death (and the talk of critics about it), Hemingway was concerned less with death than with the masculine role, which for him was always active, as the feminine was always passive. This is one reason why his protagonists, if they are unable to make love to death, if they are acted upon (as Frederic Henry is acted upon), are faced with the ultimate horror: emasculation, the feminine role. Of course the protagonist, if he is lucky enough, may find refuge with a woman who in her complete passivity substitutes her nothingness for the nothingness of death and so permits the hero to maintain his virility through an exercise of will. Death, in the novels of Hemingway, must be passive and women (in their complete passivity) must be objects; when either death or the woman forces a protagonist to exchange roles the result is emasculation; and this in turn forces him to seek out one or the other, death or the woman, as a means of repairing his sadly injured virility. Francis Macomber and Frederic Henry represent two sides of the same emotional coin: the fear of impotence.

In the work of Hemingway death is less a threat to a man's existence than to his *cojones,* and for this reason he can speak of "dying well" or "dying badly," while admitting that soldiers, as contrasted to bullfighters or fishermen, "never do die well" since they are tossed on their backs to receive rather than give the final blow. Only when a man is passive in his death does *nada* itself becomes obscene (the jackal laughs at the hunter when the hunter is dying in bed). For existentialism, on the other hand, death is always obscene, and the problem is not one of "dying well" (which is an existentialist contradiction in terms) but rather, given the inevitable and inescapable obscenity of death—in the bull ring or anywhere else—one of living well. And this is the major difference between Hemingway's *nada*—an emasculatory horror born of the World War I impact—and the nothingness of Sartre. Where the post-World War II existentialist insists that there is "no exit" from the final and obscene absurdity, Hemingway depends wholly upon ritualized action for precisely just such an escape. And when ritual fails, the individual is doomed along with his manhood. Initiative must be regained at all costs, and the demand for initiative is a clue not only to the central drama of *A Farewell to Arms*, but to the life—and the death—of Hemingway himself.[26]

" 'I refuse to have anything to do with war. . . . I won't resign myself to it,' " says Céline in *Journey to the End of the Night*—a cogent summary of the antiheroic position in general.[27] Unlike Céline, however, who is far closer to the total negation of World War II (perpetually mocking his own ineptitudes, loathing himself no less than the society from which he is alienated, and indeed loathing alienation in a verbal examination of his own absurdity), the American antihero of the Great Crusade insisted upon the possibilities of action within negation. "Life had begun with war for them," Kazin remarks of the World War I generation, "and would forever be shadowed by violence and death . . . but it was not only the war that had at once isolated them and given them their prominence; it was their sense of artistic mission."[28]

This sense of "artistic mission," and political or moral mission as well, distinguishes the antihero from both the faceless protagonist of total withdrawal on one hand and the hero of acquiescence on the other. Hicks and Mahon, for example, undergo impact and alienation, but these are only the first two stages of the antiheroic process. John Andrews, Cummings, and Frederic Henry proceed to the third and perhaps most important stage—the creation of alternatives beyond withdrawal—and so become heroes of the negative act; it is their insistence upon the imperatives of action which sets up their antiheroic role.

A basic pattern emerges: the antihero enlists for a Cause; becomes bitterly conscious of the futility of the Cause; carries on the job as a job until by its own absurdity the Cause rejects the antihero and forces his physical no less than emotional withdrawal. At this point there are the three responses: Andrews acts to achieve sacrificial gesture; Frederic Henry to regain initiative through an

[26] See A. E. Hotchner, *Papa Hemingway* (New York, 1966).
[27] Louis-Ferdinand Céline, *Journey to the End of the Night* (New York, 1960), p. 61.
[28] Kazin, *On Native Grounds*, p. 313.

exercise of will upon female passivity; and Cummings (as character) resorts to leaping waves of parody and satire, beneath which there is the serious assertion of art as an ultimate value. Claude Wheeler dies as a militarist phantom; Zorn hardens into scar tissue; Dick Savage surrenders into moral invisibility; Irwin, Fuselli, Hicks, and Mahon are totally obliterated. But the antiheroes—the heroes of the negative act—become precisely those who offer some alternative to the broken world.

VI

*War is part of the natural intercourse
of the human race.*
—General Karl von Clausewitz

*This war does not furnish the poet, the
dramatist, the novelist with the material of
literature. . . . War is an upheaval of
civilization, a return to barbarism; it means
death to all the arts.*
—William Dean Howells

*Great literary works related to war touch the
innermost existence of man, and defy the
nothingness of human life.*
—Joseph Remenyi

191

L ove, death, and war have always been the great raw materials of literature. Men still love and die in very much the same way that their ancestors—including their literary ancestors in the Homeric and epic patterns—loved and died. They do not, however, make war the same way; indeed, one might say that in the twentieth century war is made upon them. And this change has resulted in enormous problems not only for the literary artist, but for the literary critic and historian.

Traditionally, war-as-subject has been used by the artist as a framework, much like any other, for the examination of individual consciousness both in terms of environment and in relation to other individuals. The concept of war as "part of the natural intercourse of the human race" was one to which poets and novelists no less than generals assented prior to World War I, a concept which resulted in such disparate works as Tolstoy's *War and Peace* and Crane's *The Red Badge of Courage*. These books, despite wide variation of treatment, were firmly traditional in their use of war as a narrative framework. And, precisely as a narrative tool, the war environment—most particularly in the novel—offered advantages: the qualities of intensification, pathos, dramatic contrast, crisis, and action were in a sense ready-packaged to the author's hand. A framework of war or combat could also help solve certain purely mechanical problems, such as scenic focus and the definition of a temporal dimension.

Critics, however, were free to concentrate on the aesthetic structure of particular books only as long as writers themselves used war as a standard literary device. The novelist's success in rendering his environment for internal dramatic purpose; his ability to create narrative necessity without recourse to unmotivated event; his communication of meaning, even deterministic meaning, through human emotion and individual confrontation—these were valid matters for critical judgment. Quite suddenly, however, war could not be used, or was not being used, as a standard literary device at all. What J. H. Johnston noted in his study of World War I poetry applied with equal force to the novel: "Most of the poets who wrote between 1914–1918 came to realize that their work lacked certain important qualities—objectivity, comprehensiveness, clarity, proportion, and control. . . . But these poets were confronted by a species of warfare that seemed to reverse almost every ideal of heroic action."[1]

No longer one subordinate element among many contributing to a total aesthetic structure, environment—the war itself—became the chief protagonist; when this happened readers were left foundering in a situation where the traditional critical instruments simply could not be applied. One senses an authentic dilemma in the remarks of a critic like Helen McAfee who, writing in 1923, viewed with alarm environmental intrusion and the dark, external shape of "war emotion." Both, somehow, seemed quite outside the legitimate concerns of literary craftsmen. "The war," she declared, "has been useful, too useful, to novelists in turning a dangerous corner of the plot, or in getting rid of a character (always a more difficult feat than introducing one) in order to precipitate the dénouement. Some of them have also yielded to draw on the great common fund of war emotion."[2]

Miss McAfee's problem has by no means been resolved. Ever since the young writers of World War I began producing their works of literary disenchantment (a collective record of impact rather than aesthetic balance) and readers recovered sufficiently from the emotional exhaustion and moral hangover of the Great Crusade to read what the young writers were offering, the debate has continued.

Critics have first of all been concerned with the re-establishment of the war novel's aesthetic limits, attempting to reconcile traditional requirements for "the novel as form" with the apparent refusal of war writers to eliminate strictly extra-aesthetic elements from their books. After World War I this attempt took the form of warnings that sheer negativism and antiwar sentiments were violating both formal totality and literary (as distinguished from political) realism. Heywood Broun, among others, objected to the antiwar novel on the latter grounds:

In theory the iron discipline of army life was and is a force calculated to wreck almost everything in man which is free and fine. To this expression of belief we must add the attendant observation that it

---

[1] J. H. Johnston, "The Poetry of World War I: A Study in the Evolution of Lyric and Narrative Form" (unpublished Ph.D. dissertation, University of Wisconsin, 1960), *DA*, XX (1960), 4397.
[2] Helen McAfee, "The Literature of Disillusion," *Atlantic Monthly*, CXXXII (August, 1923), 225.

actually did nothing of the sort to huge numbers of men. . . . The most terrific adventure the world had ever known lifted its hordes into the air and when it set them down again vast numbers had not been changed spiritually by so much as a single hair. Having arrived at a theory of the effects of war, Dos Passos has been a little too ready to put his characters through the same emotional hopper.[3]

And Broun's point was reiterated by innumerable critics. Clennell Wilkinson, writing in the *London Mercury*, may be taken as a further example: "The amateur soldier," he said, referring to the war novelist as a type, "was filled with indignant disgust . . . ; he thought it wrong to say a word that might seem to be in favour of war. He therefore shut his eyes to half the facts—the comradeship, the self-sacrifice. Like an inverted sundial he stood on his head in mud and blood, counting only the darker hours. . . . He scarcely mentions rest billets or the exquisite pleasure of those few, fleeting days of home leave."[4]

The years immediately before and since the Second World War have compounded rather than alleviated critical confusion. The existence of a legitimate external cause prompted renewed attacks upon the "negation" and "defeatism" of the earlier writers; a necessary global conflict made the antiwar bias of the early books seem in retrospect stylistically shrill and morally irresponsible. Recent critics, certainly, have often attacked the "negation" of World War I fiction from their own historical perspective, judging according to political and military necessities which simply did not exist in the previous conflict. Counterbalancing this tendency is the work of John W. Aldridge, who in *After the Lost Generation* (1951) dismissed, with grand impartiality, the various flaws of "conservatism," "futility," and "sociology" so basic to World War II literature, pointing to the very technical sophistication of the novelists as an indication of "journalism" (prima facie evidence of superficiality). If critics, before World War II, viewed the literature of their "Big War" as though the war itself had taken place in the nineteenth century, more recently there have been persistent attempts to see the first conflict in terms of the second, or, in the case of Aldridge, to attack the literature of the second as lacking the "impact" and "discovery" of the first.

In a period of technological, political, and military chaos, stu-

---

[3] Heywood Broun, quoted in "American Army Discipline as Spiritual Murder," *Literary Digest*, LXXII (November 12, 1921), 29–30.
[4] Clennell Wilkinson, "Recent War Books," *London Mercury*, XXI (1930), 236.

dents of war literature have indeed found that there is no "still point in a turning world"; that the heresies of one generation become jejune irresponsibilities of another; that the various aesthetic dictums perfected by one generation are ridiculed by another ("I have to talk," says Saul Bellow's Dangling Man); that the sacrifices and moral gestures of one generation become the cowardice, even treachery, of another.[5] Certainly terms like "negation," "despair," "irresponsibility," "balance," "heresy," and "testimony of the total man" may be critical stumbling blocks rather than stepping stones.

It is the purpose of this section to examine major critical attitudes toward the unique combination of impact, protest, and objective withdrawal which shaped and helped define post-World War I fiction. These attitudes fall into four general categories: the humanist criticism of the interwar period; the revisionist criticism—essentially a call to affirmation—of the World War II years; the assumption, after World War II, of a circle or cycle of war acceptance-rejection-acceptance; and the nostalgic evaluation (exemplified most notably by Mr. Aldridge) of what seemed to be the brave new world of post-World War I negative creativity.

Interwar and the Humanist Protest

As the decade of the twenties drew to a close, critics on both sides of the Atlantic began massing their heaviest artillery against what Montgomery Belgion called the "School of Despair" in war literature. Certainly the initial impact of the war's technological slaughter had considerably softened; technology was already beginning to be assimilated, and the initial horror had given way to demands by literary theorists for balance and perspective— a movement paralleled by increasing formalism in the creative work of such men as Dos Passos and Hemingway. A major weapon of the critics was their repeated emphasis on "total reality," the insistence that during war—any war—"men are enriched by what

[5] Isidor Schneider, writing in 1931 ("The Fetish of Simplicity," *Nation*, CXXXII [February 18, 1931], 184–86), anticipated the rejection of Hemingwayism so obvious in the work of Saul Bellow and other post-World War II writers: "In time this style of literary conversation will seem as preposterous as the melancholy of Wertherism which soothed and flattered the generation after the Napoleonic Wars" (p. 185).

they undergo, made more human, not more mechanical."[6] For Belgion and the older critics, who looked askance at the antiwar novels as examples of false despair and unpatriotic sulking, the chief point of attack was simply that the "despair" writers were sensitive and artistic young men, and so altogether untypical as soldiers:

The chief reason why we cannot accept the . . . pacifist school of war writers as speaking for the vast majority of soldiers is that, in the very act of being a writer, the writer reveals himself as different from the common run of men. . . . Not only is he articulate where the majority are inarticulate; he must be in the habit of contemplating and analyzing his feelings, as the majority do not. Accordingly, what the majority feel and what the writer feels in any given circumstances are possibly very different. An ordinary man's feelings are possibly more spontaneous and less the product of literary associations than the writer's.[7]

Interestingly enough, Ernest Hemingway, in *Men at War* (an anthology of war stories gathered for the entertainment and edification of GI's during World War II), makes something of the same point: since the prime qualities of a soldier ("learning to suspend your imagination and live completely in the very second of the present moment, with no before and no after") are antithetical to those of a writer, it becomes all but impossible to find "good writing by good soldiers."[8] Hemingway's anthology, of course, was produced for soldiers in a war to which most men—including Hemingway himself—had already assented, and without illusions; for this reason the introductory essay is primed with all the political, military, and patriotic sloganeering so totally rejected by Frederic Henry and other World War I protagonists. For this reason also the ability to be a "good soldier" becomes a positive virtue rather than an absurdity. The suspicion here is against war writers as such, who are not likely to be military paragons; the observations of a creative artist in a war environment must be suspect.

But the writer is differentiated from the vast majority of soldiers (or bullfighters and fisherman, for that matter) by his ability to combine observations, experience, and articulation; he can both observe and articulate where the "common run of men" do not.

[6] Montgomery Belgion, "Post-War Despair," *The Human Parrot and Other Essays* (London, 1931), p. 138.
[7] *Ibid.*
[8] Ernest Hemingway, *Men at War* (New York, 1955), p. xxiv. The 1955 edition includes Hemingway's original introduction written for the 1942 "GI" edition.

Belgion's position, and Hemingway's to a lesser degree, tended to reduce the artist to some sort of eccentric jester since nothing he says can be accepted without cavil simply because he is an artist.

Offering perhaps the most reasonable defense of the artist-in-the-army, Malcolm Cowley points to the obviously atypical status of the writer and his value quite apart from his role as good soldier:

War novelists are not sociologists or historians, but neither are they average soldiers. The special training and talent of novelists lead them to express special moods. They are usually critical in temper and often are self-critical to the point of being burdened with feelings of guilt. They are sensitive—about themselves in the beginning; but if they have any imagination (and they need it) they learn to be sensitive for others. . . . In military service, many future writers were men of whom their comrades said that they were "always goofing off by themselves." They suffered more than others from the enforced promiscuity of army and shipboard life. Most of them were rebels against discipline when they thought it was illogical—which they usually did—and rebels against the system that divides officers from enlisted men. . . . Yet the war novelists were trying hard to be accurate and to tell the true story of what they saw. When we find them in substantial agreement on a number of topics, we should listen attentively to what they say.[9]

It was precisely the "substantial agreement" on the part of World War I writers that critics, especially humanist critics, found so intolerable. Along with the *ad hominem* attack upon pacifism as a product of artistic sensibility, there was fundamental criticism along humanist lines. Archibald MacLeish, in his debate with Cowley in 1933 (on Lawrence Stallings' *The First World War*, published that year), formulated a position which has since been echoed by other critics during and after World War II: a humanist attack based essentially upon the lack of "totality," "balance," and "harmony" in the novels of protest.[10]

The verse-heading to "Lines for an Interment" gives the key to MacLeish's position: "Nevertheless it is foolish to chew gall." Like Joseph Remenyi (whose essay "The Psychology of War Literature," which appeared in 1944, indicates the continuing vein of humanist criticism), MacLeish called for a dramatization of the war experience as *totality*. "It was a war of parades," he insisted,

---

[9] Malcolm Cowley, *The Literary Situation* (New York, 1947), pp. 25–26.
[10] Archibald MacLeish, "Lines for an Interment," *New Republic*, LXXVI (September 20, 1933), 159–60; and "The Dead of the Next War," *New Republic*, LXXVI (October 4, 1933), 214–16. See also Cajetan Geer's "Now It Can Be Talked About," *Commonweal*, XVI (1932), 210. Geer, like MacLeish, insisted that "the authors of our war literature have not written dispassionately enough. . . . They have told the truth too well, and with too much feeling."

in addition to a war of less pleasant moments. There were "speeches, brass-bands, bistros, boredom, terror, anguish, heroism, endurance, humor, death. It [the war] matched great cruelty with great courage. It had its fine sights and its unspeakable sights. It was a human war."[11]

In this demand for an end to "gall," MacLeish takes an orthodox humanist position: there is the lyric juxtaposition of opposites, the "balance" of negative and positive, the "harmony" of high and low. MacLeish, in short, calls for aesthetic decorum—and one remembers Hemingway's remarks in A Natural History of the Dead on precisely such a demand:

So now I want to see the death of any self-styled Humanist because a persevering traveler like Mungo Park or me lives on and maybe yet will see the actual death of members of this literary sect and watch the noble exits they make. . . . While decorum is an excellent thing, some must be indecorous, and it occurred to me that perhaps that is what these people are, or were: the children of decorous cohabitation. But regardless of how they started I hope to see the finish of a few, and speculate how worms will try that long preserved sterility; with their quaint pamphlets gone to bust and into footnotes all their lust.[12]

In view of the fact that not all humanism was sterile, Hemingway's bitterness was unreasonable. So were, in many respects, the protests of the World War I novels. But young writers were fresh from a technological slaughterhouse, from their experience of futility of cause, futility of leadership, futility of death itself; they were in no mood to be reasonable. If "Remember the Lusitania!" was a rallying cry for the bold journey into war, one might say that "A plague on all your balances!" defined the reaction, at least the literary reaction, to the war itself. For these young writers were not constructing aesthetic totalities from their experience. Even the limited formalism of Dos Passos or Hemingway, the retreat into ritualized violence, or the objective and anonymous patterns of the roman-fleuve were possible only after many intervening years had softened the initial impact and emotional chaos.[13]

[11] MacLeish, "Lines for an Interment," p. 159.
[12] Ernest Hemingway, "A Natural History of the Dead," The Short Stories of Ernest Hemingway (New York, 1953), p. 445.
[13] March's Company K, for example, appeared in 1933; Hemingway's A Farewell to Arms in 1929; Dos Passos' 1919 in 1932. Other major novels of World War I appeared earlier, of course (Dos Passos' Three Soldiers, 1921; Boyd's Through the Wheat, 1923; Cummings' The Enormous Room, 1922), but they were far less objective. One might also note that in general the World War II books were produced far more rapidly than the books of the first war.

At any rate, MacLeish's demand for a humanist war literature seemed to belong to some other war. The very point of the literature he was criticizing lay in the fact that war no longer seemed "human," that the redeeming qualities of external or internal cause were nonexistent, and that even cruelty, being machine-packaged and machine-delivered, was no longer cruelty in the "human" sense. Far from attempting to create "balance," writers were insisting upon the need for immediate and irresistible impact, for impact was what they had felt.

Of course there were good times that the writers of World War I protest tended to neglect. Reading their books, to cite but one example, one might almost assume that the sun shone in France no more than two days—or even two hours—per month. But the *impact* was there, in their work, the memory of horizons of mud and filth, influenza, mashed earth which under repeated bombardment could not even hold its dead. Granted that there were, on occasion, days when (as Willa Cather writes) "the Americans went through every village with march step, colours flying, bands playing"; this was the very expectation with which the bold journey had begun.[14] Far more emotionally shattering were those days when troops moved through towns like drenched, lice-ridden, and venereal specters before they had so much as seen combat. This is what the novelists remembered, and justly so if we consider that not all experiences are qualitatively alike. The writer, after all, must choose among experiences for the essential reality to be rendered. This reality, again, was characterized by a sense of impact rather than of balance.

Paradoxically, in attacking Stallings' negation as philosophic and antiaesthetic, MacLeish was himself the philosopher. Issuing his humanist-aesthetic demand for "totality," he failed to perceive (as have later critics, especially those conditioned by the necessities of World War II) that Stallings was making his response most immediately in art: that is, recording emotional impact as the definitive *quality* of the World War I experience. Stallings, like other war writers, had in effect made the great refusal: he had refused to force this impact into patterns limited by the abstractions of highly intellectualized aesthetic standards. These standards offered totality and balance as fixed criteria even for those works having as their artistic goals a portrait of fragmentation and imbalance. The standards were general rather than particular, and

[14] Willa Cather, *One of Ours* (1922), p. 358.

so were rejected by writers who wished to communicate a very particular experience indeed. It was MacLeish who, on philosophic grounds, was attempting to set up a concept of permissive experience—experience which could make possible those qualities of harmony and totality seen by the humanist as the ultimate criteria for art.[15]

For this reason MacLeish could decry Stallings' preoccupation with the war's impersonality and terror, criticizing his lack of heroes and his concern with mass rather than individual problems. Stallings' war, MacLeish complained, and the war of other young writers as well, "is not human. Its protagonists are not men, not even armies, but nations, continents. Its stories are not stories of men in warfare, but of beginnings, devices, forces—the greed of bankers, the rapacity of munitions makers, the starvation of nations, the death of millions, the maiming of millions." The result, for MacLeish, was simply a "dislocation of human life."[16] Operating from an aesthetic position based upon conventional attitudes toward war-as-subject, MacLeish insisted that no such war could be shown in literature with aesthetic validity.

The nonhuman impact which MacLeish ruled out as nonaesthetic, however, had to be portrayed if the particularity of this war was to be shown at all.[17] That the young writers of World War I did confront "forces" accounts not only for their negation, but also for their refusal to accept all the historically noble abstractions (including MacLeish's) which, at first believing, they found simply could not be applied to the emotional realities of their experience.

At this point the objection to negative war literature shifted to other grounds: the violation of totality through the didactic fal-

[15] MacLeish uses *The First World War* (1933), a collection of photographs with a powerful commentary by Stallings, as a departure for his attack on war protest per se.
[16] MacLeish, "Lines for an Interment," p. 159.
[17] Mary Lee, author of a war novel (*'It's a Great War!'* [Boston and New York, 1929]) whose chief interest lies in the ambitious—and unrelieved—use of interior monologue, made some pertinent comments in this connection as part of her preface: "A Book about war cannot be a romance built about an organized and neatly thought-out plot. There may be romances in it, but the Chief Protagonist is always War itself, with its stupidity, its carelessness of human life. The aims, the desires, the emotions of thousands of separate individuals who make an army are sacrificed in the enormous welter of uncontrolled events. . . . The chief characteristic of War is that human beings are powerless to achieve their ends. War is a Spectacle in which millions of lives are jostled about by mental and moral forces not their own" (p. 2).

lacy. "Art," said MacLeish, "has neither morality, nor text, nor lesson. It records those things, seen or unseen, which have actually occurred. . . . It records them regardless of their effect on the minds of the young and the minds of the old; regardless of their capacity for arousing anger against the recorder of anti-social enthusiasms directed at others."[18] MacLeish's basic implication was that the World War I novelists adopted negation—or rather, their antiwar bias—simply as a social lesson. Faced with a shift in popular mood to war repugnance, MacLeish assumed that any similar feeling on the part of the novelist must have been achieved through nonaesthetic pressures. He declared that "the artist is not and can never be an instrument of society," and then went immeasurably further, seeing any artist who did reflect current popular opinion as its instrument, and by that very fact suspect.

There is some parallel here to the attitude of some recent critics on the neoconservative element among World War II writers. MacLeish called for an affirmative totality (inclusive, despite war's horror, of nobility and glory) because the general attitude of society toward this subject (war) had become negative and therefore unbalanced. Aldridge rather wistfully looks back to negation because in our time the general attitude is either socially affirmative or philosophically futile: negation, that is, without revolutionary faith. The two positions are similar in that each tends to reduce the artist to a metronome whose direction is determined inversely according to external pressures. Neither perceives clearly that those elements which create affirmation or meaningful negation may be based upon particular contexts—contexts in which the artist no less than society is located. If Hemingway, for example, moves from World War I *nada* to what Chester E. Eisinger calls a "heightened moral consciousness," he does so not because he is being "philosophical" or attempting to follow public opinion, but rather because he is being true to the life demands of his own experience.[19] Only the theoretical critics—humanist or negativist—can attack either negation or affirmation as inherently suspicious.

Cowley, in his reply to MacLeish, emphasized that the impact of the particular horror of World War I, nonhuman both in technology and purpose, was the very quality artists wished to represent. Eliminate this negation, this nonhumanity, and the result must

[18] MacLeish, "Lines for an Interment," p. 160.
[19] Chester E. Eisinger, "The American War Novel: An Affirming Flame," *The Pacific Spectator*, IX (1955), 272–88.

be a portrait of traditional war—which was precisely what they wanted to avoid. The fate of *What Price Glory* (1924), for example, was a lesson in point: with the new, nonhuman horror edited out and the "brass-bands and bistros" edited in, the play became a vehicle for "Captain Flagg and Sergeant Quirt, urging young men by their heroic example to join the marines and sleep with foreign women."[20] Insisting that the impact of World War I could not be shaped by the absolute criteria of humanist balance (which in context produced a call for affirmation), Cowley remarked—and one feels immediately that his statement was not made through a merely "political" conviction alone—that a total revaluation of a situation of futility was essential. "It is indeed time," he said, "that we told the whole truth about the war, as Mr. MacLeish demands; my only complaint against Mr. Stallings' book is that he could not tell enough of it. It is time for us to admit that you, MacLeish, and I, Cowley, and Hemingway, Wilson, Dos Passos, Ramon Guthrie, our relatives who crashed in airplanes or died by machine-gun fire, our friends who were crippled—that all of us fought in vain."[21]

Cowley's last rhetorical flourish gave MacLeish an opportunity to shift his argument to different grounds: the concept of "generous" death (a position most recently developed by John Leslie Marsh, whose defense of "sublime absence of selfishness" will be examined later).[22] Again using rhetoric applicable only to traditional warfare, MacLeish offered death-in-battle as a nobility unto itself; following the Latin concept of *tela* ("something stern and difficult to be done, unspoiled by any completion or end in view"),[23] which men like Hemingway were to find only outside the so completely revolutionized "military necessity," MacLeish called for an aesthetic view of death for death's sake. "Is it not conceivable," he asked, "that to die generously and in loyalty to a believed-in cause is not, regardless of the success of that cause, regardless even of its validity, to die in vain?"[24]

In the new military context, however, death was futile rather

[20] Cowley, "Lines for an Interment," p. 160.
[21] *Ibid.*, p. 161.
[22] John Leslie Marsh, "A Circle of Meaning: American Novelists Face the Military Necessity" (unpublished Ph.D dissertation, University of Pennsylvania, 1959).
[23] James Gould Cozzens, *S.S. San Pedro* (New York, 1956), p. 19; first edition, New York, 1930.
[24] MacLeish, "The Dead of the Next War," p. 215.

than "generous"; the aesthetic and heroic dimensions of death were broken not alone by false reasons, but also by technologies and military absurdities which eliminated the internal no less than external cause. Cowley, continuing the debate, gives a vivid account of a military environment in which the very shape of death had changed:

Most of the ten millions killed in battle were common soldiers. Most of them served long enough to lose whatever exhilaration they may have felt in the beginning; there remained with them only a dead nausea and the hope that they could get home perhaps with the loss of a hand or foot. Some of them mutinied. I happened to be quartered for two weeks with a battalion of chasseurs that deposed its officers and marched toward Paris. From that one battalion of 1,800 men, the Germans had killed or wounded 15,000 [sic] in the course of three years fighting. . . . After the mutiny the ring-leaders were shot by the French. The survivors marched back to the front, where many of them fought with the spirit of steers driven to the abattoir—there might be a chance of life if they went ahead, but there was sure death if they ran away.
And however they felt about it, they were killed. Patriotism, love of danger, fear, boredom, disgust—all the things that went on in their heads didn't matter. The shells burst, the machines tic-tic-tacked, and presently they became the things Stallings shows in his photographs—a hand sticking out of mud, a carcass blown by flies, a unit in a pile of corpses, an entry in a ledger at headquarters. What shall we say of them now?[25]

Cowley's brief description contains a résumé of the various elements which were to make the act of dying itself negative. First, endless repetition of murderous engagements over protracted periods of time in the same extremely limited area without decisive result. Second, the concept of battle as punishment for infraction of military rules—a concept to which the military establishment itself subscribed, and one which rendered "generosity" of death absurd; third, the unparalleled situation where absolute boredom for weeks, months, even years was accompanied by extremely high casualty rates. Neither before World War I, when casualties were incurred in single great engagements continuing for no more than a few hours or days (as in the Civil War or the Napoleonic struggle), nor in World War II, when mobility had at last caught up with mechanization, did *lack* of action claim so much human life. One might almost say that *nada* was shaped in part by the "noth-

[25] Cowley, "The Dead of the Next War," pp. 215–16.

ing" and subsequent alienation which occurred in the trenches of World War I—a nothingness, however, involving casualty rates which would have cost any general his command in even the most active engagements of the second war.[26] In "Exposure," Wilfred Owen, like the American novelists we have already discussed, used alienation as the refrain and basic horror of his poem:

> Watching, we hear the mad gusts tugging at the wire
> Like twitching agonies of men among its branches.
> Northward incessantly, the flickering gunnery rumbles
> Far-off, like a dull rumour of some other war.
>   What are we doing here?
>
> Tonight, His frost will fasten on this mud and us,
> Shrivelling many mouths and puckering foreheads crisp.
> The burying-party, picks and shovels in their shaking grasp,
> Pause over half-known faces. All their eyes are ice,
>   But nothing happens.[27]

This is what MacLeish and the humanist critics could not face: the fact that internal cause had been eliminated ("what anthem for men who die like cattle?") and that this was no less a factor in the subsequent negation than the lack of legitimate external cause. It was not simply a matter of fighting a good fight in a bad cause (the *tela* concept); even such value for many men would have been comfort enough. The cause was futile, certainly, but the fight was a prolonged stench, a situation in which "one dies of war like any old disease."[28] Negation resulted not simply from political disenchantment, but from the "nothing" which reduced human action itself to passivity. Virgil could well remark: *"Furor iraque menteur praecipitant pulchrumque mori succurrit in armis"* (II 316–17). But that was in another century, and besides, such war was dead. When young writers-to-be felt *furor* in 1918 it

---

[26] Iwo Jima, the bloodiest battle of World War II, cost 5,500 casualties (both Japanese and American) per square mile and had results of considerable and obvious strategic importance. In the battle of the Third Ypres (1917), on the other hand, an engagement with no strategic result whatever, the British took 45 square miles in five months at a cost of 370,000 dead—a total of 8,222 per square mile on the British side alone (Theodore Ropp, *War in the Western World* [New York, 1959], p. 232).

[27] Wilfred Owen, *Collected Poems* (New York, 1949), p. 53.

[28] *Ibid.*, "A-Terre," p. 87. In *Journey to the End of the Night* (Boston, 1934), Céline also comments upon the "nobility" of death: "swallowing a full mouthful of Flanders mud, more than a mouthful, my face split open from ear to ear in one flash. One has surely the right to have an opinion about one's own death" (New York, 1960), p. 15.

was likely to be directed not against a gallant foeman, but against war itself.[29]

T
Critical Revisionism: World War II

he urgent necessities of World War II made the pacifism of much World War I literature intolerable on moral no less than aesthetic grounds. Many critics, writing during or after the struggle against fascism, not only reiterated and developed the terms of MacLeish's humanist attack, but also echoed his view of antiwar protest as a sort of negative propaganda. The relationship between propaganda and literature, however, is a complicated one, and more so when violent political revolutions make the virtues of one generation the vices of another. Certainly, as L. Robert Lind pointed out in his analysis of "Propaganda and Letters," it is true that "the overwhelming set of [negative] connotations" which the word propaganda recalls is connected with World War I.[30]

Propaganda, Lind believes, is virtually inevitable in any work of art communicating a political, social, or psychological conviction. He skillfully demonstrates that the work of Callinus and Solon ("war songs"), the drama of Aristophanes ("peace-propaganda"), Euripides ("humanitarian zeal"), even the poetry of Virgil ("in essence as elevated and splendid a piece of propaganda as one could desire, hymning the glories of Rome"), and numerous other works which have for a basic purpose the communication of some conviction, may be considered propaganda. The conclusion, obviously, is that the presence or absence of propaganda cannot in

[29] A. J. Liebling, replying to a J. Donald Adams' challenge to his negative review of a blood-and-guts World War II book (see "Lines from a Reviewer," *New York Times Book Review*, March 13, 1949, p. 21), bitterly denied any possibility of a "personal test" in modern warfare. This bitterness was far sharper in World War I, when the nature of machine war had not yet been assimilated. The same is true of John Steinbeck's angry denunciations of hypocrisy, stupidity, waste, and less savory aspects of American army life in World War II (see *Once There was a War* [New York, 1960], pp. i–xiv). There was more of each of these qualities in the first war, with far less expectation, and the resultant literary anger was correspondingly greater.
[30] L. Robert Lind, "The Crisis in Literature, II: Propaganda and Letters," *Sewanee Review*, XLVII (1939), 188.

itself determine the presence or absence of an aesthetic dimension in literature.[31]

Mr. Lind, of course, writing in 1939, was attempting to demonstrate that prowar literature was not necessarily propagandistic and therefore subliterary simply by the fact that it offered a conviction. The very purposes of his discussion were in themselves an indication of the vast changes which had taken place in the political and intellectual climate. For World War II necessitated a revision of the earlier, antiwar revisionists, a modification of their attack upon prowar rhetoric. To some extent, however, the revision has succeeded only too well—succeeded, that is, until the novel of protest rather than the novel of war affirmation is denounced as politically rather than artistically motivated. Mr. Lind's essay is useful for the very reason that if his insights are applied flexibly, taking into account the separate and radically different contexts of the two wars, neither the "negative" literature of World War I nor the "affirmative" literature of World War II need be attacked with a priori aesthetic or political conditions which—for one or the other of the two periods—may be quite irrelevant.

Once we grant that propaganda is not a clearly defined critical tool, however, we must still face the very basic problem that some books obviously offer a conviction without aesthetic motivation. "Propaganda," with all its negative connotations, would seem therefore to depend to a large extent upon the success of the author in terms of his craft; but this craft in turn depends upon the validity of the internal situations relating to each other, and the validity of the internal situations relating to the external. Granted, in other words, that as Belgion remarks, "every narrative is the illustration of a theory of life," hence "not the transcript of life as it is," and that "every narrative is propaganda for its theory," we as readers are still left with the necessity of choosing theories of life.[32] The aesthetic choice, however, is not to be confused with the moral or political choice, and for this reason we can—and very

---

[31] Even the attempts of specialists to offer final definitions of aesthetic (as distinguished from nonaesthetic) propaganda are likely to result in semantic obfuscations to delight the heart of a Talmudicist. Leonard W. Doob, for example, in *Propaganda, Its Psychology and Technique* (New York, 1935), offered this suggestion: "Intentional propaganda is a systematic attempt by an individual (or individuals) to control the attitudes of a group of individuals through suggestion and, consequently, to control their actions; unintentional propaganda is the control of the attitudes, and, consequently, the actions of groups of individuals through the use of suggestion" (p. 89).
[32] Belgion, *The Human Parrot and Other Essays*, p. 94.

often do—praise works whose "theory of life" may be diametrically opposed to our own.

Since any theory must be judged on the basis of how it reconciles the abstract with the concrete (i.e., "experience"), we may say that the validity of a "theory of life" in a given narrative depends upon the author's success in reconciling his own theory, or "proving" it, in terms of his own experience. Neither the theory nor the experience can be completely excised from the book and each supports the other in the total aesthetic structure. We can sharply criticize Edith Wharton's *The Marne* as art, not because it is "prowar" as such (one can, after all, maintain that in his concept of the proving ground Crane's modern classic is also prowar), but rather because its "theory" is inadequately related to its experience. A novel such as Hector Lazo's *Taps* may be sharply criticized the same way despite its antiwar bias.

Of course we can and do bring our own experience to a novel, and so—when we attack what appears to be an inadequate relationship between an author's theory and the experience which embodies it—we may actually be working from a sense of contradiction between our experience, our context, and his. In this respect one must remember that the difference between a novelist or any other creative artist and an intelligent but noncreative individual is not that the latter lacks capacity either for experience or theory, but rather that he cannot structure a narrative so that one embodies the other. The writer, in other words, is at once realizing his theory by actual experience and expanding the meaning of his experience by his theory. He explains the ways of man to man, and in so doing gives us a wider choice, a proliferation of theories of life, and indeed, a sharper realization of what our own experience was, is, or could have been given a change in context.

Objections to propaganda in art, on the simple grounds that a given work is not true to "the way it was" (or the way it could be or should have been with proper moral orientation), are inadequate; on one hand the objector overlooks the vastly complicated nature of propaganda and on the other he fails to perceive that the relation between theory of life and experience is an interaction within the book itself. The World War I novels attacked by Mac-Leish and more recent critics for not having elements of "bravery," "nobility," "selflessness," "affirmation" are products of their author's own experience—the experience of impact—upon which their theories of life are based. It is *this* experience which must be taken into account.

Among more recent critics, Joseph Remenyi and Chester Eisinger provide examples of the continuing disapproval of war literature having a basis of protest.[33] Remenyi, indeed, demands not only that war literature be "art," but that it become art by helping or permitting war to achieve "grandeur through expression." Like MacLeish, he offers totality as a fixed and perpetual virtue, regardless of context: "Unless it is the testimony of the total man, war literature is merely a documentary expression of feeling and intelligence, indifference and mental inferiority, related to social, political, economic problems. War is life in the grip of death. *This is the real meaning of war literature.*"[34] Remenyi's position is that of the humanist-aesthete: he not only asks from war the "totality" of any other experience, but insists upon "mystery of life," "grandeur through expression"; in short, one might almost say that he requires the novelist to write of modern, technological warfare as though it were another species of mountain climbing, or symbolic deep-sea fishing.

Mr. Remenyi is by no means alone in this demand. Certainly the insistence that a novelist can or should use war merely as another and quite normal subject matter has been a perennial point of criticism for decades. In 1920, for example, F. B. Kaye declaimed in the *New Republic*: "The realities of life are everywhere—on the battlefield, on the campus, in the nursery and over the counting desk . . . reality on the battlefield is not more real, but more noisy." As recently as 1962 Melvin Seiden, writing in the *Nation,* excommunicates the war novel as a literary genre. "A novelist's subject," he pontificates, boldly echoing Mr. Kaye's attack of some forty years ago, "cannot be war. . . . War is only a special set of circumstances in which people live and die. . . . Clearly it is impossible to speak of a kind of novel which is not a kind at all but owes its designation to its scene."[35] So completely has this attitude been entrenched in recent (post-World War II) years, that

[33] Joseph Remenyi, "Psychology of War Literature," *Sewanee Review*, LII (1944), 137–47; Chester E. Eisinger, "The American War Novel: An Affirming Flame."
[34] Remenyi, "Psychology of War Literature," p. 140.
[35] F. B. Kaye, "Puritanism, Literature, and War," *New Republic*, XXV (December 15, 1920), 66; Melvin Seiden, "The Hero and His War," *Nation*, CXCIII (February 18, 1961), 408.

commentators may actually refuse to acknowledge a repudiation of war even when they confront it directly, especially when looking back to a novelist's early work. John Atkins, for example, in *The Art of Ernest Hemingway*, remarks that "there are people who cry against war and spend the rest of their lives discovering a way to reject it, and theirs is an honorable way, but it is not his [Hemingway's] way. His role is to observe but, because observation is useless without understanding, also to participate. . . . He is a writer and to him war is a landscape or milieu."[36]

This became true for Hemingway, however, only when the rise of fascism made "participation" and acceptance of cause possible. But it is a long way from the Hemingway of either *Men at War* or *For Whom the Bell Tolls* to the total repudiation in *A Farewell to Arms* or the rhetorical bitterness of "Champs d'Honneur." Utilization of modern war as a "landscape or milieu," in other words, is a characteristic of World War II, and Hemingway never succeeded even in this respect; his only novel which uses rather than rejects such warfare is *Across the River and Into the Trees*. It is interesting how, under the necessities of World War II which made an antiwar position intolerable, Atkins in effect sees the early Hemingway through the shadow of Norman Mailer. And these same necessities shaped Mr. Remenyi's attack upon the "negation" of World War I novelists as a group.

The very concept of an impact so great as to destroy "totality," a situation in which war is no longer a "milieu," and in which any affirmation or "grandeur" is false because both meaning and humanity have become fragmented, is intolerable for Remenyi as it had been inadmissible for MacLeish. Ignoring the fact that aesthetic imperatives can no more be abstracted out of context than moral imperatives, Remenyi sets up his various absolutes ("totality," "mystery," "grandeur"); points to their presence as realized qualities in the work of such successful "war writers" as Euripides, Aeschylus, and Virgil; and proceeds to judge the products of World War I by these same qualities. It is, essentially, the same procedure John Leslie Marsh, in the area of military studies, follows with his "military necessity"—neither writer conceives of a situation where the absolute military morality no longer applies and the aesthetic absolute ("grandeur," "totality") no longer exists.

H. M. Tomlinson, writing in 1930, had little patience with the demand for "balance" in war literature and even less patience

[36] John Atkins, *The Art of Ernest Hemingway* (London, 1952), p. 109.

with attempts to view the war only in a framework of obsolete military moralities. "Let us imagine," he says, "that in a war every civilian concerned developed continuous neuralgia, which would ease and vanish only when 'cease fire' had sounded on the battle front."[37] Tomlinson's image is pertinent here, for the result would be quite a different concept of "totality." Neuralgia—"sallow faces wrapped in flannel"—is a most demoralizing, because sordid, suffering; it has no traditional relation to nobility, bravery, sublimity, all the qualities that humanity must use to redeem its own horrors. Given the horror without the redemptive qualities, the result would be too much; it would be "nonhuman," the ultimate futility which men cannot face. Here indeed is the jackel of Kilimanjaro and the sniggering footman of Prufrock. And given the compounded futilities of machine warfare, the humanists' refusal to tolerate negation may well be a product of their own metaphysical needs.

Remenyi attempts to judge the World War I writers by absolute criteria, which the writers themselves had previously rejected, and so—quite inevitably—he finds them wanting. He takes the position that "the sameness of the human spirit" never changes, and proceeds to offer an entire list of a prioris and affirmations which the novelists of the war had insisted could only falsify the impact of their experience, no matter how valid they might have been for Euripides. "In a psychological sense," Remenyi instructs us, "war commands man to discipline fear through consciousness":

War thus becomes awareness in action by compelling action to be aware of its own purpose. Man's capacity to endure pain is immense. Embittered and tormented humans meet blind fate with defiance and fortitude. Man does not change, but war literature celebrates man's braveness and sorrow . . . in good imaginative works we follow man's actions and reflections as an expression of total being. . . . Knowledge obtained thus brings a mental picture to the reader, resulting in emotional identification with human valor and human suffering . . . good war literature impresses upon the reader the magnificence and wastefulness of human energies. Great literary works related to war touch the innermost existence of man, and defy the nothingness of human life.[38]

Analysis of the above passage offers a good profile of the humanist position. The total effect is one of vague edification, a soaring or swelling "nobility." Key words are themselves abstractions: "disci-

[37] H. M. Tomlinson, "War Books," *Yale Review*, XIX (1930), 459.
[38] Remenyi, "Psychology of War Literature," pp. 146–47.

pline," "endure," "defiance," "fortitude," "braveness," "sorrow,"
"total being," "blind fate," "human valor," "human suffering,"
"magnificence and wastefulness." The weight of Remenyi's rhetoric, combined with a series of mutually exclusive juxtapositions,
gives the effect of a large and perfectly balanced globe. A globe,
certainly, is the most perfect of all figures. It is aesthetically pure.
And it has nothing to do with the emotional angularity or imbalance of the World War I experience.[39]

If the humanist-orientated demand for affirmation as a final
criterion for the war novel lacked perspective, the difficulty was
further compounded by the fact that neither "affirmation" nor
"negation" are constants—a consideration usually overlooked in
discussions of the World War I period. The negation of World
War I was activist in nature; it was a corrective negation accompanied by tremendous energy in the assertion of alternate
values—political, aesthetic, and experimental. Robert Heilman perceived this clearly in 1943 despite the pressures of war environment. "Through denial," he remarked, "can come affirmation. It
is only the unsophisticated who expect all affirmations to be made
with the heroic violence of a cheer-leader. But moralists and patriots alike distrust the oblique and are blind to the implicit."[40]
(World War I "denial," of course, differs basically from the total
negation to be seen in the work of a writer like John Horne Burns
[*The Gallery*, 1947]. The context of the second war resulted in
a major shift during which literary negation became passive, and
affirmation, the neoconservative movement, became activist or corrective. This factor, as I hope to demonstrate, had important effects
on post-World War II criticism, especially John Aldridge's disappointed search for "heresy.")

As recently as 1955, however, critics were still emphasizing
affirmation as a basic criterion, a constant for evaluating war litera-

[39] Remenyi singles out Hemingway's *For Whom the Bell Tolls* for particular
praise, despite its obvious inferiority to *A Farewell to Arms*. Its situation—no
longer the broken world of World War I (since Fascism provides external
cause and guerrilla war offers the possibility of internal cause)—permits some
measure of affirmation, and so Remenyi eulogizes it (listing it alongside *Song
of Roland!*) as war art which can help "retain one's sense of value." It is
the retention, not the validity of retention, with which Remenyi is concerned. In
this connection, one might note that Robert Jordan's ideological "values" are
surrounded with ambiguities. There is considerable reason for doubting whether
Hemingway had produced any sort of meaningful "affirmation" in *For Whom
the Bell Tolls*. See Stanley Cooperman, "Hemingway's Blue-Eyed Boy: Robert
Jordan and 'Purging Ecstasy'," *Criticism* VIII (Winter, 1966), 87–96.
[40] Robert Heilman, "Artist and Patria," *Sewanee Review*, LI (1943), 388.

ture. Chester Eisinger, writing primarily on the World War II novel, defended the "Affirming Flame" of the genre itself on the grounds that "in many of these books are to be found patterns of affirmation which substantially refute the contention that futility and self-destructive horror absorb the war novelists."[41] Here, more than a decade after the actual war environment had subsided, was the continued assumption that negation is perpetually invalid, that political or moral actualities of the past can somehow be recreated according to the necessities of the present, and that affirmation is the *sine qua non* of aesthetic virtue.

Perhaps the basic difficulty is that there is, at least in the twentieth century, no "war novel" as such apart from the war with which it deals. One can no more denounce the "futility and self-destructive horror" of World War I literature than one can attack the proving ground symbolism of Crane as prowar, or the sociological, political, and technological sophistication of the World War II books as a simple indication of middle-class conservatism. Again: in each case the philosophic and aesthetic validity of a novelist's attitudes must be judged by his context, or rather by his success in relating his "theory of life" to the essential quality of his particular experience.

Eisinger values in the World War II books—even in the later and more socially positive novels of Hemingway (*To Have and Have Not* and *For Whom the Bell Tolls*)—a "heightened moral consciousness . . . a way of apprehending experience that is soberly hopeful in contrast to the negativism of the twenties."[42] But this praise for "heightened moral consciousness" fails to take into account the very nature of confrontation necessities which not only were different in World War I, but which actually made "negation" the only morally conscious reaction possible for the intelligent *or* moral man. Part of Eisinger's problem here is due to an over-reliance on Kenneth Burke, who, in his theory of *circumferences*, gives Burkean restatement to an orthodox humanist concept. "A man is not only in the situation peculiar to his era or to his particular place in that era," Burke maintains, "he is also in a situation extending through centuries; he is in a 'generically human' situation, and he is in a universal situation."[43] This be-

[41] Eisinger, "The American War Novel: An Affirming Flame," pp. 272–73.
[42] *Ibid.*, p. 287.
[43] Quoted by Eisinger, "The American War Novel: An Affirming Flame," pp. 273–74.

comes true, however, only when the situation which *is* peculiar to an era has been assimilated and, to some extent, resolved. Certainly one cannot say that all historical situations are alike; granting even that the most perennial of situations (love, death, fear, poverty, etc.) become new for the individual when the individual himself confronts them, one must insist that there are historical, not individual, situations without precedent, in which the impact, the novelty, does not depend solely upon individual discovery of what is precedented.

The machine slaughter and dance-macabre absurdity of World War I, for example, had no parallel—and for this reason its impact differed in nature no less than degree from the impact of previous war experiences. Crane's Henry Fleming was in a "universal situation" and so could discover himself on the proving ground. Boyd's William Hicks, on the other hand, and the World War I protagonists as a group, found themselves in a situation which for them was in essence nonhuman and nonuniversal; there could be no "generic" recognition because the machine genre of their environment, of death itself, was without precedent.[44] Only when this machine genre had been assimilated culturally, emotionally, and imaginatively could war again become a "universal situation"; like the drawing room or office, industrial plant or courtroom, war could then—and only then—be taken simply as material upon which a drama of human values could be based.

This is why, despite Aldridge's protests, authors like Herman Wouk, Martha Gelhorn, John Hersey, and others could, in some ways like Crane, regard war as a vehicle for the sociological and metaphysical maturing of their characters. Without the assimilation, however, there was only impact and horrified negation; hence the World War I writers too often seem (from the vantage point of mid-twentieth century, when men have absorbed a genre of experience as yet unassimilated in 1914–18) so unjustifiably, almost immaturely, preoccupied with what Eisinger terms "futility and self-destructive horror." The World War I literary protest was a legitimate response to an unparalleled historical situation which has since been assimilated; a response, one might add, far more dynamic than the simple tag of "disillusion" or "negation" would seem to indicate.

[44] Burke's point is anticipated, and refuted, by H. M. Tomlinson. See "War Books," p. 450.

One indication of how completely the technological revolution in warfare has been assimilated is the fact that younger students of war literature may seem unaware that a revolution occurred at all. John Leslie Marsh, for example, uses Comte de Vigny's *Servitude et Grandeur Militaire*, together with Crane's *The Red Badge of Courage* (both, of course, nineteenth-century works), as touchstones for measuring the failure of World War I novelists to face the "military necessity."[45] He indicts "negation" no less strongly than do the humanists, but on military rather than aesthetic grounds. Marsh is a student of military environment; his failure to distinguish between the Civil War (as it actually existed and as given symbolic statement by Crane) and the military environment of World War I is symptomatic of the fact that new generations of readers may all too easily see World War I in terms of a vague identification with all that went before, rather than as the breaking point of an obsolete military tradition.[46]

So rapidly do emotional climates change in this century of total violence that the impact of such violence upon the young men first exposed to it may seem incomprehensible to the young men of the mid-century, as though a gulf of centuries rather than decades separated the two generations. Only if the enormous gap between the realities of the Civil War and the war of 1914–18 is not understood, however, can readers indict World War I literature for failing to dramatize a "sublime absence of selfishness" among soldiers. Only if the scar tissue of continuing mass war has blurred historical sensitivity can the impact of World War I be judged according to the symbolic combat values offered by Crane.

That Crane could use the Civil War for his metaphorical morality play was due in part to the fact that, as Walter Millis points out, the end of the nineteenth century was a period during which a

---

[45] Marsh, "A Circle of Meaning: American Novelists Face the Military Necessity."

[46] A parallel to Marsh's position is the statement of a soldier (Behr) in Irwin Shaw's novel of World War II, *The Young Lions:* "Last time [World War I] it was a nice, simple, European-style war. Anyone could understand it, anyone could forgive it, because they'd all been seeing the same kind of war for a thousand years. It was a war . . . of Christian gentlemen fighting another body of Christian gentlemen under the same predictable set of rules." Behr's view of the earlier conflict, like Marsh's, is an indication of how completely perspective may be lost under the pressure of continuing world crisis. The description, of course, is a catalogue of precisely what World War I was *not*—at least to the generation that fought it.

215

"Civil War legend" was formed.[47] The work of Crane, in other words, over and above its limited irony, must be seen as part of a Civil War romanticism; this is what enabled him to impose what Alfred Kazin sees as a metaphysical dimension—self-discovery, Henry Fleming as "everyman" confronting the facts of his own existence—upon the irony itself, the effective study of real fear in a real human being.[48] The symbolic detachment in Crane, however, is not altogether an act of aesthetic deliberation; it was made possible by the fact that the war with which Crane was dealing had passed into a phase of cultural and romantic memory.

World War I, to be sure, has also been used as a symbolic vehicle in the work of such men as William Faulkner (*A Fable*, 1954) and René Fulöp-Miller (*The Night of Time*, 1955). Faulkner's book, however, was essentially an attempt to erect a structure of affirmative Christian symbolism on World War I material. For this reason his book has generally been regarded as a noble failure: the gap between the material itself and the weight of symbolism was too great. Fulöp-Miller's book, on the other hand, with its symbolism-of-futility, the lemming concept of human action, is effective on the levels of both concrete action and symbolic meaning because the metaphysical dimension did not contradict but rather was part of the actualities of his material.[49] Thus symbolic realism has successfully used the World War I environment only in terms of negation rather than in terms of military affirmation.

Dealing with the Civil War, Crane could portray the ennobling of man's primary passions through combat experience; dealing with World War I, Fulöp-Miller could successfully evolve a symbolism of disorder and futility. Each writer was being true to the military context of his subject. One ignores the context and focuses completely on the symbolism only at the risk of failing to perceive that meaning, in a work of symbolic realism, must operate through before proliferating beyond the literal level of human action. Crane's "Tall Man," falling like a great oak tree in dramatic isolation, would have been out of place in the mud, amid the million corpses, the long-range barrages, and the months of useless mechanical slaughter in the single battle of Verdun.

Henry Fleming's military world was shattered in 1914; as tech-

[47] See Walter Millis, *Arms and Men* (New York, 1956), p. 127.
[48] Alfred Kazin, *On Native Grounds* (New York, 1950), p. 50.
[49] See my review of Fulöp-Miller, "Of War and Man," *Nation*, CLXXX (July 23, 1955), 80.

nological death and impact replaced confrontation, futility replaced self-reliance. Writing from the standpoint of a military historian, Walter Millis gives a vivid portrait of a military revolution whose consequences had been absorbed neither by the American people as a whole, nor by the young men setting out in 1917 to save *La Belle France* from the Hun:

> In 1861 . . . war was still personal; it was a "fight" between men, individuals, whose individual prowess, courage, and devotion counted, not a contest between men and machines. . . . It was still a personal and usually hand-to-hand encounter—a few sweating, desperately angered and terrified men engaged against their counterparts. The weapons were the tools of this personal struggle, like the broadsword or the battle-ax of the Middle Ages. . . . In 1861 war was not an engineering operation. . . . Battle was still, in the last analysis, "we-uns against they-uns," a struggle over a time period of no more than a day or two for a specific piece of ground, the possession of which would in its turn affect the course of the war, and the ability of one side physically to gain occupancy and control of the other's territory and government.[50]

Millis' last point, over and above the technological differences, refers to an element essential to the impact of World War I. Following a deliberate policy of attrition, of bleeding-the-enemy-to-death, military leaders on the Western Front carried out long campaigns of futility designed not to gain territory or immediately to affect the course of the war, but simply to inflict mass casualties. The results, again, were nightmares such as Verdun and the Somme, involving millions of casualties while month followed interminable month. As Cowley remarks, "Death, not victory was in the air."[51] Even when Crane wrote his book the single day of noble confrontation was finished and almost nobody realized it. "For many," Millis reminds us, "war was still a matter of young men 'springing to arms' and fighting the issue out with bullet, butt and bayonet in a deadly personal encounter."[52] It was from this background that Crane wrote *The Red Badge of Courage*: despite his realistic insistence upon fear and delusion as part of the process leading to ultimate affirmation, he himself, as has been pointed out, was caught up in a rapidly developing war sentimentality which gave to the Civil War an aura of legend. And it was from a continuation of this literary background that many

[50] Millis, *Arms and Men*, p. 110.
[51] Cowley, *The Literary Situation*, p. 37.
[52] Millis, *Arms and Men*, p. 157.

young men set out in 1916 (as volunteers) or 1917, fully expecting the "deadly personal encounter" if they expected to see action at all. The difference, of course, is that Stephen Crane never got to see the Western Front; the young men in 1917 did. If they rejected the affirmative symbolism of Crane, the ultimate manhood-through-confrontation achieved by Henry Fleming, it was because no such symbolism had meaning for their own experience.

But the new generation of readers who examine World War I through Crane-colored spectacles have, in turn, rejected the World War I mode of rejection. Testing protagonists like William Hicks through criteria applicable only to other wars, Marsh formulates an attitude which parallels that of Hilaire Belloc who, at the time of World War I, bitterly denounced the Germans for developing and using such indecent weapons as the submarine—weapons which ended chivalric warfare and gentlemanly soldiering.[53] Belloc blamed the Germans, Marsh the World War I novelists; Belloc could not cope with and Marsh seems unaware of a technological revolution which rendered traditional combat attitudes ludicrous. "Combat is a testing ground for Hicks," says Marsh, "as it had been for Henry Fleming, but there is this difference—before Fleming's eyes men throw themselves into certain death through a sublime absence of selfishness, while Hicks observes them motivated by their instinct for self-preservation, their individual selfishness."

In the revelatory moments of combat Hicks has come to reject the value of the combat experience as vehemently as Fleming accepted it. . . . He is not ennobled by the sight of sublimely selfless men, but besmirched by the spectacle of complete individual selfishness. . . . Men give their lives not generously, but impelled by ugly fury. They come upon the enemy not in full knowledge of what they do, but as automatons dragged into unthinking action.[54]

It is not, in other words, that Hicks was too insensitive for a revelatory moment of combat, but rather that his revelation brings into focus a violently different set of truths. This Marsh finds intolerable, and so he is forced to conclude that the change is due not to the impact of discovery, but rather to some myopic churlishness on the part of Hicks—and Boyd, as author. No less than MacLeish and the humanists in their generation, this young student of military environment in effect demands that war literature be

[53] In Louis Raemaker's *Collected Cartoons* (New York, 1917), p. 18.
[54] Marsh, "A Circle of Meaning: American Novelists Face the Military Necessity," pp. 83, 84.

218

limited to illustration of permissive experience, experience which permits an affirmation of positively creative moments in combat. Hence Methot the poet (in *Company K*) is also indicted for failing to realize the "comradeship of combat," while Cummings, who in a sense is his own protagonist, and who in *The Enormous Room* produced one of the best books to come out of World War I, is seen as deliberately "iconoclastic," as "consciously reversing" military tradition ("the manly bearing and neatness" of the soldier), as "reveling in uncouthness," as shamelessly proud of his desertion from military duty—in short, as some sort of antimilitary beatnik.[55]

Basic here is an assumption, all too frequent in critical examinations of World War I literature, pointing to a deliberate or conscious "reversal" of traditions. But novelists, Boyd and Cummings among others, were attempting to portray a war which had in effect deserted men, which had "defaulted" from every human value—including the military value of personal test—they themselves had expected. Frederic Henry, for example, had completely fulfilled his military duty (even to the extent of shooting a deserter) until the realization was forced upon him that in his particular combat environment desertion was the only sane or even manly act possible; hence his famous statement that the war had deserted him. It was the new environment, not the unmanly novelists, that rendered conformity absurd. Good soldiering could no longer be combined with moral or physical awareness, and so the men either "defaulted" like Frederic Henry, Cummings, and Andrews, or—like Zorn, Hicks, Irwin, and Mahon—conformed to the new environment at a terrible cost: the ultimate coarsening or numbing of their humanity.

Essential to the entire problem of World War I negation was the fact that the young authors-to-be, so many of whom were volunteers, in no way began their journey with some sort of perverse delight in dereliction from duty. On the contrary, they welcomed with enthusiasm their chance for military experience. Negation, certainly, did not spring fully developed like Minerva from the head of Zeus. There was a process: it was the world that showed itself to be "negative"—or, worse yet, neither positive nor negative, but totally indifferent.[56] The coward groveled in a ditch; he either

[55] *Ibid.*, pp. 136–37.
[56] See H. M. Tomlinson's vivid description of this *process* in "War Books," pp. 450–51.

survived or was killed (by a bullet if he was lucky, otherwise by the multiple punctures of shell-fragments, by decapitation or castration). The brave man groveled in a ditch; he too either survived or was eliminated in the same way. In either case there was groveling, and in either case a man was robbed of his death by the very act of dying. Hence Frederic Henry's dictum: "It kills the very good and the very gentle and the very brave impartially. If you are none of these you can be sure it will kill you too but there will be no special hurry."[57]

These young men had not yet assimilated the necessities which reduced the brave and upright soldier, with all his "manly bearing and neatness," to a creature that fought in mud and survived on all fours. And this sort of swinish combat had no true parallel in the second war, since mobility had vastly increased by 1939. The "slavery" reiterated in so many World War I novels refers not to military discipline alone; the very act of combat forced the posture of slavery on the fighting man, so that even the skirmish and patrol, with all their aura of military romance, were reduced to bloody stumbles through corpse-filled muck. Small wonder that for Hemingway the ritualized danger of the bull ring was so irresistibly attractive as a means of recapturing a sense of the dignity of death. The "military necessity" was indeed dead. It had been killed by war itself.

Because the novelists of the second war have not focused upon the impact of technological warfare as such, post-World War II readers have tended to assume that the attitude toward combat has come full cycle. Marsh, for example, postulates a "circle of meaning": acceptance (Crane), rejection (World War I), and acceptance (World War II). Charles C. Walcutt in 1947 offered a similar analysis:

From World War I to World War II there has been a cycle or pattern of attitudes toward war; this pattern appears both in literature generally and in the changing mood of particular writers. It begins with guilt, turns into fear, and purges itself in confrontation. Immediately after the first war came guilt and remorse. These were imperceptively transformed into fear of the coming war. This fear almost entirely disappeared in the literature of confrontation after the war began.[58]

---

[57] Hemingway, *A Farewell to Arms* (New York, 1929), p. 267.
[58] Charles C. Walcutt, "Fear Motifs in the Literature Between the Wars," *South Atlantic Quarterly*, XLVI (1947), 227.

The metaphor of a "cycle" or "circle" can be very misleading, however, unless we realize that in World War II it was less the act of battle that was accepted, than was the war accepted because of necessary external cause. Young men in 1941 had few illusions as to the "creative" possibilities in modern combat. Faced with the fact, the political necessities forced upon them by fascism, they approached the resulting military necessities with all the enthusiasm of a man removing a boil from his armpit.[59] It was a long cry from either Crane's "ennobling experience" or the bold journey into World War I (and the consequent impact of experience) to the attitude of Saul Bellow's Dangling Man—an attitude which would seem far closer to resignation than either to acceptance or confrontation:

'Ideally, how would you like to regard the war, then?'
  'I would like to see it as an incident.'
  'Only an incident?'
  'A very important one, perhaps the most important that has ever occurred. But, still, an incident. Is the real nature of the world changed by it? No. Will it rescue us spiritually? Still no. Will it set us free in the crudest sense, that is, merely to be allowed to breathe and eat? I hope so, but I can't be sure that it will. In no *essential* way is it crucial. . . . The war can destroy me physically. That it can do. But so can bacteria.'[60]

Even Ernest Hemingway, despite a preoccupation through most of his career with "confrontation" as a primary virtue, failed with *Across the River and Into the Trees*, his single novel of World War II. It was the general cause, not the individual act, to which Hemingway fully assented; for this reason one might seriously question whether his attitude toward war itself (in terms of individual confrontation, of *tela*) underwent any fundamental change since *A Farewell to Arms*. Individual action, of course, subsequently (and beautifully) patterned *The Old Man and the Sea*. But Hemingway had to go deep-sea fishing before he could develop a theme of confrontation in his literary work. The techniques of World War II offered nothing a man could confront as an indi-

[59] In *The Literary Situation* Cowley remarks of the World War II group: "Almost all of them agreed that Hitler and the Japanese had to be stopped, but they couldn't understand why somebody else than they, individually, shouldn't have done the stopping" (pp. 26–27).
[60] Saul Bellow, *The Dangling Man* (New York, 1944), p. 168. One might note that Bellow's novel was published while the war was very much a thing of the immediate present. Such metaphysical reservation was a World War II characteristic; it had no parallel in 1918.

vidual; only neoconservative writers like Wouk could insist upon one kind of confrontation, moral and sociological in nature, and were attacked as such by negativist critics.

One might accept Walcutt's concept of "pattern" only with the reservation that the World War II writers, while blunting the previous generation's protest, in no way returned to nineteenth-century attitudes toward war. Perhaps the pattern might be further defined as elliptical rather than circular, and for two reasons: first, the availability of external cause; and second, a long process of assimilation—the fact that total horror which is precedented becomes pain, and pain, no matter how extreme, if precedented and expected is no longer total horror. Indeed, there may even be a fascination in it. Walcutt himself remarks on the "curiosity, even absorption in the details of war" because "it was too late to prevent what had come"; and there was "the intense interest of Americans in machinery and speed and power, the eagerness of a depression-starved population for new gadgets."[61]

The "guilt and remorse" Walcutt identifies as the World War I reaction must also be seen in terms of shock, the loss of innocence and consequent transition to a new world of experience. Once these factors have been assimilated "confrontation" is again possible, especially given a valid external cause, but less as a "purge" for fear than as the result of technological assimilation. The World War II situation, in short, was not synonymous with that of World War I—but neither was it synonymous with that of the Civil War; the latter confusion is all too easily set up by the use of the term "confrontation" alone.

In suggesting "guilt, remorse, and despair" as factors which prevented action on the part of young men during the thirties, while the threat of fascism grew ("they were caught in a death-impulse of expiation"), Walcutt assumes far too deliberate a self-punishment. The issues at no time during the thirties were as clear as all that, especially for peoples who had already been exposed, and

[61] Walcutt, "Fear Motifs in the Literature Between the Wars," p. 233. Kenneth Burke makes the same point in "War, Response and Contradiction," *The Philosophy of Literary Form* (New York, 1957), pp. 201–20. See also "Reading and Fighting," *Saturday Review of Literature*, VI (April 12, 1930), 913: "Even the grimmest and most sordid of war books has an almost inevitable fascination for the inexperienced." In *Company K* March dramatizes something of this irony with the case of Private Keith, who organizes an "Anti-War Society" and is very successful until a National Guard Company is formed in town. "My disciples," he remarks, "anxious to protect their country from the horrors I had described, deserted my Society and joined in a body" (p. 158).

exposed horribly, to bombardments of atrocity propaganda, racist formulas, and all the emotional stimuli of the largest opinion machine in the history of western civilization. It was not "guilt, remorse, and fear" which prevented a revision of antiwar determination, but rather a skepticism as to the *necessities* for war, no matter how loudly these necessities were urged. The headlines of journalists, the learned analyses of professors, the bombast of politicians, the rhetoric of literary personages—all had been heard before, and none of it had been true.

It was difficult for both the World War I generation and the young men coming to maturity during the thirties to accept the change in political realities which gave to such verbiage a new dimension of truth—especially since the truth itself was couched in almost precisely the same terms which had poured forth to justify the futile butchery of World War I. There was "fear" most certainly, but not fear of technological combat; technology, again, had been assimilated as a normal part of war environment in the twentieth century. The fear came through a persistent expectation of futility. The young men of the first war had expected fulfillment and suffered the impact of futility; the World War II group, expecting futility, were unwilling and unable to embark on still another crusade. And in this connection what Lawrence Feigenbaum calls the "preliminary battles" of the Spanish Civil War, in which the Lincoln Brigade came closest to approximating the World War I sense of Crusade, with all its political ambiguities, compounded rather than alleviated a sense of futility of cause.[62] Only as it became clear that there *was* external cause, that neither the futility of World War I nor the ambiguities of the Spanish Civil War could vitiate the new violence of fascism, were young men willing or able to stand and "confront" it. But the process was gradual; resignation to twentieth-century warfare itself came as a result of reconciliation to machine civilization; affirmation of a cause for war came only when it was at last made clear that history was not repeating itself and that Nazism offered another kind of problem than the Kaiser had offered to the Entente in 1914.

Affirmation, however, provided only a doubtful solution for the World War II generation. Increasing political sophistication and the experience of a depression, with its inevitable focus upon social and economic problems, made a retreat into art or the search for

[62] Lawrence H. Feigenbaum, "War as Viewed by the Postwar Novelists of World War I and II" (unpublished Ph.D dissertation, New York University, 1950), p. 12.

a "moment of truth" in formalized danger appear rather extravagant gestures which nobody could afford in a changed historical context. Such gestures, as W. M. Frohock remarks, appeared "trival to a generation . . . compellingly impressed by the insecurity of mere physical life anywhere on the planet." And the earlier despair, Frohock continues, seemed "despair without terror. As a matter of fact the years of the great depression had already blunted its point; too many young people discovered that it is even more important to eat regularly than to feel quite in place among one's contemporaries."[63] Even the political solutions of World War I, usually collectivist, seemed doubtful: the ambiguities of the Spanish Civil War and the growth of a Soviet dictatorship (one remembers the powerful effect of the Nazi-Soviet Pact of 1939) eliminated from young collectivist thought the chance for a truly revolutionary cause; the political left had developed its own dogma. All that remained unquestioned was the external cause, the necessity, temporary and therefore nonultimate, of defeating fascism.

With nothing specific to rebel against, neither a false cause nor technology, and no clear pattern of ideology to rebel for, the serious writers of World War II had no choice but to demand a return to socially conservative values (the depression had demonstrated all too well the facts of material want and family insecurity); to examine sociological, psychological, or political problems; or to reiterate a poetry of metaphysical despair. And in each case their work demonstrated a vast increase in technological sophistication: the new warfare, the machine itself, was now part of one's normal environment, and no novelist could write of war without setting up his stage accurately.

For these reasons the attempt to view the World War I novels through the context of the second war offers serious problems of historical relevancy. Aldridge, who uses this method in *After the Lost Generation*, forgets that "heresy" is no more valid an absolute for literature than is affirmation. The legitimacy of the heresy and the validity of the affirmation must be judged according to the way each quality relates to a particular world of experience.[64]

[63] W. M. Frohock, *The Novel of Violence in America* (Dallas, 1950), p. 172.
[64] The attitude toward "heresy" as a prime literary virtue was clarified by Aldridge in his later book, *In Search of Heresy* (New York, 1956), in which Wouk was coupled with Sloan Wilson as a fair neoconservative target. Perhaps the most energetic attack upon Aldridge's negative aesthetic is Edmund Fuller's "John Aldridge and the Search for Values," *Man in Modern Fiction* (New York, 1957), pp. 45–67.

I n *After the Lost Generation* Mr. Aldridge consistently underestimates the position of the World War I group, which he remarks "had chosen to be a lost generation."[65] The very term "chosen" is in many ways characteristic of the post-World War II attitude toward the twenties, since it implies an intentional moral and aesthetic selection. Approving of the selection he believes was made by the earlier generation, Aldridge can disapprove of the World War II group as one which did not and could not "choose" authentically. Like the humanist critics, who see much to praise in Wouk in contrast to the earlier negativism, Aldridge fails to perceive that the dislocation of the twenties, coming as a result of impact lacking in the second war, depended less upon aesthetic choice than upon the realities—and lack of precedents—of an historical situation.

Neither the sense of impact within post-World War I fiction nor the explosive effect of such fiction on the reading public was due solely or even mainly to the aesthetic selection of experience to be rendered. If this sense was lacking in World War II it was because the impact, for both the writer and his audience, had long been exhausted, so that other (and to Aldridge's mind less profound) subject areas had to be used: the account of, rather than protest against, technology; the ironic examination of personal, social, or scientific causes; and the return to what Herbert Gold sneers at as "the upper-middle soap opera."[66]

Aldridge, however, persists in seeing World War I as a parallel to the later conflict. He remarks, for example, that the writers were initially "affected by the patriotic slogans and catchwords that are so much a vogue of wartime."[67] Here again is a view filtered by a World War II nostalgia; far from being a "vogue," the slogans and catchwords were accepted with total enthusiasm, complete outrage, and a tragically romantic expectation; they were accepted, indeed, even by the most sophisticated elements in American life as an ultimate cause rather than the fashionable attitude Aldridge implies. Certainly the young volunteers, some of whom

[65] Aldridge, *After the Lost Generation* (New York, 1951), p. 3.
[66] Herbert Gold, "Fiction of the Fifties," *Hudson Review*, XII (1959–60), 200.
[67] Aldridge, *After the Lost Generation*, p. 3.

were to write the novels of World War I, were searching for what Aldridge calls "the excitement of death without the experience of it"; granted too that they were looking for "romance" and thrills. But this was true not only for ambulance drivers and other volunteers; it was also true of young Americans who saw in war "the bright face of danger" and all the trappings of a romantic adventure. This is precisely what so many post-World War II readers find difficult to understand, or remember: that in 1916 Americans could combine tremendous moral seriousness, a conviction of the justice and absolute necessity of their cause, with a delighted expectation of parade, glory, and aesthetic gesture. Almost nobody, again, including the military leaders themselves, expected the slaughterhouse, and so young men could cherish both the chance for adventure and the weight of a grave public cause without any sense of contradiction.

War itself, of course, destroyed both the expectation and the cause as well. But the resulting alienation, the sense of looking on as spectators in some particularly bloody circus, cannot be equated with volunteer status alone. The "spectatorial attitude" suggested by Malcolm Cowley was produced by the war environment itself; it was not, as Aldridge insists, limited to those who came over as volunteers in auxiliary service. Placing far too much emphasis on the "volunteer" status of some novelists, Aldridge actually recapitulates the charge of older critics like Belgion that the novelists were in a very special situation, and so represented nothing but themselves:

They were outside the petty restrictions imposed upon the officers and men of a regular military organization, and owing to the nature of their work and a relaxed, almost nonexistent discipline they were able to mix in comparative freedom with the civilian population. They were fed, clothed and commanded by a government to which, since it was not their own, they owed no allegiance. They were onlookers at a struggle in which, at the time, they had no personal stake. They learned the etiquette without the experience of war, the extravagance and fatalism, the worship of courage and fear of boredom that men ordinarily learn as the price of survival; and they lost, almost by proxy, the illusions they once had had. But if the war taught them bitterness, it was a bitterness tinged with longing and detached regret, a romantic distillation of other men's despair. They were still capable of being excited by danger and the prospect of sacrificing themselves for a noble cause, stricken to exultation by death among the poppies, melted by the spectacle of love amid the ruins of a French chateau. They were special observers, immunized by their nationality and the good fortune of their service from all but the most picturesque aspects of the war.

As spectators, guests of the war by courtesy of the management, they were infected with irresponsibility, thrilled at second hand by danger, held to a pitch of excitement that made their old lives seem impossibly dull and tiresome.[68]

The implication here is that the volunteers were from the very beginning no more than military tourists; as detached and therefore unreliable observers they suffered from a sort of inbred myopia common to all tourism, the freedom which produces only superficiality and a focus upon "picturesque aspects." It was, however, the impact of the war itself which created the sense of alienation, the feeling of a lunatic combination of slaughterhouse and whorehouse. Failing to perceive clearly the unique blend of romance and emotional involvement which provided the very basis of the bold journey, Aldridge underestimates the "spectatorial attitude" as a tragic result of impact and so confuses cause and effect. The spectatorial attitude was indeed characteristic of World War I, but it was the product of the war experience no less than a preliminary condition for it.[69]

Certainly Aldridge's remark that the volunteers felt only a "romantic distillation of other men's despair" does scant justice even to the military facts involved; in the American Field Service in France alone, one out of seventeen "spectators" died.[70] Furthermore the volunteers had a very deep "personal stake" in the war precisely because their role was a product of their own choice, and their choice proved its own invalidity. Granted that their "special

[68] *Ibid.*, pp. 4–5, 10.
[69] Aldridge follows Cowley far too closely in equating the latter's concept (developed most fully in *Exile's Return* [New York, 1934]) with "amateur" soldiering. The "spectatorial" attitude is basic to the work of such combat writers as William March (American), H. M. Tomlinson (Canadian), Henri Barbusse (French), Wilfred Owen (English), and Céline (French). The sense of alienation was an international characteristic of World War I writers, by no means limited to volunteers.
[70] Out of approximately 2,100 volunteers of the American Field Service in France, 230 received the Croix de Guerre and five the Médaille Militaire as a result of their volunteer service; 127 were killed (either in ambulance service or regular assignment), making a death rate of more than 6 per cent. The casualty rate, of course, was higher. (Figures are collated from appendices to Volume III, *History of the American Field Service in France* [Boston, 1927].) It is, at any rate, necessary to distinguish between the holiday atmosphere of the bold journey and the subsequent impact of experience. See also Walter Millis, *Road to War* (Boston, 1935), p. 74.

status" did provide some freedom for observation, one must nevertheless consider that such freedom is hardly a disadvantage for the novelist, who after all is an observer to begin with. True, if Cummings were not a volunteer he would have been shot rather than sent to prison at *La Ferté Macé;* but this in no way invalidates the work which his "special status" made possible. The "irresponsibility" Aldridge notes with such condescension, far from being the result of volunteer preciosity, was the only responsible attitude possible toward a mass obscenity. William March, again, whose *Company K* is no less bitter than Cummings' book, was himself the holder of the Distinguished Service Cross. And essential to their bitterness was the fact that the volunteers were perhaps the most completely "involved," on ideological grounds, of the various groups fighting the war; far from lacking a "personal stake," their enormous Francophile and Anglophile idealism created a repugnance and despair which can hardly be described as "borrowed."[71] The reaction of Cummings, in *The Enormous Room,* or Thomas Boyd, in *Through the Wheat,* was the result of intensely personal ideological commitment.

Misunderstanding the nature of World War I impact leads to some basic distortions. Aldridge speaks of the "worship of courage" learned during the war, despite the fact that such worship was "learned" only from prewar literary sources based upon a military environment that no longer existed. Here again is confusion of cause and effect: admiration for courage as a supreme and meaningful virtue was one cause of the bold journey, but the effect of the war itself was to destroy such meaning—a point which bears reiteration since Aldridge is by no means the only critic who neglects it.

Francis Hackett in 1949 could remark of Hemingway: "The primitive mood of war gave him the chance to dig down into himself for a native primitiveness that peace had long since ruled out of bounds in American fiction."[72] The very phrase, "the primitive mood of war," demonstrates the chronic inability to see the World War I impact on its own terms. In 1927, to cite an earlier example, Edmund Wilson made much the same comment, asking

[71] The Francophile and general "cultural" impetus of many of the volunteers is indicated by the remarkable number of Ivy League men enlisting: a total of 916 (of the national 2,100) from Harvard, Yale, Princeton, Dartmouth, and Cornell—with Harvard and Yale by far the leaders.
[72] Francis Hackett, "Hemingway: 'A Farewell to Arms,'" *Saturday Review of Literature,* XXXII (August 6, 1949), 32–33.

whether the war environment was really much of a change from "Big Two-Hearted River": "Is not the principle of the life itself essentially ruthless and cruel? What is the difference between the gusto of the soldier shooting down his fellow humans and the gusto of the young fisherman hooking grasshoppers to catch trout? Ernest Hemingway is primarily occupied with these problems of natural cruelty and its inevitable obverse of suffering."[73] But the difference between the "natural cruelty" of the northwoods and the unnatural and anonymous cruelty of the war was enormous. In the northwoods, as in the bull ring, there is a direct relationship between the hunter and the hunted, and this relationship (beautifully portrayed by Faulkner in *The Bear*) is one which in a sense redeems death through love, splendor, and form. The war, as I have emphasized, made any such relationship impossible.

Certainly Hemingway made clear that the qualities he worshiped could not be kept in the trenches; only when technological warfare took on the supporting dimension of a legitimate external cause could he begin talking about "courage" again, and this not as a method of self-realization, but rather as a means to a necessary end. In *Men at War*, of course, Hemingway was writing for an audience of GI's and so the quality of political cheerleading is, perhaps, an inevitable part of his book:

But there will be no lasting peace, nor any possibility of a just peace, until *all lands* where the people are ruled, exploited, and governed by any government whatsoever against their consent are given their freedom.

We will also fight this war to enjoy the rights and privileges conveyed to us by the Declaration of Independence, the Constitution of the United States, and the Bill of Rights, and woe to anyone who has any plans for taking these rights and privileges away from us under any guise or for any reason whatsoever.[74]

It was not the virtues of courage as such that Hemingway was praising in *Men at War*, but rather the necessities of a struggle to achieve desirable political and military goals; indeed, in his attitude toward the military necessity (given the framework of legitimate external cause) he is far closer to Wouk and *The Caine Mutiny* than to the Hemingway who wrote *In Our Time* and *A Farewell to Arms*. The worship of courage-in-battle, again, was

---

[73] Edmund Wilson, "The Sportsman's Tragedy," reprinted in *A Literary Chronicle: 1920–1950* (New York, 1950), p. 99.
[74] Hemingway, *Men at War*, p. xxi, xxvii.

a pre-World War I condition and a postwar impossibility. Both the negative and affirmative World War II novelists, even while granting the necessity of the war itself, reacted savagely to any hint of the "proving ground" of combat—a concept, indeed, which provided John Hersey with his major ideological target in *The War Lover* (1959) or Joseph Heller with the comic antiheroism of Yossarian in *Catch-22* (1961).[75]

In attacking the "journalism" or "futility" of World War II novels with World War I as a touchstone, Aldridge does not take into account the fact that ultimate or ontological examinations of combat—purpose, cause, individual choice, meaning of death—are possible only when men question the ends of war. When there is agreement as to ends, the resulting examination must necessarily be limited to means, and so appears, to any demand for ultimates, as something shallow. The World War II writers, even negativists like Burns, were in the position of agreeing with the goals of political and military leaders, and so their work focused on tensions of operation rather than purpose: hence the social problems of minorities and the plight of the intellectual; the ironic and skeptical portrait of military bureaucracy; the behavior of soldiers in occupied territory. Add to this essential agreement (the novelist, almost in spite of himself, being forced into affirmation) the enormous psychological, technological, and political sophistication of the World War II group, and we see the pressures shaping the "journalistic" bias of some novels, the neoconservatism of others, and —for writers who could accept neither conservatism nor journalism—the mockery and "contrived indifference" which, in the case of Merle Miller's *That Winter* (1948), seemed to rule out high seriousness and reduce everything to an ironic we've-been-here-before.[76]

For no World War II writer could be serious in making a "separate peace"—even for Hemingway this would have been unforgiveable in the war against fascism; or in listing the horrors of machine war—he would simply describe the way it worked; or in tearing up music—Art was no longer an ultimate value and therefore

[75] In Burns's novel *The Gallery* the ghostly lieutenant demonstrates in his speech (p. 87) both the assimilation of war and the concept of war as death force. Most important here is the knowledge of who, and what, survives the proving ground. Essentially it is the cynicism of Zorn in *Soldiers March!* but with this difference: Zorn *discovers* it; the lieutenant knew it from the very beginning. The bitterness, in other words, is without process.
[76] Aldridge, *After the Lost Generation*, p. 158.

could not be an ultimate sacrifice; or in staking all on a love affair—no love affair could be a cause beyond *the* cause. Those novelists, furthermore, who remained unsatisfied by neoconservative retrenchments, broad canvas descriptions, or ironic dramatizations of means and personae, could only produce a deeper disillusion, a more metaphysical "sickness unto death" so characteristic of the work of Burns. And this illusion could no longer be explained by failure of initial expectation; it was redeemed neither by revolt (which implies countersolutions) nor by a retreat into concrete simplicities, since the simplicities of action, love, and art were no longer either simple or concrete.

Stephen H. Goode remarks that the metaphysical concerns of World War II fiction, and the resultant cynicism among writers who would not accept Woukian social retrenchment, were also true of war poetry: "His [the World War II poet's] conclusion was that war, evil as it was, is no more evil than life, for it is after all a part of life. And this was the reason for the profound cynicism throughout the poetry of the second war, a cynicism that was compounded by a realization that life itself must be changed before the problem of war might be solved."[77] The preoccupation is with metaphysical awareness rather than with social protest. "They have been driven to asking the ultimate questions," Herbert Gold says of post-World War II writers, insisting that his generation had seen too much of futile revolutions and childish confrontations. And even within the "ultimate questions" there is the combination of self-mockery and skepticism so characteristic of a protagonist like the Dangling Man: "Who am I? This question is the spinach on all our teeth. It stinks up our breath when we utter it."[78]

So too James Baldwin attacks "complaints . . . that World War II failed to produce a literary harvest comparable to that which we garnered from the first," remarking that such "idiocy" is due largely to nostalgia: "The adulation so cruelly proffered our elders has nothing to do with their achievement . . . but has to do with our impulse to look back upon what we now imagine to have been a happier time. It is an adulation which has panic at the root."[79]

[77] Stephen H. Goode, "British War Poetry of the Second World War" (unpublished Ph.D dissertation, University of Pennsylvania, 1958), *DA*, XIX (1958), 810.
[78] Herbert Gold, "Fiction of the Fifties," p. 194.
[79] James Baldwin, "As Much Truth As One Can Bear," *New York Times Book Review*, January 14, 1962, p. 1.

For Baldwin, as for Gold, Bellow, Burns, and others, the solutions of the World War I masters no longer apply; their alternatives to despair have been rendered obsolete by their very simplicity. Baldwin, typically enough, sees the "problem" of art as concerned with metaphysical rather than social good or evil, so that indignation or escape-through-action both become too thin for a new world of experience:

During World War I, we were able to be angry at the atrocities committed in the name of the Kaiser; but it was scarcely possible in World War II to be *angry* over the systematic slaughter of six million Jews; nor did our performance at Nuremburg do anything but muddy the moral and legal waters. In short, by the time of World War II, evil had entered the American Eden, and it had come to stay. . . .
   And those panaceas and formulas [of the twenties] which have so spectacularly failed . . . have also failed this country, and the world. The trouble is deeper than we wished to think; the trouble is in ourselves.[80]

Given a broad belief in the validity of external cause, the World War II disillusion was deeper because the achieved cause, while never broken by social disillusions, was futile in that it produced nothing but continuing crisis without the possibility for "panaceas." And from this futility came not the brave new social or artistic world implicit in even the bitterest World War I novel, but rather the total despair of Burns.[81] The despair was not simply created by a sense of betrayal, but rather was part of inescapable political conditions and metaphysical preoccupations. And the result was the skepticism of Bellow, the mockery of Miller, the ironic passivity of Burns, and—in reaction to these—a tendency toward conservatism exemplified by the work of such men as Herman Wouk and Sloan Wilson. Far from being the "soap-opera" ridiculed by young writers like Gold and attacked by Aldridge, the conservatism itself was based upon alternatives of constructive possibilities.

What Aldridge sees in World War I—an authentic "physical isolation and spiritual emptiness"—was, in other words, far more

[80] *Ibid.*, p. 38.
[81] Burns's narrator is able to say (of North Africa): "It's a place where all the tortures of the 20th century meet and snicker at one another" (p. 20). The narrator knows what the twentieth century is and has been, and so his negativism is total; for the World War I writer, negation was directed at nineteenth rather than twentieth-century values, and so (even in negation) there was constructive purpose. As Burns's narrator also remarks of World War I, "They hadn't yet seen the pointlessness of themselves" (p. 6).

characteristic of the negative writers of the second war.[82] For while it is true that the World War I response might be defined by a sense of deprivation and loss, countering this sense were unlimited horizons of political, aesthetic, and social discovery (or, in the case of some, a hope for social surgery). Aldridge underestimates the sense of excitement and work-to-be-done which, along with loss, was no less characteristic of the World War I generation than "disillusion" or "believing in nothing."[83] As Gorham Munson pointed out in 1932, long before the nostalgia of the fifties gave to predepression days an aura of enchantment, the post-World War I period was a time of enthusiastic and excited "muddle." There was "the war, the peace, the flare-up of liberal hopes, and extinction of them, the Lusk Committee of the Steel Strike, Bolshevism in Russia, Prohibition in the U.S. . . . It was natural for us to be in a muddle . . . we took it all in with a large and not very discriminating appetite. We heard the drums beat for a score of revolts. There seemed to be plenty of energy falling into print. . . . Revolt fitted our temper."[84] And Dos Passos—in his introduction to the 1945 edition of *Three Soldiers*—refers to the bursting sense of excitement, ideological, aesthetic, and political, which men felt indeed might "pick up the pieces" of the old world:

Lenin was alive, the Seattle general strike had seemed the beginning of a flood instead of the beginning of an ebb, Americans in Paris were groggy with the theater and painting and music; Picasso was to rebuild the eye, Stravinski was cramming the Russian steppes into our ears, currents of energy seemed to be breaking out everywhere as young guys climbed out of their uniforms, imperial America was all shining with new ideas of the Ritz, in every direction the countries of the world stretched out starving and angry, ready for anything turbulent and new.[85]

World War I writers could turn their backs on social and military values because there were goals to face, even in expatriation; *nada* itself was a means for cauterization rather than a vehicle for despair.[86] These goals, however, rapidly proved illusory, and their

---

[82] Aldridge, *After the Lost Generation*, p. 12.
[83] *Ibid.*, p. 12.
[84] Gorham Munson, "The Fledgling Years, 1916–1924," *Sewanee Review*, XL (1932), 26–27.
[85] Dos Passos, *Three Soldiers* (New York, 1921), p. 8.
[86] George Snell, in his discussion of *A Farewell to Arms*, notes the impact of World War I but sees *nada* itself as a self-conscious and romantic *assertion*; this quality was itself obsolete by the time of Burns. See *The Shapers of American Fiction* (New York, 1947), p. 164.

rate of obsolescence was speeded by political and economic factors until—by the time of a young writer like Burns—the goals became *non sequitur*. In returning to the middle class and the new orthodoxy, a novelist like Wouk could do so out of the conviction (not entirely false) that among intellectuals there had grown up a new Babbittry of leftism and expatriation. The Babbitt of the beret and bullfight could no longer serve; he had suffered his own displacement.

Nada too was obsolete, and a World War II writer like Burns, far from being proud of his "nothingness," could only suffer a sense of failure in his own alienation from a cause to which he still assented; this is in direct contrast to men like Cummings or protagonists like Andrews, for whom negation itself meant the assertion of alternate values. It is in Burns rather than in Dos Passos, or Boyd, or March, or any World War I writer, that one finds the deepest realization of *nada*—a spiritual nothingness without alternatives. Readers like Aldridge, who persist in seeing the World War I negation as an existentialist response, fail to perceive the anachronism involved in equating the World War I Hemingway with the World War II Sartre; "exits" were not only available for the earlier generation, but were opening in every direction. What Aldridge attacks as "futility" in World War II negation is a classic existential preoccupation, and the ever-present danger of futility which marks existentialism as a philosophy provides a major clue to the reasons behind the post-World War II conservative movement.

After World War I young writers saw about them an edifice of sterile values and false rhetoric; their negation was active, corrective, and for the most part socially directed. These young men, as Granville Hicks remarks, insisted that they could do something about "the evils that existed in the world"; if "they wanted to shock others" it was to expose evil and so eliminate or reduce it.[87] Aldridge underestimates this enormous social and aesthetic energy which gave to World War I negation its unique quality of enthusiastic anger and hopeful despair. In considering World War II negation, on the other hand, he attacks the "spiritual emptiness" and "utter lifelessness and sterility" without perceiving that

[87] Granville Hicks, "American Fiction Since the War," *English Journal*, XXXVII (1948), 216. See also Charles A. Fenton, "The Academy of Arts and Sciences vs. All Comers: Literary Rags and Riches in the 20's," *South Atlantic Quarterly*, LVIII (1959), 572–86.

the alternative was, indeed, the socially directed affirmation of Wouk.[88] Just as Hemingway goes from repudiation of rhetorical patriotism in *A Farewell to Arms* to a statement of patriotic rhetoric in *Men at War,* so the corrective and active position, which was negative in World War I, becomes conservative in World War II. There is, in other words, no such enormous gap between the neoconservatives and the earlier generation as is commonly supposed; on the contrary, it is the World War II negative writer—so often viewed as continuing (but failing to maintain) the earlier pattern of protest—who mocks at precisely those traditions of "lostness" which many critics have insisted he is trying to emulate.[89]

In issuing his indictment against affirmation, and in proclaiming that "the country's values are such that no writer of honesty and insight can possibly take them seriously,"[90] Aldridge makes an absolute statement that middle-class values are inherently beyond the pale of art. But his position itself merely echoes earlier patterns of protest—and the echo, moreover, is directed against a vastly changed target. By the postwar 1940's the "boob" of Liberty Bonds and Cal Coolidge no longer existed, at least not in the attitudes and values of "middle-class" writers like Wouk. Certainly Greenwald, in *The Caine Mutiny*, is not to be equated with the middle class of 1918—or 1925, for that matter. Aldridge, again, presupposes that affirmation and negation are constants; focusing on a World War I environment, he forgets that his very terminology takes on different meanings according to the social and historical environments to which it is applied. Protesting a protest which by 1948 could only result in metaphysical futility, the "middle-class" novel of World War II was far from passive in its affirmation. After World War II, indeed, it was the negative novel whose chief quality was passivity and hopelessness. Aldridge, of course, attacks both; his position would seem to imply that since World War I

[88] Aldridge, *After the Lost Generation,* p. 94.
[89] Going Aldridge one better in negativist criticism, Leslie A. Fiedler (*Love and Death in the American Novel* [New York, 1961]) attacks all war novels since Crane, dismissing the World War I books as mere sentiment, and the World War II books as simple imitations of World War I: "If the novels written after World War I seem to become clichés even as they are committed into print, the novels of World War II are echoes of these clichés, products of the minds so conditioned by the stereotypes of the earlier works that they seem never to have lived through the events of 1939–1945 at all" (pp. 441–42). Fiedler, of course, often uses negation as a stylistic rather than critical instrument. However, his second point—the view of the World War II books as merest "echoes" —is all too widely held.
[90] Aldridge, *After the Lost Generation,* p. 94.

cannot be fought again, people had better stop writing books. (And in this connection one might remember that Aldridge's despair, his prophecy of artistic doom, has precedents which in retrospect seem rather short-sighted. In 1922, for example, Robert Herrick cried out that "the art of literature is at a dead center . . . our literature has nothing it is capable of discovering. . . . Literature, like life, no longer seems to have an unhesitating conviction about anything . . . no great movement in the arts will come from a paralyzed world. . . . A new literature cannot come before another religious conversion, another certainty."[91] The situation may not, after all, be quite so hopeless as Mr. Aldridge makes out.)

The "blind alley of exile" shaping post-World War I attitudes was no true exile at all, since the "alley" itself was explosive with experiment. Politically, there was collectivism; aesthetically, there was enormous concentration on the practice of art as discipline. One cannot, certainly, describe in terms of alienation alone a generation so completely and delightedly involved in changing what it despised. In all spheres the World War I negation was corrective rather than existential; it focused upon change and a faith that people, given the facts, would respond to the ultimate amelioration of civilization.[92] The writers described by Granville Hicks as "boisterously pessimistic," and the insistence upon breaking for the purpose of building, had no parallel after the second conflict. The despair, especially in the case of war books, had its basis not in metaphysics but in social anger made possible by social faith. MacLeish, who as a humanist attacks the anger and despair for lacking totality, fails to see its ameliorative basis; Aldridge, who respects the despair, underestimates the social and artistic enthusiasms which made the World War I protest—the "exile" itself— far more closely related to the social responsibilities of Wouk than to the metaphysically ennervated futility of Burns.[93] "The American expatriots," Frohock says, "were not spoiled brats," a fact which is becoming increasingly difficult to remember.[94]

[91] Robert Herrick, "In General," *Nation*, CXIII (December 7, 1921), 658.
[92] See Randall Stewart, "American Literature Between the Wars," *South Atlantic Quarterly*, XLIV (1945), 371–83; Wallace Stegner, "The Anxious Generation," *English Journal*, XXXVIII (1949), 1–6.
[93] Malcolm Cowley, in "Two Wars and Two Generations," *New York Times Book Review*, July 25, 1948, denies that the World War I group was merely "disillusioned," and suggests "rebellious" as a more accurate term, since they had "a faith in one's ability to do things better than the people in power" (p. 1).
[94] Frohock, *The Novel of Violence in America*, p. 172.

Unlike Wouk, however, World War I writers could not use battle confrontation itself as a vehicle for the setting forth of aesthetic or social values, and this is perhaps the most basic contrast between the war literature of the two generations. Even Hemingway's "clear, never-wavering line . . . from brute violence to mass violence to obsessive recollection of violence"; his "religion of safe conduct," of total insulation, of "simple drinking, simple thinking, simple fornication"—all were methods of avoiding rather than utilizing war experience.[95] Stripping down his language partly as a reaction against the over-fleshed rhetoric so characteristic of pre-war years, he stripped down the experience to be rendered by language as well, and the result was a focus upon ritualized violence and love, the latter also controlled into a sort of violence and reduced to narcissistic singleness of dimension. These were the only real, or real-in-themselves, sources of creative raw material. But violence and love were external to war always, were not and could not be accommodated to it; the war created nothing, not even a meaningful violence. The impact was simply too great. The novelist of World War I, unlike those of the later conflict, could not use war as a given condition for their books: it was necessary either to escape from it or protest it. World War II writers, on the other hand, who had already assimilated technological impact and political ambiguities while subscribing to an external cause, could neither escape nor protest and necessarily used war as an environment much like any other for their social or metaphysical dramas.

In *The Literary Situation* Malcolm Cowley remarks of World War II that "most men in all services accepted the war as they might have accepted an earthquake, and tried to do their best in the circumstances."[96] War, in other words, was seen as a terrible but quite natural development; the possibilities had been assimilated, the horrors were expected. One does not ask, of an earthquake, if it *had* to happen; it sometimes does, and when it does, one tries to survive and to live according to whatever resources are available. Failing to accept the earthquake, however, World War I writers could function only by destroying the framework of necessity, by protesting the catastrophe or withdrawing altogether—both methods equally external to the combat situation.

[95] Aldridge, *After the Lost Generation*, pp. 26, 29, 31.
[96] Cowley, *The Literary Situation*, p. 27. Cowley perceives clearly the change in sensibility and war environment which made a change in narrative approach inevitable.

Hence Aldridge, when he remarks that World War II novelists "are faced with the same material from which Hemingway and Fitzgerald drew their artistic impetus, but are denied the dramatic values which those men found in it,"[97] neglects the fact that for the earlier writers war was either a target to be attacked or a nightmare to be eliminated; it was never, and could not be used as, an actual resource for dramatic development.

This emphasis upon similarities rather than differences relates directly to Aldridge's attack upon the technical sophistication of the World War II group. "Technique," he declares, "is the writer's instrument for discovering his subject matter."[98] It may well be, however, that the reverse is (or should be) true: that subject, or the writer's experience, shapes the technique. Certainly the experience of World War I "discovered" both the antirhetorical technique in the novel of withdrawal, and the rhetoric of indictment in novels of protest. Once we realize the enormous change in the "material" of World War II writers, the reasons for what Aldridge attacks as their over-preoccupation with literary technique and military technology become obvious: theirs was a different narrative necessity, and their subject material itself encompassed another world both particularly, in the actual combat experience, and generally, in political, aesthetic, and social attitudes.

Certainly it is dangerous to see the lack of impact in World War II fiction as due to some inherent fault of vision or art on the part of the novelists. Cowley, for example, while noting that "none of the World War II authors, not even Norman Mailer or James Jones, has had the separate impact for these times that Dos Passos and Hemingway had in the early 1920's,"[99] recognizes that "impact" depends on the shock of experience for the author himself, and on the shock of war truth (even when communicated concretely and exactly, with all of Hemingway's "sequence of motion and fact which made the emotion") for the reader. Readers, after all, were generally unprepared for a revelation of what the war experience actually involved. "After a spate of romantically presented war stories celebrating war's opportunity for private heroism and its sacred nature," George Snell remarks of *Three Soldiers*, "this novel burst like a bombshell. . . . No American had written so devastating a criticism of war's effects on the indi-

[97] Aldridge, *After the Lost Generation*, p. 90.
[98] *Ibid.*, p. 104.
[99] Cowley, *The Literary Situation*, p. 31.

vidual; no American had dared to write so candidly about the individual's real attitude toward the machine that destroyed his manhood as surely as its guns could destroy his body."[100]

With American readers still fog-bound by the war sentimentality of the Great Crusade, the reaction to Dos Passos' novel is hardly surprising. And for authors no less than readers, the impact of the war had been shaped by what they had initially expected—a different order of expectation altogether from that of young men in World War II, who had been suffering from "ideological battle fatigue" long before they had donned their uniforms.[101] Certainly Aldridge's solemn judgment that "taken as a group the novels of this war do not have the impact that those of World War I had" may be irrelevant to questions of aesthetic merit; the judgment, indeed, may be historically ingenuous.[102] For the experiences themselves have become less explosive; given the lessening of impact inherent to a situation, even the most exact rendering will produce less effect. It is a matter of what there is to be realized. And by the time of World War II the situation of combat, the technological horrors of modern war no longer had the emotional resources they possessed earlier, so that for novelists and readers alike the material Aldridge attacks as journalism or sociology was necessary to supplement a situation which by itself had lost much of its meaning.

The scope of the subject matter and flexibility of technique in World War II literature, which Aldridge sees as a precocious imposition of technology, journalism, and sociology upon the aesthetic dimensions of the novel, is singled out by Cowley for special praise. The books of World War II, Cowley says, "compose a sounder body of work. Writers of the second war have been quick to master the tools of their craft. On the average, their books are not only

[100] Snell, *The Shapers of American Fiction*, p. 250. That the "impact" of a book like *Three Soldiers* was historical rather than aesthetic is indicated by the horror with which it was received by many reviewers. Coningsby Dawson, for example, writing in the *New York Times*, October 2, 1921, attacked Dos Passos' "Calculated sordidness . . . and blind whirlwind of rage which respects neither the reticences of art nor the restraints of decency." "The book fails," Mr. Dawson continued, "because of its unmanly intemperance both in language and plot. The voice of righteousness is never sounded." In retrospect such an outburst directed at a novel like *Three Soldiers* seems almost incomprehensible; the "impact" of the book simply cannot be detached from its historical framework.
[101] Frederick J. Hoffman, *The Modern Novel in America* (Chicago, 1951), pp. 171–72.
[102] Aldridge, "America's Young Novelists: Uneasy Inheritors of a Tradition," *Saturday Review of Literature*, XXXII (February 12, 1949), 6.

more smoothly and more skillfully written than most war books of the 1920's, but are also better reporting of 'what really happened in action' to borrow a phrase from Ernest Hemingway."[103]

Basic here is the emphasis on the object-in-itself (concrete) rather than the emotion-of-the-object (abstract). The former, as Cowley rightly points out, was absorbed into the American novel under the influence of Hemingway, and for that matter, Dos Passos, who was achieving objectivity through structure while Hemingway was achieving it through language; World War II writers were influenced by both men, the Dos Passos contribution being most obvious in Mailer's "Time Machine." The war novels of the early twenties, however, gave less concern to what had happened than to the emotional shock of what had happened; theirs was a record of impact rather than an objective correlative of experience. It was not until the late twenties and early thirties, when the emotional realities of the war had already been clarified, that novelists could exercise a tighter formal and linguistic control of their material. Even in the case of World War II novels, after the long process of assimilation already noted, the early books were less objective and more rancorous than those written after 1950. This was far more intensely true of the early World War I novels because of the greater initial impact which the war represented; one need only remember Hemingway's bitter rhetoric in "Champs d'Honneur" to understand that he did not emerge from the war with a ready-packaged theory of aesthetic objectivity.

Conditioned by the later Hemingway-Dos Passos dictum of objectivity and the concrete, readers have often done injustice to works which used different tools on a different set of problems. There is some parallel here to the development of the "objective correlative" in poetics, with the result that critics, demanding "irony," "proliferation," "hard metaphor," etc., rediscovered the metaphysicals and dismissed (as they all too often still do) nonobjective poets ranging from Spenser to Tennyson. Certainly any total reliance upon "objectivity" and the concrete makes it difficult to retain perspective when we examine books written before these criteria became part of the generally accepted critical dogma. It is necessary to remember that both Hemingway and Dos Passos constructed their aesthetic positions in later work—when their own war experiences had already been softened by the process of assimilation.

[103] Cowley, *The Literary Situation*, p. 37.

Books written prior to the assimilation were necessarily less "objective," placing heavy emphasis on unabashed rhetorical statement of impact and the resultant emotion. But these qualities are total aesthetic sins only to a later generation. Cowley, for example, dismisses Thomas Boyd's *Through the Wheat* far too easily; granting that Boyd was "stressing the anxiety and rage . . . rather than the events which produced these emotions,"[104] we must bear in mind that *Through the Wheat* was published in 1923, years before the focus on event, the objective formal and linguistic modes became categorical imperatives—as they did in the later work of Dos Passos and Hemingway. And despite his lack of stylistic or formal objectivity, Boyd succeeded in making a powerful statement of withdrawal; Hicks, indeed, as a protagonist of alienation, points directly to Faulkner's Mahon and in some ways to Frederic Henry himself.

While the horror of World War I was still the prime reality of their experience, writers emphasized emotion over and above event. Only when external factors began to soften this horror could the objective aesthetic become possible. We cannot understand the effect of World War I on literature, and the effect of World War I literature on the reading public, by limiting ourselves to the more objective work produced at the end of the twenties and during the early thirties, the formal objectivity perfected by Hemingway and Dos Passos and carried on by World War II writers (who experienced even less of impact and so could concentrate on total realism not only of event, but of dialogue, politics, and sexual or social motivation).

It must be noted, however, that the war novel of rhetorical protest continued even while the various objective techniques such as cinemagraphic prose, internal monologue, and the *roman fleuve* were being absorbed into the general literary scene. Writers like Fredenburgh (1930), March (1933), and Archie Binns (1937), to cite but a few examples, maintained earlier patterns of rhetoric but showed respectively the development of emotional scar tissue, the realization of futility, and a sense of impending political tragedy. Even Mary Lee, who in *'It's a Great War!'* (1929) combined a form of the internal monologue with a heavy dose of sentimentality, demonstrates the continuation of antiwar rhetoric. This was especially true during the mid and late thirties (with books like Humphry Cobb's *Paths of Glory* [1935] and Dalton Trumbo's

[104] *Ibid.*, p. 132.

Johnny Got His Gun [1939]), when the possibility of a still greater world conflict served to reactivate the earlier and less objective attitudes. After the technically naïve rhetorical protest of the earliest postwar novels, one sees a movement first toward formal objectivity, then toward the use of objective techniques to achieve a new statement of rhetorical protest. March's *Company K* is perhaps the most memorable example of the manner in which formal objectivity—in this case the cross-sectional narrative—becomes not a device for withdrawing from rhetoric, but a vehicle for its dramatic expression.

No full perspective on post-World War I literature is possible for a reader who limits himself to Frederic Henry as an antiheroic archetype. The protest, the agony, the bitterness, the gestures, and the more verbal despair of Boyd, the early Dos Passos, Elliot Paul, or Cummings are, in their own context, aesthetically no less than historically authentic. *A Farewell to Arms* and *1919* give us the result, not the process of impact. The process itself is dramatized by the novels of rhetorical protest—a body of literature too often scorned by critics working under the imperatives of their own dogmas, and too often forgotten by readers for whom the impact of World War I has been blunted by so many years of continuing violence.

SELECTED BIBLIOGRAPHY

"A Guide to American Literature Written During World War I," *Saturday Review of Literature*, IX (October 22, 1932), 197.

Abrams, Ray H. *Preachers Present Arms*. New York, 1933.

Adams, Samuel H. *Common Cause*. Boston, 1919.

Aldington, Richard. *Death of a Hero*. New York, 1929.

Aldridge, John W. *After the Lost Generation*. New York, 1951.

————. *In Search of Heresy*. New York, 1956.

————. "The New Generation of Writers," *Harper's*, CXXCIV (1947), 423–32.

————. "America's Young Novelists: Uneasy Inheritors of a Tradition," *Saturday Review of Literature*, XXXII (February 12, 1949), 6–8, 36–37, 42.

Allen, Frederick Lewis. *The Big Change*. New York, 1952.

Allen, Hervey. *Toward the Flame*. New York, 1934.

————. *It Was Like This*. New York, 1940.

"American Army Discipline as Spiritual Murder," *Literary Digest*, LXXI (November 12, 1921), 29–30.

Andrews, Mary Raymond Shipman. *The Three Things*. New York, 1915.

————. *Old Glory*. New York, 1917.

————. *Her Country*. New York, 1918.

————. *Joy in the Morning*. New York, 1919.

————. *His Soul Goes Marching On*. New York, 1922.

Angellotti, Marion P. *The Firefly of France*. New York, 1918.

Aron, Raymond. *The Century of Total War*. New York, 1954.

Atkins, John Alfred. *The Art of Ernest Hemingway*. London, 1952.

Ayres, Leonard P. *The War With Germany: A Statistical Summary*. Washington, 1919.

Bailey, Temple. *The Tin Soldier*. Philadelphia, 1918.

Bailey, Thomas A. *A Diplomatic History of the American People*. New York, 1958.

Bainton, Roland H. *Christian Attitudes Toward War and Peace*. New York, 1960.

Baker, Carlos (ed.). *Hemingway and His Critics*. New York, 1960.

Baldwin, James. "As Much Truth As One Can Bear," *New York Times Book Review*, January 14, 1962, p. 1, 38.

Barnes, Harold Elmer. *The Genesis of the World War*. New York, 1926.

Barretto, Larry. *Horses in the Sky*. New York, 1929.

Beach, Joseph Warren. *The Twentieth Century Novel*. New York, 1932.

————. *American Fiction*. New York, 1941.

Belgion, Montgomery. *The Human Parrot and Other Essays*. London, 1931.

Bernard, L. L. *War and Its Causes*. New York, 1944.

Binns, Archie. *The Laurels Are Cut Down*. New York, 1937.

Bishop, John Peale. *Collected Essays*. Edited by Edmund Wilson. New York, 1948.

Boyd, Leonard R. "Will It Happen Again?," *Infantry Journal*, XX (1922), 145–47.

Boyd, Thomas. *Through the Wheat*. New York, 1923.

Brittain, Vera. "Books and War and Peace," *Saturday Review of Literature*, XVII (January 8, 1938), 3–4.

Brooks, Alden. *As I Saw It*. New York, 1929.

Brooks, Van Wyck. *Sketches in Criticism*. New York, 1932.

Brown, G. R. *My Country: A Story of Today*. New York, 1917.

Bullard, Robert L. *Personalities and Reminiscences of the War*. New York, 1925.

Burgum, E. B. *The Novel and The World's Dilemma*. New York, 1947.

Burke, Kenneth. "The Imagery of Killing," *Hudson Review*, I (1948), 151–67.

———. "War, Response, and Contradiction," *The Philosophy of Literary Form*. New York (Vintage edition), 1957.

Calmer, Alan. "John Dos Passos," *Sewanee Review*, XL (1932), 341–49.

Canby, Henry Seidel. *Definitions*. New York, 1922.

———. "War Books and 'All Our Yesterdays,'" *Golden Book*, XI (March, 1930), 94–96.

———. "War or Peace in Literature," *Saturday Review of Literature*, VIII (April 9, 1932), 645–47.

———. "War and Literature," *Saturday Review of Literature*, XXIV (September 20, 1941), 8.

Cantwell, Robert. "A Warning to Pre-War Novelists," *New Republic*, XCI (June 23, 1937), 178.

Cather, Willa. *One of Ours*. New York, 1922.

Caygill, Harry W. "Operations of Company M., 23rd Infantry," *Infantry Journal*, XL (1933), 131–37.

Céline, Louis-Ferdinand. *Journey to the End of the Night*. New York (New Directions), 1960.

Clark, Alan. *The Donkeys*. New York, 1962.

Coan, Otis W. (ed.). *America in Fiction*. Stanford, 1941.

Cobb, Humphry. *Paths of Glory*. New York, 1935.

Cobb, Irwin. *Thunders of Silence*. New York, 1918.

Cooperman, Stanley. "Hemingway's Blue-eyed Boy: Robert Jordan and 'Purging Ecstacy'," *Criticism* VIII (Winter, 1966), 87–96. "Of War and Man," *Nation*, CLXXX (July 23, 1955), 80.

Cowley, Malcolm. *The Literary Situation*. New York, 1954.

———. *Exile's Return*. New York (Compass edition), 1956.

———. "John Dos Passos: The Poet and the World," *New Republic*, LXX (April 27, 1932), 303–5.

———. "Two Wars and Two Generations," *New York Times Book Review*, July 25, 1948, p. 1.

———. "The Literary Atmosphere of Two Wars," *New York Herald Tribune Book Review*, September 25, 1949, p. 6.

Craig, Louis B. "First Field Artillery Brigade at Soissons," *Field Artillery Journal*, XIV (1924), 331–36.

Creel, George. *How We Advertised America*. New York, 1920.

Critoph, Gerald E. "The American Literary Reaction to World War I." Unpublished Ph.D. dissertation, University of Pennsylvania, 1957.

Cummings, E. E. *The Enormous Room*. New York, 1922.

Daiches, David. *The Novel and the Modern World*. New York, 1940.

Daniels, Jonathan. *The End of Innocence*. Philadelphia, 1954.

Davis, Richard Harding. *With the Allies*. New York, 1915.

Dawson, Coningsby. *The Glory of the Trenches*. New York, 1918.

————. *Living Bayonets*. New York, 1919.
Dawson, Loleta I., and Huntting, Marion Davis. *European War Fiction in English*. Boston, 1921.
Dawson, W. J. *War Eagle*. New York, 1915.
Deeping, Warwick. *No Hero—This*. New York, 1936.
Devine, Charles. *Cognac Hill*. New York, 1927.
Dickenson, James Franklin. "The Treatment of Military Heroism in the French War Novel." Unpublished Ph.D. dissertation, New York University, 1950.
Dickman, Joseph T. *The Great Crusade*. New York, 1927.
"Does War Produce Literature?," *Literary Digest*, XCIX (December 15, 1928), 25–26.
Doob, Leonard W. *Propaganda: Its Psychology and Technique*. New York, 1935.
Dos Passos, John. *First Encounter*. New York (Philosophical Library edition), 1945. Originally published as *One Man's Initiation*, New York, 1920.
————. *Three Soldiers*. New York, 1921.
————. *1919*. New York (Cardinal edition), 1954.
————. "Against American Literature," *New Republic*, VIII (October 14, 1916), 269–71.
————. "Off the Shoals," *Dial*, LXXIII (July, 1922), 97–102.
Dunbar, Ruth. *Swallow*. New York, 1919.
Eastman, Max. *Art and the Life of Action*. New York, 1934.
Eisinger, Chester E. "The American War Novel: An Affirming Flame," *Pacific Spectator*, IX (1955), 272–88.
Ellsberg, Edward. *Pigboats*. New York, 1930.
Empey, Arthur Guy. *From the Firing Step*. New York, 1917.
————. *Over the Top*. New York, 1917.
————. *Tales from a Dugout*. New York, 1918.
————. *A Helluva War*. New York, 1927.
"Ernest Hemingway," *Modern Fiction Studies*, I (1955), (special number, with bibliography).
Falls, Cyril. *War Books: A Critical Guide*. London, 1930.
————. *The First World War*. London, 1960.
Faulkner, Harold Underwood. *American Political and Social History*. New York, 1946.
Faulkner, William. *Soldiers' Pay*. New York, 1926.
————. *The Fable*. New York, 1954.
Fay, Sidney Bradshaw. *Origins of the World War*. New York, 1930.
Feigenbaum, Lawrence H. "War as Viewed by the Postwar Novelists of World Wars I and II." Unpublished Ph.D. dissertation, New York University, 1950.
Fenton, Charles A. *The Apprenticeship of Ernest Hemingway*. New York (Compass edition), 1958.
————. "Ambulance Drivers in France and Italy," *American Quarterly*, III (1951), 326–42.
————. "The Academy of Arts and Sciences vs. All Comers: Literary Rags and Riches in the 20's," *South Atlantic Quarterly*, LVIII (1959), 572–86.
————. "A Literary Fracture of World War I," *American Quarterly*, XII (1960), 119–32.
Fiedler, Leslie. *Love and Death in the American Novel*. New York, 1961.
Fisher, Dorothy Canfield. *Home Fires in France*. New York, 1918.
————. *The Day of Glory*. New York, 1919.
Fredenburgh, Theodore. *Soldiers March!*. New York, 1930.
Frederick, John T. "Fiction of the Second World War," *College English*, XVII (1956), 197–204.

Frederick, Pierce G. *The Great Adventure: America in the First World War.* Indianapolis, 1961.

Freud, Sigmund. "Thoughts for the Times on War and Death," *Gessamelte Werke* X, 324–55. 18 Vols. London, 1940–1952.

Frohock, W. M. *The Novel of Violence in America.* Dallas, 1950.

Fuller, Edmund. *Man in Modern Fiction.* New York, 1957.

Fuller, J. C. F. *War and Western Civilization.* London, 1932.

Gatlin, Dana. *The Full Measure of Devotion.* New York, 1918.

Geer, Cajetan. "Now It Can Be Talked About," *Commonweal*, CLXII (1932), 209–11.

Geismar, Maxwell. *Writers in Crisis.* Boston, 1942.

Gloag, John. *Word Warfare.* London, 1939.

Gold, Herbert. "Fiction of the Fifties," *Hudson Review*, XII (1959–60), 192–201.

Gold, Michael. "The Education of John Dos Passos," *English Journal*, XXII (1933), 87–97.

Gooch, George Peabody. *The Coming of War.* New York, 1938.

Goode, Stephen H. "British War Poetry of the Second World War." Unpublished Ph.D. dissertation, University of Pennsylvania, 1958.

Gosse, Sir Edmund. *Inter Arma.* New York, 1916.

――――. "War and Literature," *Living Age*, LXV (1914), 658–71.

Greever, Garland. *War Writing.* New York, 1918.

Grey, Zane. *Desert of Wheat.* New York, 1919.

Gummere, Francis B. "War and Romance," *Atlantic Monthly*, CXXVI (October, 1920), 490–96.

Hackett, Francis. "Another War: Stephen Crane's 'Red Badge of Courage,'" *New Republic*, XI (June 30, 1917), 250–51.

Hagemann, E. R. "'Correspondents Three' in the Greco-Turkish War," *American Literature*, XXX (1958), 339–44.

Hapgood, Norman. *Professional Patriots.* New York, 1927.

Harbord, James G. *The American Army in France.* Boston, 1936.

Harris, Credo F. *Where the Souls of Men Are Calling.* New York, 1918.

Harris, John. *Covenant with Death.* New York, 1961.

Harrison, Charles Yale. *Generals Die in Bed.* New York, 1930.

Hart, B. H. Liddell. *A History of the World War, 1914–1918.* London, 1934.

Hartwick, Harry. *The Foreground of American Fiction.* New York, 1934.

Heilman, Robert B. "Artist and Patria," *Sewanee Review*, LI (1943), 362–69.

Hemingway, Ernest. *A Farewell to Arms.* New York, 1929.

――――. *The Short Stories of Ernest Hemingway.* New York, 1953.

―――― (ed.). *Men at War.* New York, 1955.

Herrick, Robert. *The Conscript Mother.* New York, 1916.

――――. "War and American Literature," *Dial*, LXIV (1918), 7–8.

――――. "Telling the Truth about War," *Nation*, CX (June 26, 1920), 850–51.

――――. "In General," *Nation*, CXIII (December 7, 1921), 658–59.

Heth, Edward Harris. *Told with a Drum.* Boston, 1937.

Hicks, Granville. "John Dos Passos," *Bookman*, LXXV (1932), 32–42.

――――. "American Fiction Since the War," *English Journal*, XXXVII (1948), 271–77.

――――. "Politics and John Dos Passos," *Antioch Review*, X (1950), 85–98.

History of the American Field Service in France. 3 vols. Boston, 1920.

Hoffman, Frederick J. *The Twenties.* New York, 1949.

――――. *The Modern Novel in America.* Chicago, 1951.

―――― (ed.), with Olga Vickery. *William Faulkner: Two Decades of Faulkner Criticism.* East Lansing, Mich., 1951.

――――. "The Temper of the Twenties," *Minnesota Review*, I (1960), 46–56.

Hofstadter, Richard. *The Age of Reform.* New York, 1955.

Hotchner, A. E. *Papa Hemingway.* New York, 1966.

Hunt, E. E. *Tales from a Famished Land.* New York, 1918.

Istas, Helen. "French and German Attitudes to the First World War As Reflected in Novels and Memoirs." Unpublished Ph.D. dissertation, Indiana University, 1951.

Johnson, David. *Promenade in Champagne.* New York, 1951.

Johnson, Douglas W. *Battlefields of the World War.* New York, 1921.

Johnston, J. H. "The Poetry of World War I: A Study in the Evolution of Lyric and Narrative Form." Unpublished Ph.D. dissertation, University of Wisconsin, 1960.

Josephson, Matthew. *Portrait of the Artist as American.* New York, 1930.

Kahn, Lothar. "The Jewish Soldier in Modern Fiction," *American Judaism,* IX (1960), 12–13, 30–31.

Kaye, F. B. "Puritanism, Literature, and the War," *New Republic,* XXV (December 15, 1920), 64–67.

Kazin, Alfred. *On Native Grounds.* New York, 1942.

———. "The Mindless Young Militants," *Commentary,* VI (1948), 495–501.

Kelland, E. B. *Highflyers.* New York, 1919.

Kelly, E. M. *Over Here.* Indianapolis, 1918.

Kelly, Thomas H. *What Outfit Buddy?* New York, 1920.

Kennan, George. *American Diplomacy, 1900–1950.* New York, 1952.

Killigrew, John W. "A Critique of American Military History." Unpublished Ph.D. dissertation, Indiana University, 1952.

Killinger, John. *Hemingway and the Dead Gods.* Lexington, Ky., 1960.

Klotz, Marvin. "The Imitation of War, 1800–1900: Realism in the American War Novel." Unpublished Ph.D. dissertation, New York University, 1959.

Krutch, Joseph Wood. *The Modern Temper.* New York, 1929.

Lanza, Conrad. "Third Battle of Romagna," *Field Artillery Journal,* XXIV (1934), 334–46.

———. "The Artillery Support in the AEF," *Field Artillery Journal,* XXVI (1936), 62–86.

Lasswell, Harold. *Propaganda Techniques in the World War.* New York, 1927.

Lazo, Hector. *Taps.* Boston, 1934.

Leathem, Rev. W. H. *The Comrade in White.* New York, 1916.

Lee, Mary. *'It's a Great War!'* Boston and New York, 1929.

Lennow, Elbert. *Reader's Guide to Prose Fiction.* New York, 1940.

Levin, Harry. "Observations on the Style of Ernest Hemingway," *Kenyon Review,* XIII (1951), 581–609.

Lewisohn, Ludwig. "The Crisis of the Novel," *Yale Review,* XX (1933), 533–44.

Liebling, A. J. "Lines from a Reviewer," *New York Times Book Review,* March 13, 1949, p. 21.

Lind, L. Robert. "The Crisis in Literature, II: Propaganda and Letters," *Sewanee Review,* XLVII (1939), 184–93.

Lineberger, Paul. *Psychological Warfare.* Washington, 1955.

Literary History of the United States. Edited by Robert Spiller, Willard Thorp, Thomas H. Johnson, Henry Seidel Canby. 3 vols. New York, 1948.

Literature in America. Edited by Philip Rahv. New York, 1957.

Lloyd, V. A. T. "War in Fiction," *Fortnightly Review,* CX (November, 1918), 764–71.

Löhrke, Eugene. *Armageddon: The World War in Literature.* New York, 1930.

Loveman, Amy. "The War in Fiction," *Saturday Review of Literature,* XI (March 9, 1935), 542.

————. "Then and Now," *Saturday Review of Literature*, XXVII (August 7, 1940), 8.
————. "Then and Now," *Saturday Review of Literature*, XXVII (August 5, 1944), 45–46.
Lutes, D. T. *My Boy in Khaki*. New York, 1918.
McAfee, Helen. "The Literature of Disillusion," *Atlantic Monthly*, CXXXII (August, 1923), 225–34.
MacDonald, C. B. "Novels of World War II," *Military Affairs*, XIII (1949), 42–46.
MacLeish, Archibald, and Cowley, Malcolm. "Lines for an Interment," *New Republic*, LXXVI (September 20, 1933), "The Dead of the Next War," *New Republic*, LXXVI (October 4, 1933), 214–16.
MacQuarrie, Hector. *How to Live at the Front*. New York, 1917.
March, William. *Company K*. New York, 1933.
Marsh, John Leslie. "A Circle of Meaning: American Novelists Face the Military Necessity." Unpublished Ph.D. dissertation, University of Pennsylvania, 1959.
May, Henry F. *The End of American Innocence*. New York, 1959.
Mayo, Katherine. *That Damn Y*. Boston, 1920.
Merrill, W. P. *War Time Hymns*. New York, 1918.
Millis, Walter. *Road to War*. Boston, 1935.
————. *Arms and Men*. New York, 1956.
Mitchell, Broadus. *Depression Decade*. New York, 1947.
Montague, C. E. *Disenchantment*. New York, 1922.
————. *Fiery Particles*. New York, 1923.
Morris, Lloyd. *Postscript to Yesterday*. New York, 1947.
————. "Heritage of a Generation of Novelists," *New York Herald Tribune Book Review*, September 25, 1949, p. 74.
Muir, Edward. *The Present Age, from 1914*. New York, 1939.
Muller, Herbert J. *Modern Fiction: A Study in Values*. New York, 1937.
Munson, Gorham. "The Fledgling Years, 1916–1924," *Sewanee Review*, XL (1932), 24–54.
Nason, Leonard. *Chevrons*. New York, 1926.
————. *Sergeant Eadie*. New York, 1928.
————. *A Corporal Once*. New York, 1930.
Neibuhr, Reinhold. *Moral Man and Immoral Society*. New York, 1948.
Odum, Howard W. *Wings On My Feet*. Indianapolis, 1929.
Ogden, Archibald G. "The Book Trade in War Time," *Publishers' Weekly*, XXXVI (July 8, 1939), 94–98.
Oldsey, Stanley B. "Aspects of Combat in the Novel, 1900–1950." Unpublished Ph.D. dissertation, Pennsylvania State University, 1956.
Oppenheim, E. Phillips. *A People's Man*. New York, 1914.
————. *The Pawn's Count*. New York, 1918.
Palmer, Frederick. *America in France*. New York, 1918.
Parrington, Vernon. "The Beginnings of Critical Realism in America," Vol. III. *Main Currents in American Thought*. New York, 1930.
Pattee, F. L. *The New American Literature*. New York, 1930.
Paul, Elliot. *Impromptu*. New York, 1923.
Paxon, Frederick L. *American Democracy and World War*. 4 vols. Boston, 1936.
Penrod, John A. "American Literature and the Great Depression." Unpublished Ph.D. dissertation, University of Pennsylvania, 1954.
Perry, Ralph Barton. *Puritanism and Democracy*. New York, 1944.
Pershing, John J. *My Experiences in the World War*. 2 vols. New York, 1931.

Peterson, H. C. *Propaganda for War*. Norman, Okla., 1939.
Pfaff, William. "The Naked and the Dead and the Novels," *Commonweal* LIV (1951), 529–30.
Phipps, Frank T. "The Image of War in America, 1891–1917." Unpublished Ph.D. dissertation, Ohio State University, 1953.
Pier, A. S. *The Son Decides*. Boston, 1918.
Poling, Daniel A. *Huts in Hell*. Boston, 1918.
Posonby, Sir Arthur. *Falsehood in War Time*. London, 1929.
Pritchett, V. S. "First Person Singular in War Fiction," *New Statesman and Nation*, XXIII (1942), 291.
Raemaker, Louis. *Collected Cartoons*. New York, 1917.
Rahv, Philip. "The Cult of Experience in American Writing," *Partisan Review*, VII (1940), 412–24.
Rarey, G. H. "American Tank Units in the Forêt d'Argonne," *Infantry Journal*, XXII (1928), 389–95.
Rascoe, Burton. "What They Read during the Last War," *Saturday Review of Literature*, XX (September 23, 1939), 3–4.
Read, Herbert. *Reason and Romanticism*. New York, 1934.
Reade, James Morgan. *Atrocity Propaganda*. New Haven, Conn., 1941.
"Reading and Fighting," *Saturday Review of Literature*, VI (April 12, 1930), 918.
Remenyi, Joseph. "The Psychology of War Literature," *Sewanee Review*, LII (1944), 137–47.
Rinehart, Mary R. *Amazing Interlude*. New York, 1918.
———. *Dangerous Days*. New York, 1919.
Romains, Jules. *Verdun*. New York, 1939.
Ropp, Theodore. *War in the Western World*. Durham, N.C., 1959.
Rosenfeld, Isaac. "A Farewell to Ernest Hemingway," *Kenyon Review*, XIII (1951), 147–55.
Rugoff, Milton. "John Dos Passos," *Sewanee Review*, XLIX (1941), 453–68.
Scanlon, William. *God Have Mercy On Us*. Boston, 1929.
Schafer, Charles H. "The Causes of War in American Popular and Professional Literature, 1910–1920." Unpublished Ph.D. dissertation, University of Maryland, 1955.
Schindel, Bayard. *The Golden Pilgrimage*. New York, 1929.
Schneider, Isidor. "The Fetish of Simplicity," *Nation*, CXXXII (February 18, 1931), 184–86.
Schwartz, Delmore. "John Dos Passos and the Whole Truth," *Southern Review*, IV (1938), 351–67.
Seiden, Melvin. "The Hero and His War," *Nation*, CXCIII (November 18, 1961), 408–11.
Seldes, Gilbert. "Notes and Queries," *New Republic*, XLIV (October 21, 1925), 231.
Shephard, W. G. *The Scar that Tripled*. New York, 1918.
Sinclair, Upton. *Jimmy Higgins*. Racine, Wisc., 1918.
———. *100%: The Story of a Patriot*. Chicago, 1920.
Slosson, Preston William. *The Great Crusade and After*. New York, 1930.
Snell, George. *The Shapers of American Fiction*. New York, 1947.
Soule, George. *Prosperity Decade: 1917–1927*. New York, 1947.
Springer, June Marie. "The American Novel in Germany: A Study of the Critical Reception of American Novelists Between the Two Wars." Unpublished Ph.D. dissertation, University of Pennsylvania, 1959.
Springs, Elliott. *Nocturne Militaire*. New York, 1927.
Stallings, Lawrence. *Plumes*. New York, 1924.
———. *The First World War*. New York, 1933.

Peterson, H. C. *Propaganda for War*. Norman, Okla., 1939.

Stallman, Robert Wooster. "A Selected Bibliography of Criticism of Modern Fiction," *Critiques and Essays on Modern Fiction.* Edited by John Aldridge. New York, 1952.
Stegner, Wallace. "The Anxious Generation," *English Journal,* XXXVIII (1949), 1–6.
Stevens, James. *Mattock.* New York, 1927.
Stewart, Randall. "American Literature Between the Wars," *South Atlantic Quarterly,* XLIV (1945), 371–83.
Stidger, W. L. *Soldier Silhouettes.* New York, 1918.
Stouffer, S. A., et al. *The American Soldier: Studies in Social Psychology in World War II.* Princeton, 1949.
Streeter, Edward. *Dere Mable.* New York, 1918.
Tales of Wartime France by Contemporary French Writers Illustrating the Spirit of the French People at War. New York, 1918.
Tansill, Charles C. *America Goes to War.* Boston, 1938.
Tarbell, Ida. *The Rising of the Tide.* New York, 1919.
Tate, Allen. "Random Thoughts on the 1920's," *Minnesota Review,* I (1960), 46–56.
Taylor, A. J. P. *The Struggle for Mastery in Europe, 1848–1918.* Oxford, 1954.
"The Situation in American Writing," *Partisan Review,* VI (1939), 25–46.
Thomason, John W. *Fix Bayonets.* New York, 1927.
Tomlinson, H. M. "War Books," *Yale Review,* XIX (1930), 447–65.
Train, Arthur. *Earthquake.* New York, 1918.
Trilling, Lionel. "The America of John Dos Passos," *Partisan Review,* IV (1938), 26–32.
Trumbo, Dalton. *Johnny Got His Gun.* New York, 1939.
Tuchman, Barbara W. *The Guns of August.* New York, 1962.
———. *The Proud Tower.* New York, 1965.
Valentine, Alan. *1913: America Between Two Worlds.* New York, 1962.
Valery, Paul. *Crise de la Conscience Européene.*
Van Doren, Carl. *The American Novel, 1789–1939.* New York, 1940.
———. "American Realism," *New Republic,* XXXIV (March 21, 1923), 107–9.
———. "Post-War: The Literary 20's," *Harper's,* CLXXIII (1936), 148–56.
Van Doren, Mark. "The Art of American Fiction," *Nation,* CXXXVII (April 25, 1934), 471–73.
Venable, Clarke. *Aw Hell.* New York, 1927.
Viereck, George (ed.). *As They Saw Us.* New York, 1929.
Von Giehrl, Herman. "The A.E.F. in Europe, 1917–19," *Infantry Journal,* XX (1922), 18–23, 140–49, 292–303.
Walcutt, Charles C. "Fear Motifs in the Literature Between the Wars," *South Atlantic Quarterly,* XLVI (1947), 227–38.
Waldmeir, Joseph J. "Ideological Aspects of the American Novels of World War II." Unpublished Ph.D. dissertation, Michigan State University, 1959.
Waller, Willard (ed.). *War in the Twentieth Century.* New York, 1940.
Warren, Harold L. *With the YMCA in France.* New York, 1918.
"War's Effect on American Letters," *Literary Digest,* LII (February 19, 1916), 439.
"War's Effect on Literature," *Literary Digest,* XLIX (December 26, 1914), 1277–78.
"War's Reaction on Literature," *Nation,* XCIX (December 31, 1914), 765.
Watson, Richard L. "American Political History, 1900–1920," *South Atlantic Quarterly,* LIV (1955), 107–26.
Waugh, Arthur. "Literature and War," *Fortnightly Review,* CII (November, 1914), 766–67.

Wharton, Edith. *The Marne*. New York, 1918.

———. *A Son at the Front*. New York, 1923.

Wharton, James B. *Squad*. New York, 1928.

"What Literature Reaps from War," *Literary Digest*, L (June 5, 1915), 1330–31.

Whiting, John D. *S.O.S.* Indianapolis, 1928.

Wilkinson, Clennell. "Back to All That," *London Mercury*, XXII (1930), 539–46.

———. "Recent War Books," *London Mercury*, XXI (1930), 236–42.

"William Faulkner," *Modern Fiction Studies*, II (1956), (Special number, with bibliography).

Williamson, Henry. "Reality in War Literature," *London Mercury*, XIX (1929), 295–304.

Wilson, Edmund. "The Sportsman's Tragedy," *A Literary Chronicle 1920–1950*. New York, 1952, 96–102.

———. "Hemingway: The Gauge of Morale," *Literature in America*. Edited by Philip Rahv. New York, 1957, 373–91.

Winther, Sophus Keith. *The Realistic War Novel*. Seattle, Wash., 1930 (Chapbooks 33).

Wolff, Leon. *In Flanders Fields*. New York, 1958.

Woods, Dorothea E. "French Literature and Peace, 1919–1939." Unpublished Ph.D. dissertation, University of Illinois, 1957.

Wives, Women, and War: A Diary of Disillusionment. New York, 1926.

Wylie, Ida Alena Ross. *Towards Morning*. New York, 1918.

Zabel, Morton D. *Literary Opinion in America*. New York, 1951.

INDEX

Angell, Norman: *The Grand Illusion*, 7

Anglophilism: of Henry James, 8; of New York Times, 9; of Ambassador Page, 11; of Peterson, 28–29; in Fenton's "A Literary Fracture of World War I," 29, 35–36; in publishing, 34; mentioned, 12, 18n, 59, 82, 228

Arabic: submarine-sinking of, 11

Aristophanes, 206

Armaments. *See* Trade with Entente

Army environment: in Millis' *Arms and Men*, 77; in Céline's *Journey to the End of the Night*, 78–79; in Cummings' "Pilgrim's Progress," 83; Roppon, 83; Millis on, 83; Lazo on, 83; General Pershing on, 83; in Dos Passos' *Three Soldiers*, 83, 85, 86, 87–88; 141, 142, 143, 149–56, 175–76, 177–78; in Fredenburgh's *Soldiers March!*, 83, 86, 138–41, 142, 155–56, 163, 164; in Paul's *Impromptu*, 83, 86, 148–51, 152, 155–56, 163, 164; in Herrick's "Telling the Truth About War," 85; in March's *Company K*, 85; in Nason's *Sergeant Eadie*, 85–86; in Stevens' *Mattock*, 85–86, 145–48 *passim*; Cummings on, 86; in Faulkner's *Soldiers' Pay*, 87, 159, 162, 163; in Harrison's *Generals Die in Bed*, 88n, 157; in Kelly's *What Outfit Buddy?*, 140; in Dos Passos, *1919*, 141, 145; in Dreiser's *An American Tragedy*, 148; in Stallings' *Plumes*, 155; in Lee's *It's a Great War!*, 155; in Boyd's *Through the Wheat*, 159, 163–64; in Allen's *Toward the Flame*, 163; in Cummings' *The Enormous Room*, 163, 173, 174–75; Marsh's "A Circle of Meaning: American Novelists Face the Military Necessity" on, 203, 210, 215; in Crane's *The Red Badge of Courage*, 215–16, 217, 221. *See also* Impact of World War I; Machine war

—unrealistic: Cather on, 28, 97; in Wharton's *A Son at the Front*, 28; in Fenton's "A Literary Fracture of World War I," 29; in Gitlin's *Measure of Devotion*, 29; in Cather's *One of Ours*, 29–32; Bailey

on, 30, 42; Wylie on, 30; Andrews on, 30, 42; Adams on, 32; Empey on, 32; Dunbar on, 32; Harris on, 32; in Andrew's *His Soul Goes Marching On*, 29; in Dos Passos' *Three Soldiers*, 29; of Edward D. White, 32; in Paxon's "America at War," *American Democracy and The World War*, 32 and n; in Dos Passos' *Three Soldiers*, 33; Wharton on, 40; Fisher on, 40; in Wharton's *The Marne*, 41–43; in Lazo's *Taps*, 43–44

—training inadequate: in Ropp's *War in the Western World*, 68; in Caygill's "Operations of Company M, 23rd Infantry," 68; in Stevens' *Mattock*, 68n

—punitive executions: in Cobb's *Paths of Glory*, 78, 97; in Cowley's "Dead of the Next War," 79; in Hemingway's *Farewell To Arms*, 80, 82–83

—battle-by-compulsion: in Cobb's *Paths of Glory*, 78; in Cowley's "Dead of the Next War," 79; in Cummings' *The Enormous Room*, 80, 81; in Aldridge's *After the Lost Generation*, 81; in Cowley's *The Literary Situation*, 204

—labor: in Boyd's *Through the Wheat*, 87; in Paul's *Impromptu*, 87, 151; in Dos Passos' *Three Soldiers*, 87, 88n, 177–78

—amateur officers: in March's *Company K*, 91, 92; in Scanlon's *God Have Mercy on Us*, 91, 92; in Nason's *Sergeant Eadie*, 91; in Allen's *Toward the Flame*, 92, 93 and n; in Boyd's *Through the Wheat*, 92; in Paul's *Impromptu*, 92–93; in Cumming's *The Enormous Room*, 93

—political police activity: in Sinclair's *Jimmy Higgins*, 95; in Cumming's *The Enormous Room*, 95–96; in Dos Passos' *Three Soldiers*, 96; Paul on, 96; Binns on, 96; in Stevens' *Mattock*, 96, 147

—sex regulations: in Cummings' *The Enormous Room*, 119; in Dos Passos' *Three Soldiers*, 120, 121, 122, 123; in March's *Company K*, 120–21; in Lee's *It's a Great War!*,

121; in Stevens' *Mattock*, 122; in
Nason's *Sergeant Eadie*, 122; in
Paul's *Impromptu*, 122–23
Aisquith, Prime Minister, 37
Aron, Raymond: *The Century of
Total War*, 59
Atkins, John: on Hemingway, 196;
The Art of Ernest Hemingway, 210
Atrocities: in Reade's *Atrocity Propa-
ganda*, 13, 14n, 101; in Peterson's
Propaganda for War, 13, 15n, 101;
Bryce Report on German, 17, 25,
26, 35, 37–38, 41; in Tuchman's
The Guns of August, 17n; Wharton
on, 97; YMCA encouragement of,
127; in Cather's *One of Ours*, 133;
in Hersey's *The War Lover*, 133
—submarine, 10–18 *passim*, 27, 60,
134, 138, 218. *See also Lusitania*
—Teutonic Beast: in Millis' *Road to
War*, 15; Louisville *Courier-
Journal* on, 18; Father Bernard
Vaughan on, 18–19; Samuel
McCrea Calvert on, 19; in Stevens'
Mattock, 19, 27; in Andrews' *Old
Glory*, 25; Fisher on, 26; Train
on, 26; in Boyd's *Through
the Wheat*, 26; in Dos Passos' *First
Encounter*, 26; in Bainton's *Chris-
tian Attitudes Toward War and
Peace*, 26; in Harrison's *Generals
Die in Bed*, 27; in Dos Passos'
Three Soldiers, 29; in Schindel's
The Golden Pilgrimage, 37; in
Cather's *One of Ours*, 52–53; Dos
Passos', *1919*, 142; Lasswell on,
101; in *Raemaker's Cartoons*, 101.
See also Racism
—Sex: in Oppenheim's *Pawn's Count*,
38 and n; in Fisher's *Home Fires
in France*, 115, 117; in Dos Passos'
1919, 117; in Stallings' *Plumes*,
117; in Dos Passos' *Three Soldiers*,
118; in March's *Company K*, 118n.
See also Belgian rape
Atwater, Rev. George Parkin, 117

B

Babbitt, 156, 234. *See also* Stevens,
James; *Mattock*
Bailey, Temple: on unreal army environment, 30, 42; in *The Tin Soldier* on religious war endorsement,
19–20; on sex, 119

Bainton, Roland H:
—*Christian Attitudes Toward War
and Peace:* on Teutonic Beast, 26;
on religion and patriotism, 94; on
religious attitudes in Germany,
100; on religious war endorsement,
100, 102, 103–04
Baldwin, James: "As Much Truth As
One Can Bear," 231–32
Balfour, 60
Barbusse, 75
Baretto, Larry:
—*Horses in The Sky:* aestheticism
of, 45; Francophilism, 82n
Barnes, Harold Elmer: *The Genesis
of The World War*, 99
Barres, Maurice, 46
Barrie, J. M., 35
Belgian rape, 25, 26, 27, 52, 53, 80,
117, 118, 133
Belgion, Montgomery: 226
—*The Human Parrot and Other Es-
says*, 196–97, 198, 207–08
Bellamy, Edward, 5
Belloc, Hilaire: on Teutonic Beast,
36–37; on atrocity of submarine,
218
Bellow, Saul:
—*The Dangling Man:* Zorn as antith-
esis of, 138; impact of World
War II on, 177; aestheticism, 196;
war accepted in, 221
Bennet, O'Donnell, 26
Berillion, Doctor, 23
Bernard, L. L.: *War and Its Causes*,
72–73
Binns, Archie: on patriotism, 96
—*The Laurels are Cut Down:* on
anti-Ally feeling, 82n; on passive
combat, 88; impact of war in,
96–97; literary device of, 241
Bishop, John Peale, 9
Blackton, J. Stuart: *The Battle Cry
of Peace*, 25
Bolshevism, 95, 96, 97, 99, 146, 147, 233
Book-Trade: in Millis' *Road to War*,
34, 35; in Ogden's *Publishers'
Weekly*, 34; program of Parker,
35; in Fentons' "A Literary Frac-
ture of World War I," 35–36
Bourne, Randolph, 5
Boyd, Thomas: on religious war endorsement, 19; on adventure of
war, 30; castration images, 64; on

machine war, 66; on trench combat, 74; aestheticism of, 242

—*Through The Wheat:* Teutonic Beast, 26; machine slaughter, 61, 89; medical service inadequate, 66n; military leadership inadequate, 68; slaughter of Captain Powers, 68; racism, 82; Captain Powers as amateur officer, 92; impact of war, 98, 99, 228; army environment in, 159; machine war in, 159; Sergeant Harriman's death, 164; literary device in, 164–65; Cowley on, 241

—William Hicks: impact of war on, 32, 68–69, 162, 164–65, 189, 190, 214, 219, 234; war as purifier, 48; on passive combat, 72; machine slaughter, 84, 164; military leadership inadequate, 84; army labor and racism, 87; machine war impersonality, 89; and Captain Powers, 92; as antihero, 95; in army environment, 163–64; Marsh on, 218

British blockade, 15–16, 17, 37

Brooks, Alden:

—*As I Saw It:* on passive combat, 64 and n; military leadership inadequate, 83

Broun, Heywood, 194–95

Bryan, 12, 17

Bryce Report on German atrocities, 17, 25, 26, 35, 37–38, 41, 101

Burgum, E. B.: *The Novel and the World's Dilemma* on *A Farewell To Arms,* 181

Burke, Kenneth, on humanism, 213

Burns: *The Gallery,* 212, 230, 231, 232, 234

C

Callinus, 206

Calvert, Samuel McCrea, 19

Casualties. *See* Machine war

Cather, Willa: racism in, 28; unreal military environment, 28, 87, 97; on trench combat, 76

—*One of Ours:* on British trade, 10; unreal army environment in, 29, 32, 71; impact of war, 55, 136–37; on machine combat, 136–37; on army environment, 200

—Claude: racism, 23, 30–32; adventure of war, 30; sex, 31, 114, 130, 135; unreal army environment, 31–32; aestheticism of, 45; adventure sought, 51–53, 129; Teutonic Beast, 52–53; machine impersonality, 89; shaped by environment, 129, 130, 131; standards of, manhood, 131; Unmanned by Enid, 131–33; excited by atrocities, 133; German-American friends sacrificed, 133; erotic stimulation of war, 114, 117, 129, 130–33, 134–36, 137, 143, 155–56; relation with mother, 133–34; on machine slaughter, 135–36; army environment sweet to, 148; impact of war on, 190

Cavell, Edith, 53, 117, 133

Caygill, Harry W.: "Operations of Company M., 23rd Infantry," 68

Céline, Louis-Ferdinand:

—*Journey to the End of the Night:* machine slaughter, 62 and n; military leadership lacking, 65n; role of M. P., 78–79; eroticism of war, 117; impact of war in, 189

Chesterton, G. K., 23, 35, 36

Cinema, 14, 25

Clemenceau, 58

Cobb, Irvin, 26

Cobb, Humphrey: castration images, 64

—*Paths of Glory:* on trench combat, 75–76; machine war impersonality, 89; punitive executions, 97; on impact of war, 97; literary device in, 241

—General Assolant: on machine slaughter, 61; military leadership indicted, 78–79; pressures of press on, 78 and n; punitive execution, 78; battle-by-compulsion, 78; mentioned, 80

—Colonel Dax: machine slaughter, 63, 79; machine war impersonality, 89

Coffin, Henry Sloan, 111–12

Combat. *See* Army environment; Machine war; Manhood

Coolidge, Calvin, 235

Cooperman, Stanley: "Frank Norris and The Werewolf of Guilt," 114

of war, 55, 190; reduced by army
environment, 86; army labor and
racism, 87; on sex atrocities, 118;
army environment destroys,
149–55; prewar environment conditioned, 152, 153; manhood of,
152–55 *passim*, 159; war as proving
ground, 153; in army environment,
163, 164; and Meadville, 153, 154;
as "dog," 154; and Yvonne, 154–55;
impact of war on, 190
—*1919:* on machine war, 58, 59, 188;
fascism in, 69, 138, 141; "Unknown
Soldier" episodes in, 90; on sex
atrocities, 117; impact of war,
124–25, 180–81, 242; literary devices in, 180–81
—Richard Savage: on religious endorsement of war, 21; as vacuum,
69; on machine slaughter, 80–81,
144; degraded by army environment, 86; machine war impersonality, 89; on patriotism, 93; protests
religion, 105–06; affair with Edward's wife, 114; impersonal sex,
123–24, 143, 144; and Mrs. Powers,
123, 143; impact of war on, 141;
machine war degrades, 141–45,
155–56; and Eleanor Stoddard, 142,
145; on religion, 143; in absurd
army environment, 143–45; observes pre-Fascism, 144
—Fred Summers: impact of war on,
21–22, 97, 99, 123; on machine
slaughter, 80–81; impersonal sex,
123, 144; machine war, 144, 145;
withdraws from army environment,
145
—Ward Moorehouse: prefigured by
George Creel, 24; and Richard
Savage, 142, 143, 145
—Steve: on machine slaughter, 80–81;
impersonal sex, 123–24, 144; machine war, 144, 145; withdraws
from army environment, 144, 145
—*First Encounter:* Teutonic Beast,
26; impact of war, 43, 55, 99; on
World War II, 55; inanity of machine war, 70; on trench combat,
75; imagery in, 75, 95; war as purifier, 115; impersonal sex, 121n,
123; literary style in, 165
—Martin Howe: aesthete, 46, 176–77;
combat as proving ground, 47;

death as "circus," 95; impact of
war on, 97, 165, 169; on religion,
107–08; effect of machine war on,
142; color devices, 179 and n, 180
Doyle, Conan, 35
Dreiser: on sex, 114
—*An American Tragedy:*
—Clyde: epitome of army environ-
ment, 148
Dunbar, Ruth, 32

E

Eaton, Rev. Charles Aubrey, 103
Eisinger: "The American War Novel:
An Affirming Flame," 202, 209,
213–14
Eliot, T. S.: "The Love Song of J.
Alfred Prufrock," 211
Empey, Arthur Guy: unreal army
environment in, 32; on war as puri-
fier, 40; on YMCA and sex, 115;
on sex, 119
Eroticism of war. *See* Sex
Euripides, 206, 210

F

Facism, 69, 72, 138, 141, 144, 206,
210, 221, 222, 230
Faulkner:
—*Soldiers' Pay:* aversion to casualties, 73; manhood of Januarius
Jones, 159–60; repetitive device in,
162
—Captain Powers: killed by men, 87;
and Margaret, 114, 161; conditioning of prewar environment, 159–61;
in machine war, 161, 162; impersonal sex, 161–62
—Mahon: impact of war on, 32, 162,
165, 189, 190, 219; as antihero, 95;
creature of prewar environment,
159–62, 163; army
environment, 159, 162, 163, and
Januarius Jones, 159–60; and
Cecily, 160–61; and Margaret
Powers, 160, 163; impersonal sex,
161, 162, 163; aesthete, 162
—Margaret Powers: sex activities of,
114, 116; creature of prewar environment, 159–63; impersonal sex,
160–62; and Mahon, 160–63; and
Cadet Lowe, 114, 161; and Gilligan, 114, 161–62

War Novel: An Affirming Flame"
on, 213–14; Burke on, 213
Hyde, Charles C., 12

I

Imagery: pattern, 75n; in Dos Passos'
First Encounter, 95; in Cummings'
The Enormous Room, 106, 143, 164,
169–75 *passim*, 185; in Cather's
One of Ours, 130; in Stallings'
Plumes, 143; in Dos Passos' *Three
Soldiers*, 154, 155, 180; in Dos
Passos' *1919*, 180–81; in Hemingway's "The Snows of Kilimanjaro,"
211; in Eliot's "The Love Song of
J. Alfred Prufrock," 211; in Tomlinson's *War Books*, 211; in Faulkner's *A Fable*, 216; in Fulöp-Miller's *The Night of Time*, 216
—castration: of March, 64; of Cobb,
64; of Harrison, 64; of Boyd, 64;
of Fredenburgh, 64; in March's
Company K, 70, 97
—of mountains: in Hemingway, 75,
185; in Cummings, 75, 185; in
Barbusse, 75
—humans as animals: in Scanlon's
God Have Mercy on Us, 75n; in
Dos Passos' *First Encounter*, 75;
in Cobb's *Paths of Glory*, 79
—of mass in machine war: in Dos
Passos' early novels, 88;
in Cummings' writing, 88; in
Hemingway's *A Farewell to Arms*,
88, 89; in Harrison's *Generals Die
in Bed*, 88; in March's *Company
K*, 89; in Boyd's *Through the
Wheat*, 89; in Cobb's *Paths of
Glory*, 89; in Dos Passos' *Three
Soldiers*, 89; in Stevens' *Mattock*,
89
Impact of World War I: In Hemingway's "Champs d'Honneur," 8–9,
210; on Henry James, 8 and n;
in Dos Passos' *1919*, 21–22, 69, 97,
99, 124, 180–81, 242; in Hemingway's *A Farewell To Arms*, 32, 69,
97, 99, 127, 165, 186, 188, 189–90,
210, 219, 241, 242; in Dos Passos'
Three Soldiers, 32, 43, 55, 69, 97,
98, 99, 123, 165, 169–76 *passim*,
189, 190, 219, 233, 234; in Boyd's
Through the Wheat, 32, 68–69, 98,

99, 162, 164–65, 189, 190, 214, 219,
228, 234, 241; in Faulkner's *Soldiers' Pay*, 32, 161, 162, 165, 189,
190, 219, 241; in Fenton's "A Literary Fracture of World War I,"
40; in Dos Passos' *First Encounter*,
43, 55, 56, 97, 99, 165, 169; in Stallings' *Plumes*, 43, 69, 98; in May's
The End of American Innocence,
45 and n; in Seldes' "Notes and
Queries," 54; in Parrington's "The
Beginnings of Critical Realism in
America," 54; in Hoffman's "The
Temper of the Twenties," 54; in
Tomlinson's "War Books," 54, 211;
in Morris' *Postscript to Yesterday*,
54–55; in Cather's *One of Ours*,
55, 136–37, 190; in Fredenburgh's
Soldiers March!, 69, 97, 99, 190,
219; in Paul's *Impromptu*, 69, 97,
99, 190, 219; in Stevens' *Mattock*,
69; in Nason's *Sergeant Eadie*, 69;
Cummings on, 69; in Killinger's
Hemingway and The Dead Gods,
76–77; in March's *Company K*, 83,
97, 99, 165, 228, 234; in Binns'
The Laurels are Cut Down, 96–97;
in Cobb's *Paths of Glory*, 97; in
Cummings' *The Enormous Room*,
98, 99, 124, 165, 169–75 *passim*,
189–90, 219, 228, 234; in Lee's *It's
A Great War!*, 99, 201n; in Wharton's *A Son at the Front*, 118; in
Kazin's *On Native Grounds*, 189;
in Céline's *Journey to the End of
the Night*, 189; Howells on, 191;
in Johnston's "The Poetry of
World War I: A Study in the Evaluation of Lyric and Narrative
Form," 193–94; in McAffee's "The
Literature of Disillusion," 194;
Brown on, 194–95; in Wilkinson's
"Recent War Books," 195; Aldridge's *After the Lost Generation*
on, 195, 225–28 *passim*, 232–33,
234–35; Cowley on, 226; in
Stallings' *The First World War*,
200–01; in Cowley's *The Literary
Situation*, 204–05, 217; on Dos
Passos, 203; in Owen's "Exposure,"
205; in Owens' "A-Terre," 205; in
Walcutt's "Fear Motifs in the Lit-
erature Between the Wars," 222;
Hackett's "Hemingway: 'A Fare-

Cather's *One of Ours*, 129, 130, 131; in Paul's *Impromptu*, 149, 150, 152; in Dos Passos' *Three Soldiers*, 152, 153; in Faulkner's *Soldiers' Pay*, 159–62, 163–64
—reform: of Theodore Roosevelt, 5; of Eugene V. Deks, 5; of Henry George, 5; of Edward Bellamy, 5; in Hofstadter's *The Age of Reform*, 5; in Steffens' "Tweed Days in St. Louis," 5–6; in Flowers' *Arena*, 6; of Ida Tarbell, 6; of *The Octopus*, 6; of *The Jungle*, 6; in magazines, 5–6
—of Jordan, 7; in Angell's *The Grand Illusion*, 7; Malcolm Cowley on, 7; Jordan on, 7; in Winwar's "The World War and The Arts," 12
Purification in war. *See* Religion

R

Racism: Sir Cecil Spring Rice on, 16; in Reade's *Atrocity Propaganda*, 22, 24; in Cather's *One of Ours*, 23, 29–32; in Andrews' *The Three Things*, 23; of Dr. LeBon, 23; of Dr. Berillion, 23; in *Le Temps*, 23; of Chesterton, 23; in Hoag's *Word Warfare*, 24; in Allen's *Toward the Flame*, 24; in Fredenburgh's *Soldiers March!*, 27–28; in Hoffman's *The Twenties*, 28; in Wharton's *A Son at the Front*, 28; of Cather, 28; in Andrews' *His Soul Goes Marching On*, 29; in Gitlin's *The Full Measure of Devotion*, 29; Manifestoes on, 81; in Hemingway's *A Farewell To Arms*, 81, 82n; in May's *The End of American Innocence*, 82; in Cummings' *The Enormous Room*, 82 and n; in Boyd's *Through The Wheat*, 82n, 87; in Binn's *The Laurels Are Cut Down*, 82n; of "Y" men, 82n; in Paul's *Impromptu*, 87; in Dos Passos' *Three Soldiers*, 87, 88n; in Fisher's *Home Fires in France*, 115; in Stevens' *Mattock*, 146; Baldwin's "As Much Truth As One Can Bear" on, 231–32; mentioned, 44, 98. *See also* Anglophilism;

Army environment; Francophilism; Atrocities
—on home front: in Oppenheim's *Pawn's Court*, 38 and n; in Adams' *Common Cause*, 38–39; in Whiting's *S.O.S.*, 39n; in Heth's *Told With A Drum*, 39n; in Cather's *One of Ours*, 133
Raemaker's *Cartoons*, 18–19, 36, 37, 73, 101, 218
Reade, James Morgan: *Atrocity Propaganda*, 13, 14, 22, 24, 101
Religion: and racism, 16; Bainton on German, 100; machine weapons justified in *The Christian Herald*, 109; in Cather's *One of Ours*, 132, 133; in Dos Passos' *1919*, 143; in Stevens' *Mattock*, 145–48 *passim*; in Cummings' *The Enormous Room*, 172; in Faulkner's *A Fable*, 216; mentioned, 44, 68, 77. *See also* Racism; YMCA
—war as purifier: In Gosse's *Inter Arma*, 3, 48–49; Train on, 40, 115; Empey on, 40; in Wharton's *A Son at The Front*, 40; in Boyd's *Through The Wheat*, 48; in Stidger's *Soldier Silhouettes*, 109; Dr. Stires on, 109; Dos Passos on, 110; in Harrison's *Generals Die in Bed*, 110; in Hemingway's *The Fifth Columns and The First 49 Stories*, 110; in Dos Passos' *First Encounter*, 115; in Mary Lee's *It's a Great War!*, 127
—war endorsed by: in Louisville *Courier–Journal*, 18; of Father Bernard Vaughan, 18–19; of Samuel McCrea Calvert, 19; in Train's *Earthquake*, 19, 94–95, 127; in Stevens' *Mattock*, 19; Dos Passos on, 19, 22; Boyd on, 19, 22; Cummings on, 19, 22; Stallings on, 19; Andrews on, 19–20; Bailey on, 19–20; Wharton on, 19–20; in Andrews' *Joy in the Morning*, 20; in Bailey's *The Tin Soldier*, 20; in Dos Passos' *1919*, 21; in Cummings' *The Enormous Room*, 21; Fredenburgh on, 22; Stevens on, 22; March on, 22; Rev. Randolph McKinn, 57; in Bainton's *Christian Attitudes Toward War and Peace*, 94, 99–100, 102, 103–04; Rev. Win-

nington-Ingram on, 99–100; in
Neibuhr's *Moral Man in Immoral
Society*, 100; in Abrams' *Preachers
Present Arms*, 100, 102, 103, 104,
105; Twain on, 101–02; Rev. Para-
dise on, 103; *New York Times* on,
103; Rev. Eaton on, 103; Repper
on, 103; in Lasswell's *Propaganda
Technique in the World War*,
103n; Rev. Hughes on, 105; Rev.
Polling on, 105; in Whiting's
S.O.S., 105; in Hoffman's *The
Modern Novel in America*, 105
—war endorsement protested: in Dos
Passos' *1919*, 105–06; in March's
Company K, 106, 108; in Cum-
mings' *The Enormous Room*,
106–07; by Fredenburgh, 107; by
Paul, 107; by Lazo, 107; by Whit-
ing, 107; by Dos Passos, 107; by
Stallings, 107; in Stevens' *Mattock*,
107; in Harrison's *Generals Die in
Bed*, 107; in Dos Passos' *First En-
counter*, 107–08; in Allen's "Re-
port to Major Roberts," *It
Was Like This*, 108–09; by
March, 110
Remenyi, Joseph: on war as a literary
device, 191; "Psychology of War
Literature" on pacifist war writers,
198, 209, 210, 211–12
Review of Reviews, 3, 7
Revisionism: in Tansill's *America
Goes to War*, 17n; in Barnes' *The
Genesis of The World War*, 99;
in Lasswell's *Propaganda Technique
in the World War*, 99; in Marsh's
"A Circle of Meaning: Novelists
Face the Military Necessity," 220;
in Walcutt's "Fear Motifs in The
Literature Between the Wars," 220,
222–23. *See also* Aestheticism; Hu-
manism; Pacifism
Rice, Sir Cecil Spring, 16
Romains, Jules: *Verdun*, 5
Roosevelt, Theodore, 5, 18n, 49, 51,
71, 101
Ropp, Theodore:
—*War in The Western World*: military leadership lacking, 61; machine slaughter, 62; army training
inadequate, 68; on army environment, 83

Rosenfeld, Isaac: "A Farewell to
Ernest Hemingway," 181

S

Scanlon, William:
—*God Have Mercy On Us:* machine
slaughter, 61, 73–74, 74n; on trench
combat, 75; goat image of humans,
75n; amateur officers in, 91, 92;
on YMCA, 113
Schindel, Bayard:
—*The Golden Pilgrimage:* on ma-
chine war, 37, 70–71; on Teutonic
Beast, 37
Schwab, Charles M., 12 and n
Seiden, Melvin: "The Hero and His
War," 209
Seldes, Gilbert: "Notes and Queries,"
54
Sex: Train on, 113, 115; in May's
The End of American Innocence,
113–14, 115, 116; Dreiser on, 114;
Norris on, 114; in Cooperman's
"Frank Norris and the Werewolf
of Guilt," 114; Empey on, 115, 119;
in Hemingway's *A Farewell To
Arms*, 114, 120, 182–85 *passim*; in
Wilson's Hemingway: "The Gauge
of Morale," 114; in Dos Passos'
1919, 114; in Cather's *One of Ours*,
114, 119, 130, 132, 133, 135; in
Faulkner's *Soldiers' Pay*, 114, 116;
in Fisher's *Home Fires in France*,
115; in Nason's *Sergeant Eadie*,
115–16; in Paul's *Impromptu*, 116,
148–49; in March's *Company K*,
116, 120–21; in Stallings' *Plumes*,
116; in Cummings' *The Enormous
Room*, 119, 172; in Stevens' *Mattock*, 119; Bailey on, 119; Wharton
on, 119; in Lee's *It's a Great War!*,
119–20; in Hersey's *The War
Lover*, 130, 132; in Stevens' *Mattock*, 145, 146, 147; in Dos Passos'
Three Soldiers, 180, 181. *See also*
Army environment; Atrocities;
Belgian rape; Religion
—impersonal: in Dos Passos' *Three
Soldiers*, 22, 86, 120, 121, 122–23,
152, 154–55; in Paul's *Impromptu*,
22, 122 and n, 123, 151; in Fredenburgh's *Soldier's March!* 22, 123,
141; in Dos Passos' *First Encoun-*

Twain, Mark: "Europe and Elsewhere," 101–02

V

Valentine, Alan: 1913, *America Be-
tween Two Worlds*, 86
Van Doren, Carl: "Post-War: The
Literary Twenties," 181
Vaughan, Father Bernard, 18–19
Virgil, 205, 206, 210
von Bernstorff, Count, 51
Von Clausewitz, General, 59, 191
von Schlicht, Baron: "Life in a
German Crack Regiment," 34

W

Walcutt, Charles G.:
—"Fear Motifs in the Literature Between the Wars": on impersonal
war machine, 142; on war cycle,
220, 222–23
Warren, H. C., 106n, 111
Warren, Herbert, 73
Warren, Robert Penn, introduction
to Hemingway's *A Farewell To
Arms*, 182n
Wharton, Edith: on religious war en-
dorsement, 19–20; George Snell on,
40; on atrocities, 97; on sex, 119
—*A Son at the Front:* unreal army
environment in, 28, 40, 71; impact
of war in, 118
—*The Marne:* on pacifism, 3, 42–43;
Francophilism in, 81; unreal army
environment in, 41–43; aesthetic
structure of, 208
What Price Glory?, 203
White, Edward D., 32
Whiting, John D.: on racism, 39n; on
religion, 107
—*S.O.S.:* on religious endorsement
of war, 105
Wilkinson, Clennell: "Recent War
Books" on antiwar novels, 195
Wilson, Edmund: "Hemingway: The
Gauge of Morale," *Literature in
America*, 114, 181, 186; "The
Sportsman's Tragedy," 228–29
Wilson, Sloan, conservatism of, 232
Wilson, Woodrow, 6, 7, 9, 11, 12,
24, 51, 58, 60, 83
Winnington-Ingram, Rev. A. F., 99–
100

Winwar, Frances: "The World and
the Arts," *War in the Twentieth
Century*, 12
Woods, General, 18n, 51, 59
World War II: genocide of, 24; impact of, 33, 61, 76, 189; in Dos
Passos' *First Encounter*, 55, 56,
181n; in Miller's *That Winter*,
181n; mobility matched mechanization, 204; mentioned, 200, 202,
220, 222, 223
—accepted: in Bellow's *The Dangling
Man*, 177; in Hemingway's *Men
at War*, 197, 229; in Hemingway's
*Across the River and into the
Trees*, 210, 221; Marsh's "A Circle
of Meaning: Novelists Face the
Military Necessity" on, 220; Walcutt's "Fear Motifs in the Literature Between the Wars" on, 220,
222–23; in Wouk, 222, 231, 232,
234, 236, 237; Frohock's *The Novel
of Violence in America* on, 224;
Aldridge's *After the Lost Generation on*, 225–28 *passim*; in Wouk's
The Caine Mutiny, 229; in S. Wilson, 232; Cowley's *The Literary
Situation* on, 237; Hoffman's *The
Modern Novel in America* on, 239;
by Hemingway, 230–31
—literature generally: in Aldridge's
After The Lost Generation, 195,
212, 214, 224, 225–28 *passim*, 230,
232–33, 234–38 *passim;* in Gold's
"Fiction of the Fifties," 225, 231,
232; in Aldridge's "America's
Young Novelists: Uneasy Inheritors
of a Tradition," 239
—literary disillusion: on Bellow's *The
Dangling Man*, 221, 231, 232; in
Burns' *The Gallery*, 230, 231, 232,
234, 236; in Miller's *That Winter*,
230, 232; Goode's "British War
Party of the Second World War"
on, 231; Baldwin's "As Much
Truth as One Can Bear" on,
231–32. *See also* Aestheticism;
Humanism
Wouk, Herman: war as literary device, 214; conservatism of, 222, 231,
232, 234, 235, 236, 237; war accepted in *The Caine Mutiny*, 229,
235
Wylie, Ida Alma Ross, 30

designer : Gerard A. Valerio

typesetter : Maple Press

typefaces : Waverly

printer : Maple Press

paper : Mohawk Tosca Text

binder : Maple Press

cover material : G. S. B. s/535 #096 Silver Black